1001728292

NELL

COMMUNICATION AT WORK

Donation

COMMUNICATION AT WORK

Listening, Speaking, Writing, and Reading

Kathleen S. Abrams
North Central Technical Institute

Eric P. Hibbison, consulting editor

Prentice-Hall, Inc., Englewood Cliffs, New Jersey 07632

Library of Congress Cataloging in Publication Data

ABRAMS, KATHLEEN S.
  Communication at work.

  Includes index.
  1. Communication. I. Title.
P90.A237 1986   001.54   85-3381
ISBN 0-13-153826-8

Editorial/production supervision and
  interior design: Dee Amir Josephson
Cover design: Lundgren Graphics, Ltd.
Manufacturing buyer: Harry Baisley

Printed in the United States of America

10 9 8 7 6 5 4 3 2 1

ISBN 0-13-153826-8   01

Prentice-Hall International (UK) Limited, *London*
Prentice-Hall of Australia Pty. Limited, *Sydney*
Editora Prentice-Hall do Brasil, Ltda., *Rio de Janeiro*
Prentice-Hall Canada Inc., *Toronto*
Prentice-Hall Hispanoamericana, S. A., *Mexico*
Prentice-Hall of India Private Limited, *New Delhi*
Prentice-Hall of Japan, Inc., *Tokyo*
Prentice-Hall of Southeast Asia Pte. Ltd., *Singapore*
Whitehall Books Limited, *Wellington, New Zealand*

For my partners, Larry and Nathaniel

COMMUNICATION AT WORK

CONTENTS

PREFACE TO STUDENTS

Emperor Frederick, a thirteenth-century Roman ruler, set up an experiment to find out what language had been spoken in the Garden of Eden. He designed a garden which as closely as possible recreated his image of that first garden, and there he placed a group of newborn infants. Planning to let the babies' speech develop naturally, he ordered that no one be allowed to talk to the infants. Wet nurses took care of the babies' physical needs, but they did not speak to the infants or to each other while they were in the garden. The result of Emperor Frederick's experiment? All the infants died.[1]

Although this test did not satisfy the emperor's curiosity about the first language spoken, it does point out the importance of communication. Lack of communication can evidently be fatal.

Our need to communicate is substantiated by modern experiences. A 1977 British court case described a two-year old girl and her one-year-old brother whose mother thought they should grow up without adult intervention. Although she took care of the children's physical needs, she did not talk to them or respond to their attempts to communicate. This lack of communication between mother and children slowed the children's development. The one-year-old could not sit up alone and the two-year-old's language consisted of unintelligible noises.[2]

Communication is obviously a vital part of our daily lives. From the time we wake up in the morning until we go to sleep at night, we communicate. Reading the paper, watching the morning news, discussing problems with our co-workers, and making plans with our families all involve communication. We com-

[1]Joseph Dahmus, *Seven Medieval Kings*, Doubleday, 1967, p. 224.
[2]David Lewis, *How to Be a Gifted Parent* (New York: Berkley Books, 1979), p. 156.

municate by talking, listening, reading, and writing. The way we dress, stand, sit, walk, and look at each other relays messages. Some people say we even communicate while we sleep. Someone watching a person sleep can tell whether that person feels peaceful or restless.

Although for most of us a lack of communication may not result in anything as drastic as mental retardation or death, it can contribute to failures at work and unhappiness at home. According to John C. Crystal, career development expert, one of the most common reasons for the firing of an employee is "that the employee just doesn't see eye to eye with the boss. Something has gone wrong with their relationship."[3] Lack of communication has also been mentioned as a major factor in divorce. Herbert A. Glieberman, domestic relation lawyer, says the "inability to talk to each other" is the main reason couples split up.[4] Evidently, losing a job or a spouse may be the serious result of ineffective communication.

When we think of communicating, we often think of talking or writing, in other words, telling people what we think. Communication, however, is an ongoing process involving both a sender of a message and a receiver. It includes four activities: listening, speaking, reading, and writing. The amount of communicating time the average person spends daily in each activity is illustrated by the following graph:[5]

You can see that each area of communication plays an important part in our lives. Although we spend a large amount (45%) of our time listening, we also spend 55% of our communication time in the other three areas. Even writing, which typically takes up the least time, accounts for 9%. Therefore, if you want to be an effective communicator, you must develop skills in all four areas of communication.

These four communication activities are interrelated. You will notice from looking at the graph that the amount of time we spend listening is closely related to the time we spend speaking, and the time we spend reading relates closely to the time we spend writing. You can imagine that many of the factors of speaking and writing such as word choice and audience analysis are similar, and awareness of the presenter's style is important whether you are reading or listening.

[3]"If the Boss Says: 'You're Fired,'" *U.S. News & World Report*, Inc., March 12, 1979, p. 59.
[4]"Why So Many Marriages Fail," *U.S. News & World Report*, Inc., July 20, 1981, p. 53.
[5]Theodore H. Wright, *Tuning In* (Stamford, Conn.: Xerox Corporation, 1973–74), p. 4.

Although we sometimes tend to underestimate the importance of the connection—we might talk when no one is listening or might hide the poetry we write in a drawer—we have long been aware that communicating means sharing. In fact, the Japanese character for "listen" is their symbol for ear placed within their symbol for gate, indicating that we must put ourselves in the speaker's place in order to listen effectively. The listener has as much responsibility for absorbing the message as the speaker has for presenting it.

Because communication is an ongoing process involving both sender and receiver, this book emphasizes all four areas of communication. As you study the text, you will notice how these activities interrelate. For example, the listening section discusses techniques for interpreting a speaker's body language, and the speech section tells you how to use gestures and facial expression to help listeners understand your meaning. The writing chapters stress the importance of keeping your audience in mind, and the reading section helps you learn how to adapt your reading skills to the different styles writers use.

How well we actually read, write, speak, or listen is related to our understanding of skills. For that reason each section of the text includes three areas: information about the communication process, a discussion of the skills involved in carrying out that process, and suggestions for using the information and skills you have learned in actual situations.

Some skills, such as word choice, logical thinking, and information gathering, are necessary for all types of communication. For that reason, these areas are discussed first and make up the opening section of the text.

Most important, you are preparing for employment. You will want to use this text to help you acquire the skills necessary to achieve success on the job. Successful workers use their communication skills in three ways: (1) to do a job, (2) to understand their co-workers, and (3) to maintain an enjoyable and relatively stress-free personal life. Because on-the-job success is usually a combination of these three areas, the activities and examples in this book are planned to help you understand how communication skills relate to each of these situations. As closely as possible, the activities in this text represent real-life experiences.

Much emphasis is placed today on job seeking and other work-related skills, and current textbooks tend to approach the discussion of communication from that viewpoint. Although the importance of skillful on-the-job communication is also emphasized here, this text presents a more diversified approach to the study of communication. Effective communication skills can help you to establish a satisfying personal life and to become a contributing member of your community. These skills are necessary for a well-rounded life.

The concluding chapter of the book brings all these communication skills together by applying them to an important activity: job seeking. We will discuss how to apply reading and writing skills in the job search, resume, and application letter process and how to apply speaking and listening skills in the interview process. The information in this text will help you use the communication skills you have learned here to take the first step in finding a satisfying job.

As advanced technology plays an ever-increasing role in the workplace and at home, the need to refine our interpersonal communication skills also increases. A successful business deal may hinge on how accurately you can listen to a telephone conversation or how well you understand word connotations when you write a letter. One source estimates that communication has changed more rapidly in the 40 years since World War II than it did in the 1,800 years before that. Our need to keep pace with the changing demands of communication is obvious when we consider the types of jobs available today. In 1950 people without high school diplomas could do approximately one-third of all the industrial jobs in the United States. By 1980 that figure had dropped to 5%. Today fewer than 5% of all the industrial jobs in the United States can be done successfully by people without high school diplomas.[6]

The message is clear. Jobs in our advanced technological society require highly trained people. An important part of that training is the development of communication skills. This text will help you understand the basics of the communication process in listening, speaking, reading, and writing. Use it to learn how to communicate effectively in many different work-related and personal situations.

[6]Lloyd Dobyns, "The Decline of American Productivity: If Japan Can, Why Can't We," *Training and Development Journal,* August 1982, p. 56.

PREFACE TO
THE INSTRUCTOR

A successful communicator knows how to listen as well as speak, read as well as write. Communication is an integrated process involving both sender and receiver. For that reason, Communication at Work presents all four areas of communication skills: listening, speaking, writing, and reading. The purpose of the text is to help students develop skills while showing them how these skills interact throughout the entire communication process. A speaker's effectiveness, for example, is enhanced by interpretation of the listener's body language; familiarity with the writing process helps the reader understand written messages better.

Keeping that purpose in mind, the author begins the text with an overview of the communication process as it applies to both spoken and written messages and concludes the text with a chapter on job-seeking skills which shows how the four areas of communication can be integrated in practical application.

The main part of the text is divided into the four areas of communication. The sections have been arranged as you might teach them, beginning with listening to start the semester, then speaking, writing, and reading. Each section, however, is a full discussion of the skill and may be used individually at any time during the semester. Nevertheless, listening and speaking have been placed together, as have writing and reading, to emphasize their interrelatedness, and it is probably best to teach them in this pattern.

The book also includes a section on preparing. Because certain skills such as research, logical thinking, and effective word choice are basic to all areas of communication, a section on these three skills follows the overview of the four areas of communication. Students who understand the necessity for and the techniques of research will send more interesting, compelling messages. Students who know how to think logically to solve problems will send more organized, persuasive messages. Students who adapt their word choice to their receivers will send more readily understandable messages. These qualities of interest, organization, and intelligibility are essential to all communication; therefore the skills that will help your students incorporate these qualities into their messages are discussed first. However, each chapter within the preparing section is a complete unit and you may decide to disperse these chapters throughout the text.

The main emphasis of the text is on using the skills presented to improve on-the-job performance. Many of the examples used to illustrate concepts are taken directly from business and industry. Report writing, for example, is illustrated with an annual report from Sentry Insurance. Examples in the reading chapters are taken from manuals and trade journals typical of on-the-job reading. The application activities that conclude each chapter are intended to simulate work experiences.

The author also believes that an efficient employee sustains a happy personal life; therefore, some of the activities also relate to interaction with spouses, friends, and neighbors. They are intended to help students apply communication skills to their lives at home and in their communities.

The belief that a successful communicator understands all areas of communication as they relate to both personal and on-the-job experiences comes from the author's fifteen years as a communication instructor in schools and for business and industry. She is experienced in teaching specialized courses for business and industry as well as in meeting the needs of the traditional student. The text is a practical guide for instructors who want to relate traditional concepts of communication skills to their students' primary focus of interest: the world of work.

ACKNOWLEDGEMENTS

Many people helped with the writing of this book from the initial proposal stage to final copy. I thank especially my husband Larry Abrams who has always encouraged my writing efforts, book rep Kris King who first showed this proposal to Prentice-Hall, and editor Eric Hibbison who patiently guided the book from rough draft to finished copy.

I also thank the many librarians and other resource people who helped with cross references, obscure sources and appropriate examples. They were important in the successful completion of this book.

No author writes a book alone. The encouragement of my husband and son, the interest of my friends and the cooperation of fellow professionals were invaluable as I worked to complete this formidable task.

1

THE COMMUNICATION PROCESS

You cannot speak of oceans to a well-frog—the creature of a narrow sphere. You cannot speak of ice to a summer insect—the creature of a season.
Chuang Tzu, *Autumn Floods,* 4-3 Century B.C. trans. Herbert Jiles

After studying this chapter you should understand:
1. The communication process
2. How barriers can prevent us from communicating
3. Similarities between spoken and written communication
4. Differences between spoken and written communication

THE COMMUNICATION PROCESS

Nathan Miller, American author and journalist, has said, "Conversation in the United States is a competitive exercise in which the first person to draw a breath is declared the listener." Although you may chuckle at Miller's statement, you probably also see the truth in his observation. People often seem more interested in hearing themselves talk than in maintaining a constant flow of ideas with other people. Whether we are speaking or writing, we tend to think of communication as a linear process starting with the sender's comments and ending when someone receives the message.

$$\text{sender} \xrightarrow{\text{message}} \text{receiver}$$

However, communication is actually an ongoing process involving both the speaker and the listener. This process is best described by a circular diagram.

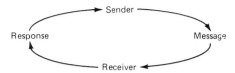

"To communicate" comes from the Latin "to make common." When people communicate, they relate to each others' experiences; in other words, they share something "in common."

This sharing process can best be illustrated with a diagram developed by Wilbur Schramm in the 1950s. Schramm showed communication occurring when the "fields of experience" (knowledge, attitude, values, etc.) of the sender (encoder) and receiver (decoder) overlap.[1]

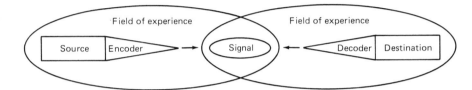

This model, or symbolic drawing, illustrates several important aspects of the communication process. All communication begins with a source or a stimulus. This stimulus gives us a reason to communicate. We interpret (encode) that stimulus within the context of our own experience. Then we send the message (our interpretation of the stimulus). The receivers of our message decode (translate) it within the context of their own experiences. We hope they will decode the message in the way we expect. When the encoding of a stimulus and the decoding of the message are similar, the sharing process is complete.

Let's say you and a friend are canoeing down a river. From your vantage point in front, you notice that the canoe is headed for a large rock. This observation is a stimulus. You interpret (encode) the rock as danger so you yell to your canoeing partner, "Rock ahead." If your partner receives the message and also decodes it as danger, the two of you will work together to avoid the rock. In this case an accurate sharing of ideas has been achieved because you and your friend have had similar experiences with rocks. The pattern of your communication looks like Diagram A.

Diagram A

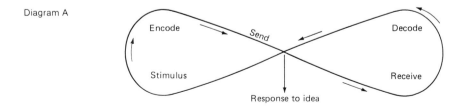

Now let's say that your canoeing partner had a different attitude toward rocks than you did. Perhaps your friend thought it was fun to bash the canoe into rocks to see how much of a beating it could take. Therefore, when you yelled, "Rock ahead," your friend deliberately directed the canoe toward the rock. Your partner decoded your message differently. To your partner "Rock ahead" meant excitement rather than danger; therefore, your partner's response was the exact opposite of the one you expected. In this case, the pattern of your communication would look like Diagram B.

Diagram B

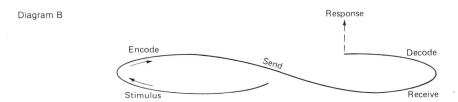

Because the message is decoded (understood) differently, you do not share the same idea with your friend.

COMMUNICATION BARRIERS

When people do not accurately share ideas and information, we say that communication breaks down. Although you may use a lot of words and people may respond to them, the communication process is completed only when your receiver shares the meaning of your message.

Many factors prevent us from understanding each other. Prejudice against the sender or topic, failure to hear the message, or misunderstanding of the language used are only a few of the barriers to communication. Like roadblocks on a highway, these barriers cause us to change directions when we are communicating or to stop communicating entirely.

Barriers may occur anytime during the communication process, and they may result from either environmental conditions such as excessive noise or unpleasant weather (these are called *external barriers*) or from personal distraction such as prejudice against the speaker or preoccupation with other ideas (*internal barriers*).

We have already seen what happens when your friend decodes a message differently than you encoded the stimulus. We can use diagrams to show other ways communication could be broken down between you and your friend during your canoeing adventure. Remember that although we are using spoken communication here to illustrate these ideas, the process applies equally to spoken or written communication. Can you think of ways a written message would break down in each of these situations?

In Diagram C you see the rock, interpret the stimulus as danger and yell, "Rock ahead." However, the sound of the rushing river prevents your partner from hearing you. Your message is not received.

Diagram C

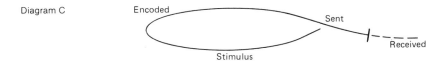

In Diagram D you see the rock and interpret the stimulus as danger, but a bear on the opposite shore distracts you and you forget to yell, "Rock ahead." You do not send the message.

Diagram D

In Diagram E you see the rock but you do not interpret the stimulus as danger so you don't mention the rock to your friend. Communication breaks down in the encoding.

Diagram E

Finally, you may not see the rock at all, so you do not receive the stimulus to send a message. In that case, the communication process would look like Diagram F.

Diagram F

Diagram B illustrates an internal barrier to communication. Your friend does not have the experience with rocks that you do and therefore does not interpret the stimulus as danger. Diagram C shows an external barrier to communication; the river (an environmental factor) is making too much noise for your friend to hear you. An external barrier is also present in Diagram D. The bear distracts you and you forget to send the message. In Diagram E an internal barrier prevents you from encoding the stimulus as danger. This internal barrier may be a reluctance to acknowledge the danger or some other factor which prevents you from encoding the rock as danger. In Diagram F, you may have been prevented from receiving the stimulus by either an external or an internal barrier. Your friend, sitting in front of you, may have blocked your view (external barrier), or you may have been preoccupied with your thoughts and tuned out your environment (internal barrier). From this description of the diagrams you can see that many factors may hinder communication.

Now let's look at Diagram A again. Remember, in this instance your friend decoded your message as danger and worked with you to avoid the rock. Because you and your friend shared the same interpretation, we say communication was completed.

However, this communication process can also be completed even when the receiver's response is not what the sender expects. Let's say, for example, that your partner decoded your message as danger but decided to hit the rock anyway. You and your partner shared the same experiences with rocks but your friend chose to act differently than you. It is important to remember that the communication process can be completed even when people react differently. You may understand a speaker's message perfectly, but you may choose to respond to that message differently than the speaker hoped you would.

The communication that occurs during political campaigns is a good example of this situation. You may understand perfectly well the reforms a candidate hopes to make in the social security system, but that understanding may become a reason for you *not* to vote for the candidate rather than to respond as the candidate had hoped. As long as you share an idea in common with the speaker (regardless of how you respond) the communication process is complete.

SIMILARITIES BETWEEN SPOKEN AND WRITTEN COMMUNICATION

This communication process applies equally to spoken and written communication. Whether you are writing a letter or making a telephone call, your reason for communicating begins with a stimulus, and the message is sent to people who act according to their individual interpretations.

Spoken and written communications have other similarities as well. Conversations, letters, formal talks, and reports all have a beginning, middle, and ending. The composing process may be lengthy, as in reports, or brief, as in many phone conversations, but the message is always introduced, discussed, and restated. In the following chapters we will discuss in detail how this three-step process can be applied to individual types of communication.

Whether you are speaking or writing, you should gather information about your topic. Make sure your facts are correct before you send your message. Apply logical thinking to situations requiring problem solving, and use effective argumentation when you want to persuade your audience.

Although you usually do not face your audience when you send a written message, audience analysis is as important in written as in spoken communication.

Find out as much as you can about your audience before you begin composing the message. Choose words and discussion details that relate to your audience. We will discuss audience analysis in detail in the sections on speaking and writing.

When we think of speaking and writing, we think of sending verbal signals in the form of written or spoken words, but our spoken and written messages are also conveyed through nonverbal signals. The way you stand, gesture, and look at your audience when you are talking sends nonverbal signals to your listeners. Similarly, the way you type your letters, use white space in a report, and spell are all nonverbal signals that send messages in written communication. You must be as aware of the nonverbal signals you send as you are of your verbal signals. For that reason, throughout this text we will concentrate on improving your nonverbal as well as your verbal communication skills.

DIFFERENCES BETWEEN SPOKEN
AND WRITTEN COMMUNICATION

Although the processes of written and spoken communication are similar, there are also some significant differences.

In spoken communication listeners and speakers interact more closely than they do in written communication. When you are talking, your listeners can say: "Wait a minute! I don't understand." When you send a letter, however, your readers cannot question you directly if your message is unclear.

Similarly, when you are talking and your listener's attention wanders, you can change your emphasis or modify your language to hold your listener's attention. You can even say, "Hey, listen to me!" When you send a letter, however, the written message must have enough impact to hold the reader's attention. If you lose that attention, you do not have a second chance to establish contact.

These differences may make you think that talking and listening are easier than writing and reading, but there are some additional factors to consider which tend to offset the differences we just discussed.

When you talk to a group of people, you set the pace of the discussion. The listener has limited control over how fast or slowly you present your ideas. You may talk too rapidly for the listener to follow everything you say; you may talk too slowly for the listener to maintain a constant interest in your discussion. Usually, listeners cannot choose the times when they will listen. They must receive the message as the speaker sends it. If they are hot, tired, or preoccupied, they cannot say, "I'll listen to this later when I feel better."

This factor can make the speaker's task difficult. You must be especially attuned to your listeners' needs and adapt the pace and timing of your message as much as possible to meet those needs.

Readers, on the other hand, can set their own pace. They can reread as often as they need in order to understand the message. If they are ill or worried, they can put the reading aside and pick it up again when they can concentrate better.

Awareness of these differences will help you send written and spoken messages more efficiently.

SUMMARY

Communication is an ongoing process involving both the sender and the receiver. When people communicate, they share ideas and experiences. This process is best described by a diagram developed by Wilbur Schramm[1] which shows communication as occurring when the "fields of experience" of the sender and receiver overlap.

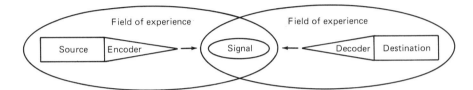

Both internal and external barriers can prevent the completion of this process. External barriers may be noise, discomfort, or other distractions that divert your attention or prevent you from hearing. Internal barriers may be prejudice against the speaker, the topic, or the occasion, anxiety, or other factors that cause receivers to close their minds to the communication situation.

Similarities and differences exist between written and oral communication. Some of the similarities are: (1) each has a beginning, middle, and ending, (2) each requires accurate information and audience analysis to be effective, and (3) each uses both verbal and nonverbal signals to complete the message.

One of the main differences between spoken and written communication is that readers set their own pace and timing whereas listeners must adapt to the pace and timing of the speaker.

REVIEW QUESTIONS

1. Summarize Schramm's communication model. Do you agree that we must share experiences in order to communicate? Use reasoning and examples to support your opinion.
2. Which do you think prevent communication more: internal or external barriers? Support your opinion with reasoning and examples.
3. What barriers to communication have you encountered today? How did you cope with those barriers?
4. What are some of the similarities between written and spoken communication? What are some of the differences? How do these similarities and differences affect the way you send a message?

ACTIVITIES

1. Recall a time when communication broke down between you and another person. Write a paragraph identifying the place in the process where your communication broke down. What barriers caused this breakdown? Be prepared to share this paragraph with your class.
2. Using the same situation you described in number 1, write a paragraph explaining how you could have prevented this communication breakdown. Be prepared to share this paragraph with your class.
3. Listen carefully to a conversation between two people (teacher/student, parent/child, husbana/wife, employer/employee). Diagram the communication process as you listen. Was communication complete? If not, where did it break down and what caused the breakdown?

PART I Preparing

SCENARIO

After three years in the Word Processing Department of Pillar Insurance, Theresa has recently been promoted to assistant supervisor. Her first assignment is to write a report.

"We have to decide how to make the best use of our word processors," Mrs. Wilson, word processing supervisor, tells her. "Right now all our word processors are in a central area. Employees bring their work to our area. But a lot of people think we should decentralize the word processing department. They want individual units placed in specific work areas.

"I'm meeting with an advisory committee to discuss decentralizing our department. Can you work up a report discussing the pros and cons of decentralization for me in time for that meeting?"

"Sure," Theresa says, eager to get started on her first assignment. "When do you need it?"

"The meeting is two weeks from today," Mrs. Wilson says. "I'll need the preliminary so I can look it over before the meeting."

Theresa draws in her breath sharply. "Two weeks from today," she says surprised. "That doesn't give me much time. I'll have to get started right away. I'll need some more information from you. When can we get together?"

"How long will it take?" Mrs. Wilson says, looking at her pocket calendar.

"At least an hour," Theresa tells her.

"I don't have any time until Friday afternoon," Mrs. Wilson says. "But that should be soon enough. You'll have a whole week to work up the report."

"Who else should I talk to?" Theresa asks.

"I'll leave that up to you," Mrs. Wilson says. "You're the assistant supervisor now."

As Mrs. Wilson leaves, Tom Kasper from the Claims Department sits down at Theresa's table.

"How's the new job going?" he says cordially.

"Oh, just fine," Theresa answers absent-mindedly. "I just got my first big assignment."

"Great," Tom says. "What's it on?"

"Decentralizing the word processing area," Theresa tells him.

"Sounds like a good idea," Tom says. "The boss has a word processor in his office. Why shouldn't we have one in our area?"

"Are you talking about decentralizing the Word Processing Department?" Jane asks as she joins them.

"What else does anyone talk about around here?" Tom says.

"What do you think we should do?" Theresa asks Jane.

Jane thinks for a minute before answering. When she does answer, she seems to have given the idea careful thought.

"I look at it this way," Jane says. "Either we decentralize the word processors

9

immediately or we'll have to lay off a lot of people in the spring. A centralized system is just too expensive. You have to spend so much time running downstairs with your typing that you never get anything done."

"In other words, you're saying that the centralized system has caused a decrease in production around here."

"I guess you could say that," Jane agreed hesitantly. "I'm not quite sure it's that simple, but. . . ." She stops talking as she sees Theresa stuffing her notes in her jacket pocket.

"Thanks a lot for the information," Theresa says happily. "It sure sounds like a centralized unit is inconvenient."

"You bet it's inconvenient," Tom adds. "You never know who's going to type your material. Some of the girls do good work and some don't. There's one girl in the pool whose brother has been fired from three different jobs in the last year. How can you expect a girl with a brother like that to do good work?"

From then on, whenever Theresa sits down next to someone, she asks the person about decentralizing the Word Processing Department. Then she tries to remember the people's responses until she can find a quiet minute to write down what they have said.

By Friday afternoon she has a pile of scraps of paper, each scrap with a few notes scribbled on it.

"Let's see," she thinks, as she looks over her notes. "I've talked to five people about decentralizing the word processor. That should be enough. I guess I'm ready to write this report.

Finding a quiet place to write is a problem, but by the next Friday she has something on paper. She types all weekend, and early Monday she turns the typed report into Mrs. Wilson.

"Thanks, Theresa," Mrs. Wilson says. "I'll look it over and get back to you before the meeting."

Here is Theresa's report:

```
     The purpose of this report is to ascertain the feasibility of
modifying our word processing system.  Currently we are utilizing a
centralized system, but numerous personnel in this company are of the
opinion that a decentralized system would be preferred.  They refer back
to the days when each office controlled its own affairs.  In this report,
the writer will define the methodology of utilizing a decentralized unit.
The writer will then compare the advantages of the centralized system
currently in use with the decentralized unit being proposed.

     In a decentralized system, the girls in the pool would be sent to
individual work areas.  Each girl would be given a screen and a keyboard.
Personnel would take copy to their girl for processing.  When she had run
it through, they could proof it immediately and send it on out.

     This would save personnel a lot of time.  Of course, the company
would save a tremendous amount of money because interoffice mail would be
reduced.

     It is apparent that a decentralized system will be more efficient to
utilize.  When one sends his material to a centralized unit, he does not
```

have the privilege of determining who will type it. We all know some of
the girls do better work than others.

The machines will also work better decentralized. Most of the
problems experienced by personnel result because of the centralized
system. A decentralized unit would keep the work load better controlled
and the assignments more manageable. Either we modify our approach to
include a decentralized system or we will have to lay off some workers
next year as a way of compensating for the inefficiency of the centralized
unit.

One must ask himself why this question should be deliberated.
Maynard Implements has always had a decentralized system and it works
fine for them.

Personnel must consider how they will be benefited by the change.
After all, the billing procedure has just been modified to better meet the
needs of Sales; therefore, the word processing system should be modified
to better meet personnel's needs. It's a good principle to keep
everything equal.

It has come to the writer's attention through research that most of
the personnel in this company want a decentralized system. Since everyone
prefers a decentralized system, it is the writer's judgment that the
centralized system should be replaced by a decentralized system.

If there are any noticeable errors in this report, it is because the
writer had limited time to prepare it.

DISCUSSION OF SCENARIO

What comments do you think Mrs. Wilson made about Theresa's report? Do you think she
took Theresa's report to the committee or asked her to rewrite it?

Before studying the introductory section on information gathering, logic, and word
choice, read the report again and indicate problems in these three areas. You can mark
the error on the report, then write a one-page evaluation explaining in detail specific problems
with Theresa's report.

Be sure to consider Theresa's use of logical reasoning and her choice of words.
As you evaluate the report, include comments about the research techniques she used to
gather information for the report. When you have finished your evaluation, compare it
with Mrs. Wilson's evaluation on page 12.

EVALUATION

Mrs. Wilson's comments point out three problems with Theresa's report.

First, she did not analyze the problem carefully, nor outline the criteria she would
use to evaluate the problem. You will remember she questioned people randomly when she

met them in the hall and recorded their casual observations as fact. As a result, she did not give her readers enough information to make a decision. "How can I decide without knowing the cost?" Mrs. Wilson asks.

This paragraph contains jargon, repetition, and wordiness.

negative connotation

What basis?

The purpose of this report is to (ascertain) the feasibility of modifying our word processing system. Currently we are (utilizing) a centralized system, but (numerous) personnel in this company are of the opinion that a decentralized system would be preferred. They (refer back) to the days when each office controlled its own affairs. In this report, the writer will define the (methodology) of (utilizing) a decentralized unit. The writer will then compare the advantages and disadvantages of the centralized system currently in use with the decentralized unit being proposed.

In a decentralized system, the girls in the pool would be sent to individual work areas. Each girl would be given a screen and a keyboard. Personnel would take a copy to (their) (girl) for processing. When she had run it through, they could proof it immediately and send it on out.

This would save personnel (a lot of time.) Of course, the company would save a (tremendous amount) of money because interoffice mail would be reduced.

It is apparent that a decentralized system will be more efficient to utilize. When one sends his material to a centralized unit, he does not have the privilege of determining who will type it. We all know some of the girls do better work than others.

The machines will also work better decentralized. Most of the problems experienced by personnel result because of the centralized system. A decentralized unit would keep the work load better controlled and the assignments more manageable. Either we modify our approach to include a decentralized system or we will have to lay off some workers next year as a way of compensating for the inefficiency of the centralized unit.

One must ask himself why this question should be deliberated. Maynard Implements has always had a decentralized system and it works fine for them.

Personnel must consider how they will be benefited by the change. After all, the billing procedure has just been modified to better meet the needs of Sales; therefore, the word processing system should be modified to better meet personnel's needs. It's a good principle to keep everything equal.

It has come to the writer's attention through research that most of the personnel in this company want a decentralized system. Since (everyone) prefers a decentralized system, it is the writer's judgment that the centralized system should be replaced by a decentralized system.

hasty generalization

generalizations

source?

shaky comparison

shaky comparison

Did you talk to everyone?

Second, Theresa does not evaluate the reasoning of the people she interviews. She repeats illogical reasoning and uses it to draw inaccurate conclusions that confuse the reader. When Jane said a centralized system is costly and would contribute to layoffs, Theresa did not ask her to support her statement with facts. Instead she inferred that the centralized system had caused a lack of production.

In the same way she did not question the faulty reasoning Tom used when he compared one of the typists to her brother and drew the conclusion that since the brother had been fired, the girl's work was also inadequate. Theresa did not identify faulty reasoning when she listened to people. As a result, she incorporated it in her report and caused Mrs. Wilson to ask, "What are you hinting at?"

Third, Theresa does not ask Mrs. Wilson who will be reading the report. Because Theresa writes in technical jargon—"define the methodology of utilizing a decentralized unit"—Mrs. Wilson worries that some readers from nontechnical areas will be confused. Also, some of her wording such as "Personnel would take a copy to their *girl* for processing," would insult many readers.

Theresa's word choice and reasoning skills need improvement, but her listening skills are also inefficient. She does not question the logical reasoning of any of the comments she hears, and when she is talking to Jane, she draws an illogical conclusion from her statement.

Theresa ignores all the techniques of skillful research and logical reasoning when preparing this report. She also ignores her audience and often chooses words that either confuse or insult them.

HOW WOULD YOU RATE YOURSELF ON THESE SKILLS?

Does Theresa's situation remind you of times when you could have reasoned more logically, expressed yourself more accurately, or researched a problem more carefully? Whether we speak or write our ideas, we must pay attention to our reasoning, word choice, and research techniques.

In the next three chapters we will discuss research techniques, logical reasoning, and word choice as they apply to spoken and written communication. As a pretest to this section on preparing, use the following rating scale to evaluate your comments about Theresa's report. After you have studied these three chapters, you will have a chance to think about Theresa's report again.

Rating Scale

Give yourself the points indicated for each of these items that you discussed in your evaluation.

1. Theresa's research techniques are haphazard. She talks to anyone who is convenient rather than finding authorities on the subject. She takes notes on scraps of paper without any clear organization, and she bases her entire argument on one source of information—personal interviews. (5)
2. She does not think through the problem first or decide on the area she should discuss in the paper. (5)
3. She does not listen critically to her sources. She repeats illogical reasoning:

". . . either we decentralize the word processors immediately or we'll have to lay off a lot of people in the spring." (5)

"There's one girl in the pool whose brother has been fired from three different jobs in the last year. How can you expect a girl with a brother like that to do good work?" (5)

4. She draws inaccurate inferences:

"In other words, you're saying that the centralized system has caused a decrease in production around here." (5)

Jane's statement that centralization will contribute to layoffs is not the same as Theresa's statement that it contributes to a general lack of production.

5. She uses illogical reasoning and hasty generalization in her report:

"numerous personnel in this company are of the opinion that"
(Theresa interviewed only five people) (5)

"We all know some of the girls do better work than others"
(Based on Tom's comment which Theresa takes at face value) (5)

"Most of the problems experienced"
(Not supported with detailed evidence) (5)

"Maynard Implements has always had a decentralized system"
(On what basis does Theresa compare Maynard Implements with Pillar Insurance?) (5)

"The billing procedure has just been modified . . . [so] the word processing system should be modified"
(Another shaky comparison) (5)

"Everyone prefers a decentralized system"
(Theresa talked to only five people) (5)

6. Her word choice is poor.
   Elaborate wording such as: (5)

ascertain
feasibility
utilize
it is apparent
modify our approach
one must ask himself

   Vague wording and redundancies: (5)

machines will work better
refer back

   Negative connotations: (5)

their girl

Total: 70 points

65–70: Excellent
60–65: Very good
53–60: Good

2

GATHERING INFORMATION

Writing comes more easily if you have something to say.
Sholem Asch

After studying this chapter you should understand how to gather information from the following sources:
1. Library, including how to take notes on printed material
2. Interviewing
3. Observation
4. Personal experience

"What can I write about?" "What should I say?" are often the first questions we ask ourselves when we have to write a report or talk to a group. In the same way, when we are reading a report or listening to a talk, we evaluate the content with comments like: "She really knew what she was talking about; she backed up all her opinions with concrete information" or "This report is full of details; the writer really knows his subject."

A major portion of the time you spend in the writing process should be taken up with research and planning. The same emphasis holds true when you are preparing a talk. Gathering materials is a vital part of preparing to communicate. If Theresa (in our opening scenario) had researched her topic thoroughly, she would have written a more effective report. Readers and listeners will judge the worth of your ideas by how accurately you relay supportive details, statistics, examples, quotations, and other types of information. When preparing to present your ideas, you should plan to research the topic carefully. Although some people seem to think of research as a "waste of time," it can make other parts of the communication process easier. Thorough research will give you many ideas and concrete information. This background will help you feel confident when you write or talk about your topic.

Because researching is an important part of the communication process, we will discuss in detail four sources for gathering information: library and other printed materials, interviews, observation, and personal experience. For clarity we will follow one topic—dressing for success in the business world—and will use examples related to that topic throughout the chapter.

LIBRARY SOURCES

When confronted with a topic to research, we usually think first of the library. With its collection of books, magazines, films, and other recorded and printed media, it is an excellent place to begin gathering information.

Card Catalog

Your first stop will probably be the card catalog. Here all the books, records, films, filmstrips, and video tapes collected in the library are listed in three ways: by subject, by author, and by title. You will probably look under the subject for your report (clothing, for example) unless you are familiar with a particular book on the subject or a person who has written a lot about your topic.

Figure 2-1 contains examples of entries found in the card catalog for *Success Book* by Barbara Coffey. The first one is a subject card. Notice the subject "clothing and dress" is printed in capitals to set it apart from the rest of the information. The capital letters tell you that it is the subject and not the title of the source. You can see that the information on each card is the same, but the heading for each card is different; the title card begins with the book's title, and the author card begins with the book's author. As a result, you can find the book easily in any one of the three sections of your library's card catalog.

Each card in the card catalog will give a brief description of the source it represents. Read this description carefully. After reading the description, you have to try to decide whether the book will be helpful to you. In our example, "effective dressing on the job" tells you that part of the book discusses the way to dress for on-the-job success.

If you think the book has information you can use, write the entire call number (the number in the upper-left hand corner of the card) and the title down on a slip of paper so you can find the book in the stacks later. When you are reading the description, remember to take note of the copyright date. Generally, you will want

Figure 2-1

646.34   CLOTHING AND DRESS
C654   Coffey, Barbara
           Success book: effective dressing on the job,
      at home, in your community, elsewhere/by Barbara
      Coffey, and the Editors of Glamour.—New York:
      Simon and Schuster, c 1979.
          190 p.: ill.

Subject card

646.34   Coffey, Barbara
C654   Success book: effective dressing on the job,
      at home, in your community, elsewhere/by Barbara
      Coffey, and the Editors of Glamour.—New York:
      Simon and Schuster, c 1979.
          190 p.: ill.

Author card

646.34   Success book
C654   Coffey, Barbara
      Success book: effective dressing on the job,
      at home, in your community, elsewhere/by Barbara
      Coffey, and the editors of Glamour.—New York:
      Simon and Schuster, c 1979.
          190 p.: ill.

Title card

to use material that goes back no more than five years. Exceptions to this are books that give good background or historical material. When you are using sources older than five years, be sure to validate everything with current material so you have the most up-to-date information possible.

Guides to Magazines

Another important library source is the *Reader's Guide,* which is a listing of magazine articles. Updated ten times each year, this guide indexes many of the most popular magazines published in the United States. Look under subject headings to find articles on your topic.

For our topic, "Dressing for success in the business world," we first look under "Clothing and dress" in the March 1982–February 1983 guide (Figure 2–2). Here all the articles published on the subject during that time are listed. Read through the list, noting those articles that pertain to your subject.

Clooney, Rosemary
  Clooney sings Porter. P. Reilly. il por Stereo Rev 47:100 O '82 •
  Rosemary Clooney. S. Pileggi. il pors People Wkly 18:119-20+ D 13 '82 •
Clore, Alan
  When a high roller is left holding the bag. Bus Week p49+ O 25 '82 •
Close, Bill
  Keeping calm in a crisis at KOOL-TV, anchorman Bill Close persuades an angry gunman not to turn killer. D. Sheff. il pors People Wkly 17:80-1 Je 28 '82 •
Close, Glenn
  Garp's mom Glenn Close handsprings to stardom. M. Shindler. il pors People Wkly 18:138-9 O 25 '82 •
  It's time for Glenn Close. W. Wolf. il por N Y 15:50-1 Ag 2 '82 •
Close-up on the Kirov [television program] See Television program reviews—Single works
Close-up photography. See Photography, Close-up
Closed circuit television. See Television, closed circuit
Closed-end funds. See Investment trusts
Closets
  Cedar closet for out-of-season clothes. W. J. Hawkins. il Pop Sci 220:119 Ap '82
  A closet full of clothes and nothing to wear. il Mademoiselle 88:166-7+ My '82
  How to line your closet with cedar. R. Spangler. il Pop Mech 157:158-9 Ap '82
  Spring cleanout. il Teen 26:44 Ap '82
  Yes, it's possible. A teen-ager's closet is neat. il Sunset 169:130 N '82

Equipment
  Getting organized! il Redbook 158:100-1 Ap '82
  Mail-order closet organizers. K. Brookhouser. il Better Homes Gard 60:66+ Ap '82
  Shaped-up closets. il Better Homes Gard 60:96 Je '82
Closing of schools. See High schools—Closing; Public schools—Closing
Clotfelter, James
  Why peace movements fail. Christ Century 99:790-2 Jl 21-28 '82
Clothes dryers
  Buying a washer and dryer. M. Cubisino. Work Woman 7:132-3 Ap '82
  Clothes dryers. il Consum Rep 47:31-7 Ja '82

Maintenance and repair
  Can you give the GE dryer a Quick Fix? il Consum Rep 47:33 Ja '82
Clothes pins. See Clothespins
Clothes racks
  Personalized coat racks. M. Gregory. il Workbench 38:116-17 Ja/F '82
Clotheslines

Anecdotes, facetiae, satire, etc.
  Requiem for the washline. D. S. Pizano. il World Press Rev 29:36 Ap '82
Clothespins
  Magic to make with clothespins [home made clowns, soldiers and ballerinas] il McCalls 110:116-17 D '82
Clothing, Cold weather
  See also
  Ear muffs

  Button up your overcoat. B. P. Quinby. il Mademoiselle 88:65 Ja '82
  Cold comfort. N. A. Bond, Jr. il Technol Rev 85:78 Jl '82
  Cold weather cruising gear—on ice. S. Mitchell. il Mot Boat Sail 150:36-9 N '82
  Fine new fibers fight the cold. B. McKeown. il Pop Mech 158:108-9+ O '82
  Kit it together [outdoor clothing] L. Bignami. il Creat Crafts 8:32-6 O '82
  Thermal insulating capabilities of outdoor clothing materials. W. C. Kaufman and others. bibl f il Science 215:690-1 F 5 '82
  Warm winter hunts. S. Netherby. il Field Stream 87:103-6 N '82
  Winter's on the way (we think) [ed. by Dodi Schultz] V. E. Pomeranz. il Parents 57:102 O '82
Clothing, Protective
  See also
  Arms and armor
  Clothing, Cold weather
  Clothing, Waterproof
  Helmets

  Make a pair of brush-buster britches. B. Mathson. il Mother Earth News 76:86 Jl/Ag '82
Clothing, Secondhand
  See also
  Clothing stores

  Vintage passion... il Vogue 172:452+ S '82
Clothing, Waterproof
  Accessories: rainsuits [motorcyclists' gear] B. Buzzelli. il Cycle 33:75-80+ Ap '82
  Wet suits. S. Netherby. il Field Stream 86:58+ Mr '82

Clothing and dress
  See also
  Aprons
  Bathing suits
  Clothing industry
  Clothing stores
  Collars
  Costume
  Dress accessories
  Fashion
  Fashion designers
  Fashion shows
  Footwear
  Foundation garments
  Fur coats, wraps, etc.
  Hats
  Headgear
  Hosiery
  Kimonos
  Leather garments
  Models (Persons)
  Neckties
  Pants
  Scarves
  Sewing
  Shirts
  Sleepwear
  Sweaters
  Tailoring
  Vests

  Are you still dressing for your mother? J. Thurman. Mademoiselle 88:244 S '82
  Booty from the boys' department [clothes for women] il Glamour 80:46 Ag '82
  Cameleon clothing. S. Wood. il Mother Earth News 74:112 Mr/Ap '82
  Clothes that are going places [traveling clothes] il pors Harpers Bazaar 115:138-41 F '82
  Cruising chic [pareos] S. Mitchell. il Mot Boat Sail 149:58-61 My '82
  Dos & don'ts. See issues of Glamour
  Dressing for your office party. il Glamour 80:66+ D '82
  ✓ Dressing on the job [black women] il Essence 12:104-13 Mr '82
  Experts' views on shopping [ed. by J. Weir] il Vogue 172:239+ F '82
  ✓ Fall fashion [businesswomen] il Work Woman 7:104-9 O '82
  Fashion questions. See issues of Glamour
  Fashion resolutions. il Glamour 80:110-17 Ja '82
  Get yourself in shipshape! il Teen 26:61-75 Ap '82
  ✓ A Glamour special report: clothes and clout—some real-life stories [business clothes] il Glamour 80:240-7 O '82
  Good looks. See issues of McCall's
  Heat wave fashion. il Ladies Home J 99:90-1+ Jl '82
  How to dress rich—even if you're not. A. Meyer and C. Pierre. il Mademoiselle 88:109-17 O '82
  How to hide your figure flaws even in summer clothes. il Ladies Home J 99:59-62 Je '82
  How to manage a fashion budget: what to splurge on, what to save on. M. Lynch. il Ladies Home J 99:125-8 Mr '82
  How to stretch your fashion dollar. S. Anawalt. Ladies Home J 99:131-3 Mr '82
  ✓ Image building for execs. il Work Woman 7:116-18 My '82
  Keep your cool! [summer clothes] il Seventeen 41:10 Jl '82
  ✓ Making a statement [black businesswomen] E. Pattner and J. Paris-Chitanvis. il Work Woman 7:64-7 Jl '82
  The mini strides back into style. B. Hurowitz. il Macleans 95:48-9 Ap 12 '82
  Nobody's perfect. See issues of Glamour
  Nobody's perfect [how to hide flaws in your figure] il Harpers Bazaar 115:240-51 My '82
  P.M.—women's choices [evening clothes] il Vogue 172:312+ Mr '82
  Put on a personal touch! il Teen 26:51-7 F '82
  Ready to wear. J. Thurman. See issues of Mademoiselle
  ✓ Ready-to-wear [businesswomen] il Work Woman 7:108 N '82
  Return of the mini. M. Demarest. il Time 119:66-7 Mr 22 '82
  Short-circuiting the short skirt. C. Donovan. il N Y Times Mag p94-5+ Ap 25 '82
  Skirts, the American way [New York showings of fall and winter clothing] L. Langway. il Newsweek 99:90-1 My 3 '82
  Success for the dress. J. Weir. il N Y Times Mag p86+ F 7 '82
  A summer cover-up for people who hate to sew [Polynesian pareu] il Mother Earth News 75:132-3 My/Je '82
  The super wardrobe [mix and match clothes] E. Cho. il Ladies Home J 99:102-5 N '82
  The thighs have it, as Betsey Johnson designs a return to mini madness. L. Marx. il por People Wkly 18:75-8 Ag 30 '82
  This summer's best looks. M. Lynch. il Ladies Home J 99:84-7 My '82

Figure 2-2 In this example references have been checked so that you can see them easily.

Clothing and dress—*Continued*
Update your looks. il Teen 26:66-73 S '82
What fashion changes tell us about the U.S.
L. D. Maloney. il U S News World Rep 93:
60-1 O 11 '82
What went wrong here? How to make it right.
See issues of Mademoiselle
When did you start wearing your self? [personal style] M. Peacock. il por s Ms 11:53-4+
Jl/Ag '82
Why you have nothing to wear [excerpt from
Clothes wise] A. Meyer and C. Pierre. il Mademoiselle 88:160-5 My '82
A working woman's guide to successful dress.
C. Tuhy. il Money 11:144-6+ Ap '82
Wrap-and-go fashion. il Good Housekeep 195:126-
7+ Jl '82

Care
See also
Leather garments—Care

Caring for holiday wear. Teen 26:48 D '82

Celebrities
The best-dressed actresses in all-star black. il
Harpers Bazaar 115:160-9 My '82
Big names in jeans—not the famous designers,
but famous wearers. il Mademoiselle 88:119-23
Je '82
For better or worse, these 30 people change our
styles. il People Wkly 18:38-48 S 20 '82
Who lusts after celebrity shoes? These are the
kinds that buy men's soles (and women's
too). K. Cassill. il People Wkly 17:34-5 F 8
'82

Children
See also
Chesebrough-Pond's Inc. Health-Tex Division
Children's Place (Firm)

Back to school in style. A. Skinner. il N Y
Times Mag p44-9 Ag 22 '82
Booty from the boys' department [clothes for
women] il Glamour 80:46 Ag '82
Classic clothes you can sew [children's holiday
wear] K. Benton. il Parents 57:152+ N '82
Winter's on the way (we think) [ed. by Dodi
Schultz] V. E. Pomeranz. il Parents 57:102
O '82

Dyeing
See Dyes and dyeing

History
Points of origin. M. Olmert. il Smithsonian 13:
130+ Je '82
See also
Bibs

Infants
Chesebrough-Pond's Inc. Health-Tex Division
Diapers

For the baby who has everything [tuxedos] il
Newsweek 100:65 Ag 23 '82

Maternity clothes
Dresses perfect for a pregnant princess and you,
too. L. MacCallum. il Glamour 80:50 Ap '82
From her favorite designers, a maternity wardrobe for mother-to-be Diana. A. Parkinson.
il por Good Housekeep 194:132-3+ Mr '82
Great looks for a total pregnancy wardrobe.
il Glamour 80:266 S '82
Stepping out with my baby. J. Cocks. il Time
119:56-7 F 22 '82

Men
See also
Coats
Reagan, Ronald—Clothing and dress
Sweaters
Underwear

Executive suit [Savile Row tailors] L. Minard.
Forbes 129:156-7+ My 24 '82
How to dress for your body type. il Esquire
98:56-7 O '82
A man's guide to dressing well for business.
C. J. Rolo. il Money 11:84-5+ F '82
A preview of next fall. J. Duka. il N Y Times
Mag p98-103 My 2 '82
Report from Europe: breaking with tradition.
K. Probst. il N Y Times Mag p56-9+ Ag 29
'82
The seersucker suit. J. Berendt. il Esquire 98:30
Ag '82
Tampering with the traditional [Italian designs]
C. Churchward. il N Y Times Mag p68-70 Ja
17 '82
The wing collar. J. Berendt. il Esquire 97:32
Mr '82

Anecdotes, facetiae, satire, etc.

Uncivil liberties [tuxedos] C. Trillin. il Nation
236:8 Ja 1-8 '83
Upper class blues. W. Hamilton. Harpers 264:64
Mr '82

Psychological aspects
Clothes make the lineup [research by Rod
Lindsay and Harold Wallbridge] H. Goodman.
il Psychol Today 16:90 D '82
Clothes power. H. Dienstfrey. il Psychol Today
16:68-73 D '82
Designer jeans—a sign of insecurity? [views of
Chaytor D. Mason] il USA Today 110:12 Ap
'82

Size
How the right suit can shape your body image.
il Redbook 159:94-7 S '82
A short story [businesswomen] E. Pattner and
A. Kelvin. il Work Woman 7:82-5 F '82
Taller-than-ever spring look-ahead. il Harpers
Bazaar 115:122-9 F '82
You don't have to change your body to look
thinner, shapelier—simply changing the fit of
your clothes can make a difference [excerpt
from Great looks] P. Swift and M. Mulherne.
il Mademoiselle 88:220 Ag '82

Sports clothes
See also
Needlecraft (Firm)
Uniforms, Sports

Accessories: rainsuits [motorcyclists' gear] B.
Buzzelli. il Cycle 33:75-80+ Ag '82
Camping—weather or not. S. Curtis. Field Stream
87:27+ My '82
Cold weather cruising gear—on ice. S. Mitchell.
il Mot Boat Sail 150:36-9 N '82
Fashion in action! energy, vitality, adventure!
il Harpers Bazaar 115:66-73 Jl '82
Italians are in the game to win [tennis wear]
R. DiGennaro. il N Y Times Mag p30-1 Jl
'82
Kit it together [outdoor clothing] L. Bignami.
il Creat Crafts 8:32-6 O '82
Making a statement [ski clothes] G. Lichtenstein. il Skiing 35:210+ N '82
See-Me Vests [for motorcyclists] il Cycle 33:150
Mr '82
Skiwear [cont] H. Brooks. il Skiing 35:143-7
S; 130-3 O; 168-71 N; 115-17 D '82
The tennis racket [Italian tenniswear manufacturers] B. Kanner. il N Y 15:18+ S 6 '82
The tennis sweater. J. Berendt. il Esquire 97:
38 Ap '82
Warm winter hunts. S. Netherby. il Field Stream
87:103-6 N '82
What's behind the high cost of Italian tennis
wear? D. Lott. il World Tennis 29:32-4 My
'82

Students
Dress codes make a comeback. il Ladies Home J
99:102 S '82

Work clothes
Gifts that will dress them for the job. il Sunset
169:92 D '82

Youth
Clothing and the preadolescent. J. P. Comer.
il Parents 57:88 Ja '82

Clothing industry
See also
Amalgamated Clothing and Textile Workers
Union
Anne Klein and Company
Belle France (Firm)
Carole Little for Saint-Tropez West (Firm)
CB Sports (Firm)
Chesebrough-Pond's Inc. Health-Tex Division
Dan River Inc.
French Creek Sheep & Wool Co.
Harbour Knits (Firm)
Hart Schaffner & Marx
International Ladies' Garment Workers' Union
Jonathan Logan Inc.
Levi Strauss & Co.
Manhattan Industries, Inc.
Needlecraft (Firm)
Oxford Industries, Inc.
Palm Beach Incorporated
Phillips-Van Heusen Corp.
Puritan Fashions Corp.
Tailors
Underwear industry
V. F. Corp.
Warnaco Inc.

Her classy clothes for kids make Florence
Eiseman a perennial star under the Christmas
tree. B. K. Mills. il por People Wkly 18:154-5
D 20 '82
Lookout [swimwear designer D. Weiss] il por s
People Wkly 17:116-17 My 24 '82
No one needs to be shiftless this summer, thanks
to Lilly Pulitzer of Palm Beach. L. Marx. il
por s People Wkly 17:45-6 Je 7 '82

Acquisitions and mergers
"I see undervalued assets" [Limited Stores acquisition of Lane Bryant] B. Gallanis. il por
Forbes 130:45 Ag 2 '82
Limited Inc.: expanding its position to serve
the Rubenesque woman. il Bus Week p56+ N
22 '82

For help in understanding the listings, use the brief explanation in the front of any *Reader's Guide* issue. Information in each listing for an article includes:

(Title of article)

Making a statement   [black businesswomen]

(Author)   illustration

E. Pattner and J. Paris-Chitanvis.   il

(Magazine)

Work Woman   7:64-7   J1   '82

(volume) (pages) (month) (year)

When you find articles you think will be important to your research, write down the name and date of the magazine (libraries usually have special forms for this purpose) and request the magazine from the librarian. You should also record the page number of the article, because this information will help you find the article more easily when you have the magazine. If your library does not have the magazine you need, the librarian can sometimes request it for you through an interlibrary loan service.

Other magazine guides are also available in most libraries. The *Education Index* and the *Business Periodicals Index* are organized like the *Reader's Guide,* but they include education, business, or technology articles.

Figure 2–3 shows the listings on our topic in the *Business Periodicals Index.* First we look under "Clothing and dress" as we did in the *Reader's Guide.* One article, "Man's guide to dressing well for business," seems to fit our topic. Then we return to the "see also" listing. Here one topic—Executives—Clothing and dress—is a good lead. Turning to that heading (Figure 2–4), we find two articles that pertain to our topic: "Dressing for Success: how do security managers measure up?" and "Man's guide to dressing well for business."

Other Indexes

Another excellent library resource is the vertical file. This is a collection of newspaper clippings and pamphlets, usually organized by subject in a series of file drawers. The vertical file is a good source of current materials and materials of local importance.

Your library should also have indexes for some state and national newspapers and magazines of wide distribution, such as the *New York Times Index.* You can use these newspaper and magazine indexes just as you use the more familiar magazine indexes.

CLOTHING and dress
See also
Coats
Department stores—Dress departments
Executives—Clothing and dress
Fashion
Jeans (clothing)
Sportswear
Tariff—United States—Clothing
Underwear
Uniforms
Used clothing

Silver linings: tailors turn men off, but suit women just fine. G. Gray. Can Bus 54:17-18 Jl '81
Soft goods: footwear ahead but undies show style. Prog Grocer 61:68+ Ja '82
Success begins with the way you dress. J. Gray, Jr. Super Mgt 27:2-8 F '82

Children
See also
Department stores—Children's departments
Golf is boring, anyway [Children's Place] L. Rohmann. Forbes 129:104-5 F 1 '82

Men
See also
Department stores—Men's departments
Shirts
Cycles of men's wear. H. Bragman and others. Adv Age 52 sec2:S 12 S 14 '81
Esquire binds in its fashion guide. S. Emmrich. Adv Age 53:40 Mr 15 '82
✓ Man's guide to dressing well for business. C. J. Rolo. il Money 11:84-5+ F '82
Selling menswear in Paris with a French accent. R. Hamilton. il Bus Am 5:24-5 Ap '82
Special sizes for special men: big! L. A. Spalding. il Stores 63:23-4+ Jl '81
Suiting up in Hongkong. A. Conti. Inst Invest 15:25-6 O '81

Size
Petite sportswear: s-o-o-o- big! M. Ondovcsik. il Stores 63:20-3+ O '81
Small clothes are selling big. Bus W p 152+ N 16 '81

CLOTHING factories

Employees
See Garment workers
CLOTHING industry
See also
Garfinckel, Brooks, Brothers, Miller & Rhoads, Inc.
Genesco, Inc.
Hart Schaffner & Marx
Lane Bryant, Inc.
Levi Strauss & Company
Oshkosh B'Gosh, Inc.
Salant Corporation
Tailors and tailoring
Warnaco, Inc.

Apparel industry need: more textile knowledge. F. Fortess. Textile Ind 145:91+ F '81
Awareness in the textile-apparel interface. F. Fortess. Textile Ind 145:78+ O '81
Marcade: not only a new name, but a total overhaul of Unishops. Bus W p83+ S 21 '81
Textile snags: apparel productivity. L. E. Seidel. Textile Ind 145:72+ S '81

Advertising
Buttoning up the shirt market with television [Arrow] R. Clark. Broadcasting 101:24 Ag 17 '81
Crazy Horse dresses up for first effort. P. Sloan. il Adv Age 52:55 O 5 '81
Fashion marketing [special report] Adv Age 52 sec2:S 1-S 19 S 14 '81
Hirsh, Fisher reunion near? P. Sloan. Adv Age 52:3+ O 26 '81
Jeans stretch across Europe: but the right advertising approach creates a dilemma. A. Michalowska. il Adv Age 53 sec2:M2-M3 Ap 12 '82
Kids' clothes-buying role a marketer's dilemma. P. Sloan. il Adv Age 53:24 Ap 5 '82
Levi zipping up world image. D. Chase and E. Bacot. Adv Age 52:34+ S 14 '81
Retail and fashion advertising's influence on television ads. J. Myers. Broadcasting 102:24 Ap 19 '82
Style and You split Formfit. Ayer. P. Sloan. Adv Age 52:98 N 2 '81

Communication systems
Computerized PBX helps I. Magnin maintains its touch of class image. il Comms N 18:36-7 Jl '81

Exhibitions
Selling menswear in Paris with a French accent. R. Hamilton. il Bus Am 5:24-5 Ap 19 '82
Textile-apparel interface at Bobbin Show 81 [Atlanta] F. Fortess. Textile Ind 145:58+ D '81

Export-import trade
See also
Tariff—United States—Clothing
Linkages: missing link in world competitiveness. R. I. Miller. Textile World 132:38+ F '82
US apparel exporters go south, explore growing Latin markets. R. S. Edwards. Bus Am 5:12-13 Ja 11 '82

Finance
Cloak and suit: the strange case of Donnkenny. M. Brody. Barrons 62:13+ Ap 5 '82

Management
Jordach's new executive look. Bus W p 121-2 N 2 '81
Manhattan Industries: saving its shirt with higher-priced apparel. Bus W p 117-18 Ag 17 '81

Marketing
Can Levi's get back into jeans saddle? J. Pendleton. il Adv Age 53:4 F 15 '82
Fashion marketing [special report] Adv Age 52 sec2:S 1-S 19 S 14 '81
Frayed Palm Beach tries to patch itself up. Bus W p 161+ My 24 '82
Great jeans jitters. M. Blakstad and G. Foster. il Mgt Today p67-73+ My '81
How a jeans vendor is responding to customers' new timing needs: ship fresh, fast! [Sasson] Stores 64:23 Ap '82
It's back to basics for Levi's. Bus W p77-8 Mr 8 '82
New sweet bedtime story: sleepwear. L. G. Berliner. il Stores 63:20-9 N '81
Resilient Raab charts growth course for Hook. P. Sloan. il Adv Age 53:4+ My 10 '82
Small clothes are selling big. Bus W p 152+ N 16 '81
Strategies for merchandising tailored clothing [sports coats] R. DeGennaro. Stores 64:66-70 Ja '82
Translating consumer shifts. L. E. Seidel. il tab Textile Ind 145:44-5 Ap '81
Woolrich weaves style with tradition. S. Mintz. Sales & Mkt Mgt 127:40-2 O 12 '81

Securities
Big brand era: so sales, earnings of Warnaco are picking up. J. Greenwald. Barrons 61:33+ Ag 31 '81
Designer look: it's given Oxford Industries stylish operating results. M. Gordon. tab Barrons 62:40-1 Ja 18 '82
Jeans and things: VF Corp. has fashioned a stylish growth record. M. Gordon. tab Barrons 61:34-5 Ag 17 '81
Low-cost kid on the block: Minnesota Fabrics changes its image and gains yardage. J. Greenwald. tab Barrons 61:64-6 D 7 '81
Perry Ellis to Frank Masandrea: high fashion pays off for Manhattan Industries. Barrons 62:62-4 My 10 '82
Rags to riches. C. Davenport. Barrons 61:9+ D 14 '81
Skirting the slump: Russ Togs, shunning fads in apparel lines, looks for record year. J. Kennedy. tab Barrons 61:45+ Ag 10 '81
Sporting a new look: Cluett, Peabody cashes in on middle of the road fashions. J. Greenwald. tab Barrons 62:42-3 Mr 15 '82
Why apparel stocks are in style. A. L. Morner. Fortune 104:113+ Ag 24 '81

Statistics
Apparel. See issues of Survey of Current Business; section Current business statistics
Apparel [Forbes yardstick, 1981] J. A. Byrne. il Forbes 129:216-17 Ja 4 '82
Textile/apparel. Ind W 212:55 Mr 22 '82

Suits and calms
Legal woes hit Bonjour. P. Sloan. Adv Age 52:3+ Ag 24 '81

Canada
Blue-collar couturier [Work Warehouse, Canada] S. Zwarun. il Can Bus 54:52-6+ S '81
Hustlers of the bottom line [jeans] W. Collins. il Can Bus 54:78-82 O '81
Silver linings: tailors turn men off, but suit women just fine. G. Gray. Can Bus 54:17-18 Jl '81

Europe, Western
Cycles of men's wear. H. Bragman and others. Adv Age 52 sec2:S 12 S 14 '81
It's a question of style. il Adv Age 52 sec2:S2+ S 14 '81

Figure 2-3 In this example references have been checked so that you can see them easily.
Source: *Business Periodicals Index*. Copyright © 1981, 1982, 1983 by the H. W. Wilson Company. Material reproduced by permission of the publisher.

EXECUTIVES—Attitudes—*Continued*
Plateaued versus nonplateaued managers: career patterns, attitudes, and path potential. J. F. Veiga. bibl(p576-8) tabs Acad Mgt J 24: 566-78 S '81
Rating the gurus of Wall Street. M. Much. Ind W 211:75-6+ O 19 '81
Singing the small business blues. Mgt R 70:56 Je
Still for free trade—but with pressure on Japan [Harris poll] Bus W p 13 My 3 '82
Survey reveals growing interest among managers in phased retirement. Mgt R 71:34-5 Ja '82
Top executives don't escape inflation, either. Ind W 209:90 Je 1 '81
Unreasonableness, coupled with the ability to dream, may be necessary attributes of the really effective, dynamic administrator. D. B. Norris. Adm Mgt 42:101 N '81
What men are saying about women in business. A. S. Baron. Bus Horizons 25:10-14 Ja/F '82
Will he—or won't he—work with a female manager? A. S. Baron and K. Abrahamsen. Mgt R 70:48-53 N '81

Certification

Bill Kinney, CAM—profile of progressive management. L. Pilla. Mgt World 10:18-20 N '81

Clothing and dress

Dressing for success: how do security managers measure up? Sec Mgt 25:12-13+ Ag '81
Executive suit. L. Minard. il Forbes 129:156-7+ My 24 '82
Man's guide of dressing well for business. C. J. Rolo. il Money 11:84-5+ F '82

Compensation

See Executives—Salaries, pensions, etc.

Demotion

Falling superstars. F. R. Beaudine. Nations Bus 69:64-5 S '81

Employment contracts

See also
Executives, Dismissal of
Surge in executive job contracts. J. Perham. Duns Bus M 118:86-8 O '81; Same cond. Compens R 14 no2:68-71 '82

Expenses

See Expense accounts

Financial counseling services

See Financial services

Foreign assignments

Attitudes of host-country organizations toward MNC's staffing policies: a cross-country and cross-industry analysis. Y. Zeira and M. Dania. tab Mgt Int R 21 no2:38-47 '81
Can your marriage survive an overseas transfer? P. Berlin. Int Mgt 37:45 F '82
Global gamesmanship: how the expatriate manager copes with cultural differences. T. P. Cullen. Cornell Hotel & Restau Adm Q 22:18-24 N '81
How I learned to love the Middle East. J. R. Arbose. il Int Mgt 36:27-9 D '81
How to pick expatriates. C. Raffael. Mgt Today p58-61+ Ap '82
Influence of expatriate nationality and regional location of the overseas subsidiary on participative decision making. E. L. Miller and others. bibl tabs Mgt Int R 21 no3:31-46 '81
Mutual perception of managerial performance and style in multinational subsidiaries. B. W. Stening and others. bibl tabs J Occupa Psychol 54:255-63 D '81
Nigeria tops cost league for expatriates. tab Int Mgt 36:4 My '81
Repatriation: an ending and a beginning. D. W. Kendall. map Bus Horizons 24:21-5 N/D '81
Selection and training of personnel for overseas assignments. R. L. Tung. bibl tabs Columbia J World Bus 16:68-78 Spr '81

Health and safety

Away from it all. J. Walsh. Director 34:32-3 Ap '82
Beyond Freud: widening choices in executive mental health. Bus W p 128-9+ S 28 '81
Coping with crime. Mgt R 70:6 My '81
Coronary comebacks: executives with heart. B. Horovitz. Ind W 211:72-6 O 5 '81
Executive fitness: shape up [special report] il Sales & Mkt Mgt 126:53-86 My 18 '81
Executive health: fitness counselling at work keeps executives trim. Int Mgt 36:47 My '81
Executive health [special report] Director 33: 103-8 Ap '81
Executive stress and you. J. L. Hayes. Sec Mgt 26:16-17 Ja '82

Health begins at home. N. Tyrer. Director 34: 70+ Mr '82
Is blubber blunting your career? R. Whitehead. Ind W 210:49-50 Ag 24 '81
Looking out for the executive alcoholic. W. Kiechel, 3d. Fortune 105:117-18+ Ja 11 '82
Male menopause—a real condition or just a myth? D. Delvin. Int Mgt 36:47 Je '81
Many US executives fear kidnapping, other crimes. Int Mgt 36:3 Jl '81
Obesity: an obstacle to managerial success [interview with M. Winick] S. Auerbach. Comp Decisions 14:166+ Ja '82
Preventing executive disorders. D. Norfolk. Mgt Today p37+ Ap '82
Putting prevention before diagnosis in the company medical. A. Melhuish. Int Mgt 36:39 Jl '81
Super clinics—meccas for executives. B. S. Moskal. il Ind W 210:4-5+ S 21 '81
Terminal tempers and office hassles. T. G. Harris. Ind W 212:19 F 22 '82
What the boardroom needs to know [director's health] H. B. Wright. Director 34:68-9 Mr '82
What the doctors say about stress. M. E. Miller. Super Mgt 26:35-9 N '81
When executives burn out [Canada] R. Levinson. Can Banker & ICB R 88:52-8 D '81

Kidnapping

See Kidnapping

Loyalty

See Organizational loyalty

Pensions

See Executives—Salaries, pensions, etc.

Personality

See Executives—Psychology

Press relations

Are you ready to face 60 minutes? B. Hunter. Ind W 212:74-6 Mr 8 '82
External pressures on the CEO: worse than an Excedrin headache. D. H. Simon. Pub Rel Q 26:9-12 Wint '81/'82
How to deal with the press when times are troubled. Sav & Loan N 102:102-3+ Ag '81
Meeting the press. Mgt R 70:7 Je '81
Preparing for a broadcast appearance. M. D. Meeske. Pers J 60:686-7 S '81
Showtime for the CEO. R. Poe. Across the Bd 18:39-45+ D '81

Promotion

See Promotions

Psychology

Burnout: a real threat to human resources managers. O. L. Niehouse. Pers 58:25-32 S-O '81
Career success and personal failure: alienation in professionals and managers. A. K. Korman and others. bibl tabs Acad Mgt J 24:342-60 Je '81
Coming to grips with executive burnout. M. D. Glicken and K. Janka. Int Mgt 36:27+ O '81
Conversation with a successful man [excerpt from book, Making good] J. Adams. Across the Bd 19:47-52 Ap '82
Design of the corporate budgeting system: influences on managerial behavior and performance. K. A. Merchant. bibl(p827-9) tabs Acct R 56:813-29 O '81
Dropouts: chucking the corporate life-style. G. Johnson. il Ind W 209:40-2+ Je 15 '81
Facing up to executive anger. W. Kiechell, 3d. Fortune 104:205+ N 16 '81
Getting a good fit. Mgt R 70:7 My '81
How to say no to your boss. T. Blakely. Can Bus 54:64-6 S '81
Interactionist approach to measuring anxiety at work. R. L. Payne and others. bibl tabs J Occupa Psychol 55:13-25 Mr '82
Isolated executives. D. B. Thompson. Ind W 210:36-9+ Ag 10 '81
Managers can avoid wasting time [job related anxiety] R. N. Ashkenas and R. H. Schaffer. Harvard Bus R 60:98-104 My/Je '82
Managers should adapt skills, practice individual approach. Train & Devel J 36:9 Ja '82
New manager: male and female. Mgt World 11: 24 Mr '82
Note on sex-role identity effects on managerial aspirations. G. N. Powell and D. A. Butterfield. tab J Occupa Psychol 54:299-301 D '81
Opportunities in doubt. J. L. Hayes. Mgt R 70:2-3 Ag '81
Participation in budgeting, locus on control and organizational effectiveness. P. Brownell. bibl(p858-60) tabs Acct R 56:844-60 O '81
Peers and power: a delicate imbalance. M. Price. Ind W 213:50-1+ My 17 '82
Personality could be the key to business success [interview with S. Lecker] G. Bickerstaffe. Int Mgt 36:23-4 My '81

Figure 2-4 *Business Periodicals Index.*
Source: Copyright © 1981, 1982, 1983 by the H. W. Wilson Company.
Material reproduced by permission of the publisher.

22

Additional Sources of Printed Material

Pamphlets and brochures are another good supplement to library material. Often a company will prepare a pamphlet describing a product or a service. The pamphlet gives pertinent information in easy-to-read style. You can usually pick up these brochures from local stores and offices that handle the product or supply the service. Your librarian can help you find addresses of national and local corporations and of local, state, and national government agencies.

Government agencies are another excellent source of these materials. Local, state, and federal agencies prepare many pamphlets and brochures on a wide variety of subjects as a public service. You can probably find a listing of these materials in the library. They are usually sent to you free of charge when you request them.

You can also sometimes go to a local agency connected with the topic you are researching. In that office you will usually find a conveniently located selection of brochures and pamphlets. Ask if you can take the ones that apply to the area you are researching.

TAKING NOTES

When you have selected the material that you think will be most helpful to you, you should read it carefully (perhaps several times) and take notes on the material as you read. Writers differ on the methods they find most effective for note taking; some use 3 x 5 cards and others use legal pads. You may even have read about successful authors who jot down ideas and information on facial tissue and dinner napkins. Although you may occasionally get a good idea as you finish lunch and quickly jot it down on the first piece of paper available, you will probably find the writing process easier if you use one of the more traditional methods of note taking. On the next few pages are some examples of note taking techniques. Compare them and decide what process will work best for you.

Characteristics of Good Notes

Whatever method of note taking you decide to use, you should remember that good notes have several things in common.

First, good notes are clear and easy to read. Don't cram numerous items on one page. Make your facts and ideas stand out. Leave space between each statistic or quote that you record and underline or label important materials. Print names and terms that you may have trouble spelling later. In handwriting an *i* can often look like an *e*, an *l* may be nearly impossible to distinguish from a hurriedly crossed *t*, and an *o* and an *a* may look the same. When you write your report, you will want each name and term to be spelled correctly. Printing them in your notes will save you the time of checking the spelling later.

Completeness is a second characteristic of good notes. Don't say, "That's such a good idea I'll remember it." Write it down. Each item you record should also have the source recorded with it. There are a variety of time-saving ways to indicate sources as you research. On the following pages, you will see some of them. Although you may think that recording the sources is too time-consuming, you should remember that you will be required to give credit in your report to people from whom you quote or to sources of statistics or unique or controversial ideas. A little extra time while you are taking notes will save you hours of checking on sources later.

A third characteristic of good notes is that they are just that—notes. They are not pages lifted verbatim from sources. They are not whole paragraphs copied longhand into a notebook. Usually, they are not even sentences. Notes are phrases, words, and numbers written in outline form. Their purpose is to give you information quickly which you can then transcribe into sentences and paragraphs of your own design.

Reasons for Taking Notes

There are several very good reasons for taking notes rather than copying long passages from varied sources. The first reason is that when you begin to write the report, it is difficult to remember if a particular paragraph is your own wording or someone's else's. You will want your report to be written in your own words, so you may end up checking sources again.

A second reason for taking notes is that they are much quicker to read. You have already read and perhaps reread books and magazines with lengthy sentences and paragraphs. Now you need to remember and find quickly those important facts you found in your reading. You do not need to take the time to read through a lot of extraneous words yet a third time.

The third reason for taking notes is the time factor. Note taking is much faster than copying material verbatim. In every paragraph there will be a lot of linking words, phrases, and examples that you will not want to include in your report. Weed those items out as you take notes. Your writing will be accomplished a lot more easily and faster if you use good note-taking skills while you are researching.

Using Note Cards

You can use two kinds of cards when you take notes: source cards and information cards. A *source card* gives bibliographical information. An *information card* contains facts, quotes, or ideas that you can use in your report.

The following example of a source card shows how to record bibliographical information.

```
                                            1
                    Carrie Tuhy, "A Working Woman's Guide
              to Successful Dress," Money April 1982,
              p. 144–148.
```

You will have only one source card for each source you use in your report. However, you will probably have many information cards for each source card. For that reason you need an easy way to identify the source for each information card. Some people number their source cards and put that number on their information cards (see example below). Other people write the author's last name on each information card; then they can relate their information cards to a particular source card by the author's last name.

An information card should contain only one item of information. Be sure to record the number of the page where you found the information. Even though a lot of space probably remains on the card, do not fill it with other facts and ideas.

A page from the Tuhy article is shown in Figure 2–5. Here is an information card based on that page.

```
              Tuhy                                    1
              p. 146  Guidelines for better dress
                        1. Buy fewer pieces but best you
                           can afford
                        2. Choose good natural fabrics first
                        3. Choose good fit
                        4. Choose basic color as a pivot
                           for your wardrobe
```

When it comes time to write your paper, you will first prepare an outline. Then you will organize your cards in stacks according to the topics of the outline. In other words, you will play solitaire with your information cards. Then you will write your paper from the information in each stack of cards. If you have more than one item on each card, you may find that a single card belongs in two different stacks. This makes the writing process more complicated. That is why you should put only one item of information on each information card.

Taking Notes on Legal Pads

You can also use legal pads or a spiral notebook to take notes. In that case you write the complete source at the top of the page and record information below it. Page numbers are placed in the margin. Many people prefer this method over

Figure 2-5   *A well-made wool suit at $300 is a better value than a dress
on sale at half the price.*

RULE ONE: *Buy fewer pieces, but buy the best you can afford.*
    When contemplating a purchase, consider not just the initial price but also the
cost per wearing—the price divided by the number of times you expect to wear the
article of clothing. A well-made wool suit will probably cost between $250 and $300, but
it's a better value than a dress on sale at half the price. Although dresses are once again
popular, buying one is hard for a working woman to justify. The few good dresses made
usually sell for more than $200, and in any case they lack the flexibility of a blazer and
skirt or a suit. If you wear a dress more than once a week it will be noticed, but you can
change the look of a suit simply by wearing a different blouse, scarf or jewelry or by
combining the jacket with a different skirt.
    Superior fabrics and workmanship are the essence of quality. Traditionally,
men's clothing has been better made than women's largely because male fashions
change infrequently and the patterns used by manufacturers have been perfected over
the years. Now that men's wear manufacturers such as Arthur Chapnik, Stanley Blacker
and Southwick are making women's clothes, the quality is improving. These makers use
the same tightly woven fabrics in women's suits that they do in men's, and do more hand
stitching than is usual in women's wear. Hand-stitched garments have softer, more
natural contours than those that are machine sewn. Details can also indicate top
quality: horn buttons, a silk or fine rayon lining that allows the material to drape properly,
a zipper that lies flat.

RULE TWO: *Choose good natural fabrics when you can; choose good synthetic blends
when you can't.*
    Natural fabrics look better and wear longer than most synthetics. Because they
breathe, they are better suited to year-round wear. Lightweight worsted wool, wool
gabardine, wool crepe, linen, cotton and silk are good fabric choices for year-round
clothes. If you work in an office, you will probably never need a fabric as heavy as a
double-worsted wool or a hearty flannel. Silk is often criticized as fragile and fussy, but
it can be nearly indestructible and is easily cared for.
    To be sure, fabrics made of natural fibers can vary radically in quality. The
difference is evident in a tightly woven gabardine that wears well for years and one
that gets shiny after only a few outings. The quality of silk is determined by its density
of weave and weight. A simple blouse made of an adequate-weight silk costs around $90.
A cheap, almost transparent Korean silk is far inferior to a more substantial one from
Italy or even to a high-grade polyester. Synthetics like polysilk, polyester and rayon are
acceptable alternatives, especially for blouses, if you can't afford a good silk.
    If your job requires travel, you should also consider how well your clothes will
survive packing. Wool crepe and linen wrinkle easily. You may want to look for blends of
natural and synthetic fibers that resist wrinkles or give the fabric body.

RULE THREE: *Be certain of fit, be aware of proportion.*
    Even an exquisite suit looks awful if it fits poorly. Chances are you will never
be lucky enough to pull a suit off the rack and have it fit perfectly, so you'll need
expert tailoring services. Some women's wear retailers now provide tailoring for their
customers. Most stores charge for the service, but it's usually well worth it if you're
investing in a good-quality garment. It may cost $6 or so to lengthen a sleeve, $15 to
let out the waist and $8 to shorten a hem. To minimize alteration costs, if necessary
you should look for suits where the jacket and skirt match but can be bought in separate
sizes.

If you must buy the suit as an ensemble, choose the size in which the jacket fits you best. A jacket should lie smoothly across your back; when buttoned, it should not buckle in front. Full-busted women should avoid tailored styles for this reason; they should consider instead the classic boxy fashion popularized by Chanel. In any style, the armholes should be ample. Sleeve lengths, like skirt hems, are a matter of personal taste. Most women wear their sleeves no shorter than their wrist bones and no longer than two inches below them.

Unlike men's jackets, which come in short, regular and long, women's jackets usually are cut only one way. Some men's wear manufacturers who have crossed over to women's wear have not yet perfected their women's patterns. As a result, a man-tailored women's jacket may taper beneath the armholes instead of at the waist, producing an awkward fit. Or it may be too long, outlining the derrière unflatteringly. The new short-length jacket, which falls three to five inches below the waist, looks attractive on most figures.

Proportion is important in assuring that clothes look well on you. A tall woman or one with a long neck would do well to wear a jacket with gently puffed sleeves or a bowed blouse to focus attention closer to the face. Proper proportion can also camouflage figure flaws. A woman with sloping shoulders looks best in a jacket with slight padding or one made from stiffer fabric that shapes the garment better.

RULE FOUR: *Use color to build and expand your wardrobe.*

The contents of your closet should not resemble a rainbow; instead, your clothes should have a concentrated color scheme. A basic color you like and can wear is the pivot of a wardrobe. Whether you choose navy, black, burgundy or another color, you should buy your major pieces—a suit, a blazer, a skirt—in it.

C. Tuhy, "A Working Woman's Guide to Successful Dress," *MONEY* (April, 1982) p. 146.

note cards. It seems faster to them and it is more familiar, because people are used to writing on sheets of paper rather than on note cards. The disadvantage to taking notes this way is that you can't shuffle the items of information when you are organizing your report. You have many items on one page. This makes the writing process slower. In order to make the writing as easy as possible for yourself, you may decide to put your extra time into preparing the note cards.

Figure 2–6 shows how to use a legal pad to take notes. On the left you can read the article and compare it with the notes taken as they are shown on the right.

Underlining Copies

A third way of taking notes has become more popular as copy machines have become standard items in most libraries. With this method you make a copy of a magazine article or a page from a book and underline important material.

This method works well when you intend to quote directly from the source. It can save you time you would otherwise spend copying the quote and it ensures that you repeat the material accurately. Underlining copies should not be used for information other than quotes, however. Lifting material verbatim from other sources is too easy when you use underlined copies. Soon the report is a

Figure 2.6

A MAN'S GUIDE TO
DRESSING WELL FOR BUSINESS

Here's an easy-to-follow system
that will enable you to look your best and get top mileage
from your clothing dollar.

by Charles J. Rolo

"Costly thy habit as thy purse can buy,
But not express'd in fancy;
  rich, not gaudy;
For the apparel oft proclaims the man."
Shakespeare, *Hamlet*

"A well-tied tie is the first serious step
in life."
Oscar Wilde,
The Importance of Being Earnest

In contrast to Europeans, Americans have traditionally disdained men who display a pronounced preoccupation with clothes. A man dressed with noticeable chic risks arousing suspicions that he's snobbish, phony or effete—perhaps a smarmy social climber or a retired mobster with an English valet. The only irreproachable American form of dandyism is the rugged elegance of the cowboy, a style incongruously emulated by teenagers, urban dudes and jet-setters around the world. But being pragmatic, Americans accept the idea of dressing well in order to succeed in business.

Last fall, some 200 M.B.A. students at the University of Pennsylvania's prestigious Wharton School crowded into a day-long seminar on executive dress. And Wharton isn't the only academy that has seasoned its curriculum with a dash of sartorial advice. Some corporations—Equitable Life and Fluor, for example—make available to their executives professional advice on business attire. These firms recognize that, for business and professional men, presenting a properly tailored image isn't the simple matter that it used to be. The breakdown of dress codes in the 1960s freed urban executives from a stodgy and unvarying uniform—dark suit, white shirt, conservative tie and plain black shoes with laces—only to land them in a different pickle. Today the clothing industry offers them a bewildering array of choices, and designers have compounded their problem by introducing rapid and radical changes of fashion.

In the universe of powerfully promoted "designer" clothes, suit lapels, collars and neckties widen to proportions suitable for a gorilla, then shrink to dimensions becoming only to a bean pole or a shrimp. "Planned obsolescence" empties a shopper's pocketbook and fills his closet with outmoded apparel. How then should a man go about building a business wardrobe that will make him look his best and give him good mileage for his clothing dollar?

Sensible, tasteful and easy-to-follow answers to that question are provided by Mortimer Levitt in his recent book, *The Executive Look: How to Get It—How to Keep It* (Atheneum, $16.95). The author has been telling men how to improve their appearance for 45 years. Now 74, he has amassed the wealth of a minor oil sheik by selling modestly priced custom-made shirts. He opened his first Custom Shop Shirtmakers in Manhattan in 1937, charging $2.15 for a custom-made shirt; today he owns a chain of 42 stores in 21 cities and charges $22.50 and up—slightly more than you might pay for readymade shirts of comparable quality.

Levitt's advice is timeless. Says he: "Fashion is an industry rip-off. Forget it! Stay with the classics." While he thinks that it's false economy for businessmen to skimp on their dress budget, Levitt doesn't address himself to would-be Beau Brummells with money to burn. At current prices, the total cost of the major annual clothing purchases that Levitt suggests for business dress amounts to about $1,200. His list: two suits ($590), five shirts ($125), five ties ($75), two pairs of shoes ($180), one overcoat ($240). Since men normally don't buy an outercoat and two pairs of dress shoes every year, Levitt's budget has some built-in flexibility.

Most men dress haphazardly and don't know what to wear with what. Levitt's remedy for the chaotic approach is a system that clothes businessmen in a professionally conceived outfit—in effect, a "uniform" but one that doesn't suppress individuality and provides a large variety of choices. The Levitt system's cornerstones are four prescriptions:

RULE ONE: *Wear two plains but only one fancy.* With a striped, checked or otherwise patterned suit, both your shirt and tie should be plain. With a fancy shirt, wear a plain suit and a plain-colored tie. Two pronounced patterns conflict, like ice cream and pickles.

RULE TWO: *Wear a base color—Oxford gray, navy or brown—with a brighter "accent" color (which might be red, yellow or blue).* Your suit is *always* the base color; the accent is provided by your shirt and/or tie. If your suit is plain gray and the accent color chosen is blue, you might

Charles J. Rolo., "A Man's Guide to Dressing Well for Business," *MONEY* (February 1982) p. 85.

Charles J. Rolo.   "A Man's Guide
to Dressing Well for Business."
Money, February 1982, 84-92

p. 85   How to "dress for success" - economically

quote   "Fashion is an industry rip-off.
Forget it! Stay with the classics."
— Mortimer Levitt   author   of
The Executive Look: How to Get It -
How to Keep It

Levitt's budget
2 suits ($590)
5 shirts ($125)
5 ties   ($75)
2 pairs shoes ($180)
1 overcoat ($240)

Levitt's 4 "rules" of dress

1. "Wear two plains but only
one fancy." i.e. patterned
suit - plain shirt + tie
2. "Wear a base color - Oxford
grey, navy or brown - with a
bright "accent" color (which
might be red, yellow or blue.)"

hodgepodge of other authors' styles rather than your original use of the material. In lengthy reports underlined copies can also be expensive. Therefore, this method of note taking should supplement one of the other methods mentioned rather than be the main way of note taking.

INTERVIEWING

Interviewing is another means of information gathering you may use when researching your topic. Person-to-person contact with people who have experience in the area you are researching can be especially helpful. To get the most information from an interview, you should understand the interviewing process.

What Is an Interview?

An interview has three characteristics: (1) it involves two or more people, (2) it is well-planned by at least one of the people involved, and (3) both the interviewer and interviewee(s) take turns talking and listening. The key to a successful interview lies in the second part of this definition: it is well-planned. The following discussion will help you plan your interviews effectively.

Prepare for Interview

Before you actually sit down to talk to the expert you have chosen to interview, you should decide on an exact purpose for the interview. Ask yourself: "Why have I chosen to interview this person? What do I hope to learn during the interview?"

Keeping your purpose firmly in mind, plan the questions you will ask during the interview. Some background information on the topic and the position of the person you are interviewing will help you plan these questions. Write down those questions and take them with you to the interview. With written questions in front of you, you will be sure to cover your main points and get the information you need even if you feel nervous or hurried during the interview.

Types of Questions

The amount of information you get from an interview depends partly on how you phrase your questions. Basically, questions are divided into two categories: open questions and closed questions. *Open questions* are worded to encourage the respondent to express an opinion or give detailed information:

"How should a salesperson dress in your company?"

This question invites a description of clothing appropriate for a salesperson in that company.

On the other hand, the answer to a *closed question* reveals limited information.

"Do you require your salespeople to wear suits?"

This question can be answered "yes" or "no." If it is answered "yes," you do not know if the suits must be subdued business suits or if more casual suits and sports coats are also appropriate. If the answer is "no," you know only that suits are not required. The answer does not give you an indication of the employer's preference in dress.

Word your questions so you get as much information from your respondent as possible.

Questions can also be worded to draw out a specific kind of answer from the respondent. These are called *leading questions*. One way to guard against leading questions is to be aware of personal biases you may have on the subject and try to keep those biases from showing during your questioning. For example, if you favor a four-day work week, you might ask the question:

"Don't you think a four-day work week has distinct advantages over the traditional five-day work week?"

With this question you are leading your respondent to support your opinion.

If you want an accurate idea of your respondent's opinion, you should use neutral wording to phrase your question:

"What is your reaction to the idea of a four-day work week?"

Even when you plan your questions carefully and ask open questions that encourage your respondent to express individual thoughts, you may have trouble getting all the information you need during the interview. If your respondent is reluctant to answer your questions completely, you may have to probe for the information you need. Repeat a question or ask the respondent to elaborate on an answer. Silence is also an effective probe. Give the respondent time to reflect and you will often have a more complete answer to your question. You can also branch off from your prepared list of questions when this will help you get more information. React to information the respondent gives you and use it to explore areas of your topic more completely. Your prepared questions should be used as a guide: they should not be the only questions you feel free to ask.

Setting Up the Interview

When you know your purpose for the interview and have decided with whom you want to talk, you should set up an appointment for the interview. Be sure to call first. Most people who are experts in their fields—and therefore likely candidates for an interview—are often busy. They may be too busy to talk to you if you just drop in on them. Even if the people you want to interview have plenty of time, however, calling them is a courtesy that will pave the way for a successful interview.

When you call to set up the appointment, give the person some background information about your project and explain why you want the interview. This will help the respondent prepare for the interview by brushing up on specific items or gathering information for you ahead of time.

Choose a time and place that is convenient for the respondent and indicate how long you expect the interview to take. These measures show the respondent that you value time and help you both plan your schedule more efficiently.

Conducting the Interview

Like other types of written and oral communication, an interview has a beginning, a middle, and an ending.

Establish a comfortable atmosphere at the beginning of the interview. Introduce yourself to the person you are interviewing. Most people talk more freely to people they know. Even a little information about yourself will help the person you are interviewing feel comfortable talking to you. Explain what kind of information you need and why you need the information. Most people talk more freely when they understand the purpose of the interview.

In the middle of the interview you ask the questions you have prepared. Start with the easier questions on your list; save the challenging or controversial questions until later in the interview. Doing this also helps put the interviewee at ease. Persons are more likely to answer difficult questions later in the interview after they have warmed up to the subject and gained confidence in the interviewer.

Write down the answers the person gives you. Interviewing an authority can be a tense experience. Don't think you will remember everything that is said. Also remember you must quote the person accurately. The only way to make sure you are accurately repeating the information given you is to write it down or record it on tape (if the person approves).

As the interview draws to a close, review the main points of the discussion. Make sure you understand the respondent's answers and have quoted accurately. Clarify anything you do not understand and probe for additional information if necessary. Be sure to thank the person for the time spent discussing the topic with you.

Through interviews you can often gain important firsthand information from people who have practical experience in the area you are researching. An interview is also an excellent opportunity to clarify ideas you may not have understood thoroughly from your reading and to add valuable material to your library research.

Taking Notes During the Interview

Taking notes during an interview can tax your energy and your patience, but accurate notes are essential to a successful interview. A few guidelines will help you record your respondent's comments efficiently.

1. Before you interview, write out on a legal pad the questions you want to ask. Leave spaces between the questions so you can write in the answers during the interview.
2. Record the respondent's full name, title, and the date of the interview for your source reference.
3. Write down only the facts the respondent gives you. Do not try to record complete sentences unless you plan to quote the person.
4. Star information the respondent emphasizes. These stars will help you recall the important items later.
5. Be sure you spell all names correctly and record all numbers accurately. Ask the respondent to repeat if necessary.
6. Read over your notes as soon as possible after the interview. Fill in words and thoughts to clarify the notes while the interview is still fresh in your mind.

You may also decide to tape the interview. Taping is acceptable as long as the respondent agrees to be taped and knows when you are taping the conversation. Even if you do tape, however, you should not depend solely on the recording. Many things can go wrong during taping. The speaker's voice may not record clearly or the recorder may run out of tape. Another problem with taping is that the person you are interviewing may not speak freely while the tape is running. For these reasons you may prefer notes. Certainly, you should take notes as a backup even if you are recording the interview.

OBSERVATION

Observation is a third way to collect information. It is firsthand information that helps verify material you have gathered from other sources. Observation can also be used to help you and your audience picture a product or situation in detail. It gives on-the-scene information which often lends realism to material you have gathered through books and interviews. It can be a casual way of noting particular things or it can be a more structured study of those same conditions.

For example, if you wanted to add to your information about the proper way to dress for success on the job, you could tour a place of business and generally note the way the people are dressed in different work areas throughout the building. This would be casual observation.

You could also prepare a list of employees and organize that list according to the promotion route within that company. Then, if company policy permits, you could visit work areas and record the dress of the workers on each level from entry jobs to executive positions. You could repeat your observation several times to see if the dress you observed on the first visit is consistent with that seen in subsequent observations. A comparison of the dress at various job levels will help you determine the way to dress for success on the job in that particular company.

PERSONAL EXPERIENCE

Personal experience can also be an effective way to add information to your research. Ask yourself, "What experience have I had related to this topic?" Use that experience to expand on or emphasize information you have received from other sources. Avoid the tendency to overuse personal experience, though. Sometimes our own experiences seem so compelling to us that they may overshadow information from other sources. We may also become so involved in relating a personal experience that we forget to find out what has happened to other people. Nevertheless, personal experiences are effective attention getters. They also help your audience relate to nationally based statistics or quotes from public figures. However, they are seldom effective as the primary basis of your discussion.

For example, you can quote Mortimer Levitt (from our library research) as saying, "Fashion is an industry rip-off. Forget it! Stay with the classics"; then you can relate that quote to your audience (who may never have heard of Mortimer Levitt) with a personal experience. You can say:

> I learned the truth of Levitt's statement the hard way. The first year I worked I spent a fourth of every paycheck on clothes. I wanted to be "in style" so I bought the most current fashions. Now I have a closet full of leather boots and prairie skirts which nobody wears this year. If I had bought traditional skirts and blazers I would have an appropriate wardrobe for the next several years.

The personal experience alone would probably not convince your audience to abandon "high style" for traditional wear, but when you couple it with the quote from an expert, you give your personal experience clout and bring the quote close to home. The two sources of information complement each other and work effectively together.

SUMMARY

Gathering information is an important part of the communication process. Whether you are talking or writing, you should research your topic thoroughly. You can gather information from library and other printed materials, interviews, observations, and personal experience.

Library sources are indexed in the card catalog (for books, films, filmstrips, tapes, and videos) and periodical indexes such as the *Reader's Guide* and the *Guide to Business Periodicals* (for magazines). Be sure to take careful notes on these library sources. Good notes are: (1) clear and easy to read, (2) complete, (3) phrases, words, and numbers written in outline form.

A second way of gathering information is to interview experts in the subject you are researching. Plan these interviews carefully. Before going to the interview define your purpose and prepare questions. As a general rule, avoid closed and leading questions and concentrate on open-ended questions that encourage the respondent to give detailed information. Before the interview, call the respondent and explain your purpose so the person you are interviewing can also prepare for the meeting. Start the interview with nonthreatening, easy-to-answer questions that put the respondent at ease; then move into the middle of the interview, where you concentrate on gathering information. Conclude the interview by summing up the main points and clarifying vague comments. Be sure to take accurate notes during the interview.

Observation and personal experience are other ways of gathering information. Observation lends realism to material you have gathered through the library and interviews. Use observation and personal experience to expand on or emphasize information you gather from other sources. Although they are usually not effective as the only sources of information, they can be used to get the audience's attention and help them relate to issues of national concern.

REVIEW QUESTIONS

1. What guides help you find material in the library? When you want to find books, what do you use? When you want to find magazine articles, what do you use?
2. What are the characteristics of good notes?
3. Why should you prepare your questions for an interview in advance? What types of questions will help you gather information? What types of questions will limit the information the respondent gives you? Use examples to illustrate your answer.
4. For an interview, what method of note taking—pen and paper or tape recorder—do you prefer? What are the advantages and disadvantages of each method? How can you best overcome the disadvantages and make use of the advantages?
5. How can observation add to your knowledge of the topic?
6. What is the best way to use personal experience? Explain your answer, using an illustration.

ACTIVITIES

1. Choose a topic and research it using all four methods of information gathering.

   First, use the library to find five sources including at least one book, two magazine articles, and one newspaper article on the topic. Take notes on these sources, using one of the techniques discussed in this chapter.

   Second, identify an expert on your topic and set up an interview. Prepare for the interview using the techniques discussed in this chapter. Before going to the interview, exchange the questions you have prepared with a classmate. Ask your classmate to look for closed or leading questions and to comment on how thoroughly your questions cover the topic. You, in turn, should evaluate your classmate's questions for the same items. Then interview the person you have chosen, using the techniques of a good interview discussed in this chapter.

   Third, supplement your research with observation.

   Fourth, use some personal experience to expand on or emphasize part of your other information.

When you have finished the research activities, write a paragraph evaluating the four kinds of research. What kinds of information did you learn from the library materials? How did the interview add to the library material? How would you use the observation and personal experiences in your talk or report? Did you need all four sources of information? Why or why not? Be prepared to discuss your observations in class.

2. Choose a factual article from a trade magazine in your field. As closely as possible, identify the sources of information (library, interview, observation, or personal experience) the author used to develop the ideas. How did each of the sources used complement each other? Do you think the author used enough sources? What information-gathering techniques, if any, would have improved the article? Be prepared to discuss your article and observations about it with your class.

3. Attend a lecture (other than a class lecture) given by an authority in your field. As closely as possible, identify the sources of information (library, interview, observation, or personal experience) the speaker used to develop the ideas. How did each of the sources used complement each other? Do you think the speaker used enough sources? What information-gathering techniques, if any, would have improved the talk? Be prepared to discuss the talk and your observations about it with your class.

3

SOLVING PROBLEMS THROUGH LOGICAL THINKING

Logic is the art of making truth prevail.
LaBruyere

After studying this chapter you should understand:
1. The definition of a problem
2. Convergent and divergent problems
3. The parts of a problem
4. The processes of problem solving
5. Pitfalls to problem solving
6. The definition of logical reasoning
7. Inductive reasoning and deductive reasoning
8. The difference between statements of report and statements of opinion
9. Fallacies of the reasoning process

Dr. Alexander Fleming studied the bacteria culture in the petri dish. A mold was growing in the middle of the culture. All around the mold the bacteria were dissolving. The only place the germs seemed to grow was around the edge of the petri dish, far away from the mold.

"Why don't germs grow near the mold?" Dr. Fleming wondered. He took some of the mold and put it in another petri dish where bacteria were growing. The bacteria dissolved in that dish, too. Wherever he put the mold, it dissolved bacteria.

In this way, through logical reasoning, Dr. Fleming discovered penicillin, an effective antibiotic.

All of us apply the logical reasoning process daily to help solve work-related and personal problems.

Am I ready for the expert ski trails?
Do airbags significantly reduce injury during car accidents?
What causes the carburetor on this customer's car to stick in cold weather?

These are examples of problems you can solve through logical thinking. Whether you are talking or writing, an understanding of the logical reasoning and problem-solving processes will help you make effective decisions.

This understanding will also help you evaluate other people's ideas. Theresa, in the opening scenario, would have written a more accurate report if she had understood how to evaluate the comments she heard.

In this chapter we will show how to tackle problems. We will also discuss reasoning processes you can use to solve these problems.

WHAT IS A PROBLEM?

When you have a goal in mind but don't know how to reach that goal, you have a problem. In our opening scenario, Theresa had to analyze the placement of the word processors in her company. Her goal was to decide whether a centralized or a decentralized system was more efficient. Her problem was how to gather adequate information about both systems and analyze her data.

Theresa's goal was assigned to her, but not all goals are as clearly stated. When Dr. Fleming began experimenting with molds, his goal was less directed than Theresa's. Dr. Fleming did not set out to discover penicillin; his goal was to learn why the mold repelled the bacteria. In the process of solving that problem he discovered penicillin.

CONVERGENT AND DIVERGENT PROBLEMS

There are two kinds of problems, *convergent* and *divergent.*

Convergent Problems

A convergent problem is one that has only one correct solution. Let's say you are an American traveling in Canada. You stop at a restaurant to eat. When your bill for $10 comes, you realize you have only American money. The U.S. dollar is worth 25% more than the Canadian dollar. How much American money will you give the cashier? This is a convergent problem. There is only one correct answer: you will give the cashier $7.50, 25% less than you would if you were paying in Canadian money.

Divergent Problems

A divergent problem, on the other hand, may have several correct answers. Some of these answers may provide more efficient solutions than others, but each answer is adequate. Let's say, again, that you are traveling in Canada. Since the U.S.

dollar is worth more than the Canadian dollar, you must solve the problem of how to deal with the difference. You can choose from a variety of solutions: (1) you can convert all your American money to Canadian money at the border, (2) you can convert your money at local banks as you travel, or (3) you can pay in American money, converting it each time you buy something. How you deal with the rate of exchange between U.S. and Canadian money is a divergent problem. It has many solutions. Depending upon your outlook, you will probably find one solution more appropriate than the others, but each solution can be applied to solve the problem.

THE PARTS OF A PROBLEM

Each problem, whether it is convergent or divergent, has three parts: givens, operations, and goals. Understanding these three parts will help you solve problems effectively.

Givens

The information you have as you set out to solve the problem is called the *givens*. In the first example of paying a $10 restaurant bill in Canada with American money, the givens are: (1) the $10 bill, (2) the American money you must use to pay the bill, and (3) the 25% rate of exchange.

Operations

The way you solve the problem is called the *operations*. In this example, the operations would be mathematical. You would reduce the $10 Canadian bill by 25% to make it equal to the American money you are using.

Goals

The last part of a problem is the *goal*. Knowing your goal will help you solve the problem. In our example, your goal was to equalize the Canadian and American money so you could pay the Canadian bill with U.S. dollars.

Problem-Solving Practice

Now, let's look at another problem. Before you solve it, identify the givens, operation and goals.

Problem: If a shirt and jacket cost $110 and the jacket costs $100 more than the shirt, how much does the jacket cost?

Discussion: Did you decide that the jacket cost $100 and the shirt $10? Let's look at the problem again. It says that the jacket costs $100 more than the shirt. The difference between $100 and $10 is $90; however, not $100. Therefore the jacket must cost more than $90 and the shirt less. The jacket costs $105 and the shirt $5 because $5 subtracted from $105 leaves $100. What are the givens to this problem? The operation? The goals?

Problem-Solving Guidelines

Before trying to solve a problem, be sure you understand all the givens. Don't assume things about the information you have or gloss over vague material. To solve a problem effectively, you must have adequate, accurate information.

Next, be sure you know what operations are required and how to use them. Can you multiply, subtract, or divide? Do you know how to use a drill or climb a tree? Can you express yourself effectively? Know what skills your problem requires and evaluate your abilities to perform those skills. Also, be sure you have explored all the operations that you may use to solve the problem. Several different methods may be used for any one problem. Let's say, for example, you have locked yourself out of the house. You may decide to climb a ladder and pry open an upstairs window, but if you are afraid of heights or not strong enough to pry open the window, that operation will not work for you. You will have to look for alternate operations such as cutting a screen or squeezing through a basement window. You choose the method of solving the problem that works best for you.

Finally, know the goal you want to reach. If your goal is to get into your house at all costs, you will break a window, cut a screen, or damage a door. You will overlook the damage done because your primary goal is to get into the house as quickly as possible. If, on the other hand, you want to get into the house without damaging anything, you will look for an operation that allows you to satisfy the goal even if that operation is sitting outside on the front step for several hours until your spouse comes home with a key. Your primary goal influenced the operation you chose to solve the problem.

THE PROCESSES OF PROBLEM SOLVING

When you know the parts of your problem, you are ready to solve it.

Solving a problem is usually easier if you break it into several smaller problems and solve each of those problems first. Then you can link the solutions to the individual problems together to form a solution to the large problem. The following example illustrates this process.

Problem-Solving Practice

Problem: You are the personnel director for a large insurance company. Because of the tightened economy, the company is streamlining its staff. When an opening occurs, you try to fill it with someone who can do several different jobs.

Today you are reviewing applications for an assistant to one of the vice-presidents. There are 100 applicants. Of these 100, 10 applicants have had no training on the computer and no training on the dictaphone; 70 have had some computer experience and 82 have had some dictaphone.

How many applicants have had both computer and dictaphone experience?

Discussion: This problem becomes easier if you break it into smaller problems.

First ask yourself: How many applicants have had no experience on the dictaphone or the computer? Your answer to this problem is: 10.

That means you are left with 90 applicants. Next ask yourself: How many of these applicants have not had experience on the computer? Your answer to this problem is: $90 - 70 = 20$. Then ask yourself: How many applicants have not had experience on the dictaphone? Your answer is: $90 - 82 = 8$. Now add the 20 with no computer experience to the 8 with no dictaphone experience and subtract your answer, 28, from the 90 applicants you were considering. That means you have 62 applicants to consider carefully for the assistant's position.

Often diagraming the problem will help you see the solution.

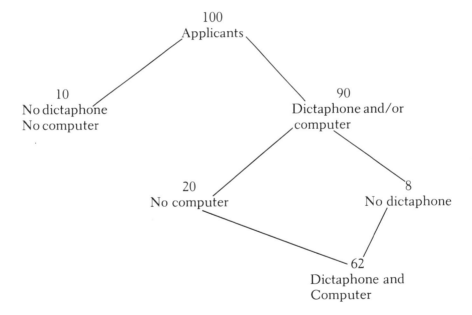

Solving Divergent Problems

Thus far we have used convergent problems to illustrate problem-solving techniques. The same process also applies to divergent problems. Let's think back to our example of the Canadian rates of exchange for U.S. money. We have already suggested several solutions for that divergent problem. Here's how a diagram would help us reach a solution.

Problem: How to use U.S. money in Canada

Exchange at border	Exchange at banks along the trip	Convert U.S. currency as you purchase
|	|	|
Advantages	*Advantages*	*Advantages*
|	|	|
Have Canadian money	Have Canadian money	Convenient
|	|	|
Best rate of exchange	Best rate of exchange	Don't have to plan ahead
|	|	|
		Disadvantages
	|	|
	Only a limited amount of money on hand	People may not know rate of exchange
	|	|
Disadvantages	*Disadvantages*	May not get best rate
|	|	
Lot of cash to travel with	Must find bank	
	|	
	Be there during banking hours each time you need cash	

Which solution would you choose? The diagram helps you see clearly the comparison among the solutions.

PITFALLS TO EFFICIENT PROBLEM SOLVING

Even when we know the parts of a problem and follow the problem-solving process, we may reach incorrect or unworkable solutions. One reason we reach inaccurate solutions is that we set our mind in one direction and see or hear only what we expect to. This mind set is illustrated by the following example. Read this sentence:

**In our office the
the heat is on.**

Did you read one *the* or two? Because we expect to read only one *the*, most of us will see the sentence that way. We have set our minds and that mind set prevents us from seeing the information as it really is.

Another pitfall to efficient problem solving is our tendency to follow only traditional paths when seeking solutions. Some problems can be solved more effectively with less usual approaches. The following problem shows how some problems can be solved best by unique approaches.

Problem-Solving Practice

Problem:

A merchant with a beautiful, loving daughter owes money he cannot repay to an ugly old moneylender. The moneylender likes the daughter and makes the merchant this offer:

All three will meet on a path in the moneylender's yard, a path covered with black and white stones. A black stone and a white stone will be taken from the path. The daughter must reach into a bag and select a stone. If she picks the black one, she must marry the moneylender and her father's debt is cancelled. If she pulls out the white one, she is free and the debt is cancelled. If she refuses to select either, her father will go to jail.

The father agrees, and he and his daughter go to the moneylender's yard at the appointed hour. As the moneylender stoops to pick up the stones, the daughter sees him slip two black stones into the bag—and no white stone at all. This is unfair, but accusing the moneylender will only anger him and land her father in jail. She notices the moneylender smile in triumph as he carefully watches her prepare to reach into the bag.[1]

What do you think she should do? Remember to search for unique ways to solve this problem.

Discussion: Traditional approaches will not work here. The girl cannot accuse the moneylender of putting two black stones in the bag because this will make him even angrier with her father. She cannot choose a stone, because regardless of the one she chooses she will have to marry the moneylender. Only a unique approach will solve the problem. This is what she does:

Without revealing that she has seen the moneylender's trick, the daughter reaches into the bag and pulls out a stone. As she does so, she fumbles with the stone and drops it on the path, where it is lost in all the other black and white stones.

"My goodness," she says in a sweetly apologetic voice, "how clumsy of me! But you can tell which stone I picked by the color of the one left in the bag."[2]

Some of the problems you face will also require these nontraditional paths for a satisfactory solution.

Understanding the process of problem solving is only one part of efficient decision making. To solve problems effectively, you must apply logical thinking to

---

[1] Xerox Corporation, "Creativity in Thinking and Writing," © 1971, pp. 1–2. Reprinted by permission of Xerox Education Publications.

[2] "Creativity in Thinking and Writing," p. 4. Reprinted by permission of Xerox Education Publications.

the problem-solving process. In the second part of this chapter, we will discuss logical reasoning.

WHAT IS LOGICAL THINKING?

Logical thinking is the search for relationships between items of information. When you think logically, you gather information on the subject and you think about how those facts relate to each other; then you use the relationships you have found to make your decision. Dr. Fleming, for example, put the mold in many bacteria cultures. When it dissolved the germs each time, he saw the relationship among the incidents and concluded that the mold prevented bacteria from growing. We call this logical thinking process *reasoning*.

Inductive thinking and deductive thinking are the two ways to reason effectively.

INDUCTIVE REASONING

Definition

One way to accomplish effective reasoning is to gather specific items of information and use these specifics to reach a general conclusion. For example, you can say: 1,000 college students at Northwoods College were given a measles vaccine. Of those 1,000 students, 999 did not get measles during the recent epidemic; therefore, the measles vaccine is effective in preventing measles. You have used the relationship among a number of specific items of information (1,000 vaccinated students, 999 of whom did not get measles) to reach a conclusion about the measles vaccine (it is effective in preventing measles). We call reasoning from specific items of information to a general conclusion *inductive reasoning*. Dr. Fleming used inductive reasoning when he put the mold in many bacteria cultures and watched the germs dissolve in each one.

Guidelines

To use inductive reasoning effectively, you must follow certain guidelines. First, you must make sure the specific items you use are numerous enough to support your conclusion. For example you could say:

My two friends, Mary and Pete, each had a measles vaccination. They didn't get measles. If I have the vaccine I won't get measles either.

You have followed the processes of inductive reasoning, but the specifics you used were not numerous enough to support your conclusion. The fact that two of your friends were vaccinated and did not get measles does not necessarily mean that the measles vaccine is 100 percent effective.

Second, make sure your information is accurate. Validate your information and try to eliminate hearsay. Use facts that appear in several sources or data that you can document. Don't depend on remarks that begin with "Jack told me . . ." when you are collecting data.

Third, make sure your specifics are typical of the problem you are trying to solve. Let's say you have never had measles and you are trying to decide whether you should be vaccinated. You will collect information about people like yourself: those who did not have measles as children. You will find out how many of those people were vaccinated and how many of those vaccinated escaped the last measles epidemic. On the basis of that information you will be able to decide whether you should be vaccinated.

Fourth, look for major items of information that do not fit with the specifics you are collecting. Let's say you are doing a follow-up study on the 1,000 college students who were vaccinated at Northwoods College. You learn that 999 of the 1,000 did not get measles. Southwoods and Eastwoods Colleges report similar results. It seems to follow that the vaccine is effective against measles. Then you learn that at Westwoods College 1,000 students were vaccinated and 500 of those students came down with measles. This is a significant factor that does not fit the pattern established by the other three colleges. Why did those 500 vaccinated students come down with measles? This evidence seems to indicate that the vaccine is not as effective as you had at first thought. It casts doubt on your previous conclusion that the vaccine prevents measles. You must explain why those 500 cases of measles occurred before you can generalize from the other data you have collected.

If you follow these guidelines:

1. Take an adequate sampling
2. Use verifiable information
3. Make sure your examples relate directly to the problem you are trying to solve
4. Consider major factors that deviate from the data you are collecting

you should be able to use the inductive reasoning process to reason effectively.

DEDUCTIVE REASONING

Definition

The second method of effective reasoning is called *deductive reasoning*. When we use deductive reasoning, we start with a general statement and use it to arrive at a specific conclusion. For example, you can say:

All students at Northwoods College have been vaccinated against measles.
Tom is a student at Northwoods College.
Tom is vaccinated against measles.

We start with a general statement about the students at Northwoods College (they have all been vaccinated against measles). Then we relate one specific student (Tom) to our general statement about the students and we use that relationship to reach a specific conclusion about Tom (he has been vaccinated against measles).

Dr. Fleming also used deductive reasoning. His thought process probably went something like this:

Organisms grow only in friendly environments.
These organisms aren't growing.
Therefore, the mold is not a friendly environment.

Syllogism

You will notice that we used three distinct steps to reach the conclusion. This three-part process is called a *syllogism*. The syllogism is a tool for analyzing deductive reasoning. It is a pattern of thought we use to show relationships.

Each part of the pattern is given a name. We call the first general statement (*All students at Northwoods College have been vaccinated against measles*) a *major premise*. A premise is the statement of an idea. A major premise is the main idea on which the rest of your thinking is based—an assumption, an accepted principle, or an established pattern of facts.

The second part of the syllogism is called a *minor premise*. This is the statement that shows relationship between a large population and an individual person or item (*Tom is a college student at Northwoods College*).

From this relationship we draw a *conclusion* (*Tom is vaccinated against measles*). This conclusion is the third part of the syllogism.

Guidelines

The syllogism we have just developed about Tom's vaccination is called a *categorical syllogism*. That means we use a category of things like people, retail stores, or insurance companies as the basis for our reasoning. In order for reasoning from this type of syllogism to be valid, you must follow certain guidelines. First, the category must be all-inclusive. In other words, the major premise must state that all the members of the category are the same. We must say, "All students were vaccinated," or "None of the students was vaccinated." Words like *all, every,* and *none* are indicators that the major premise includes every member of the category.

If the category is not all-inclusive, we cannot reach a definite conclusion. For example, if we say:

Most students at Northwoods College were vaccinated against measles.
Tom is a student at Northwoods College.

we can only speculate as to whether Tom has or has not been vaccinated. The word *most* leaves room for other students who were not vaccinated and Tom may have been one of those students.

The second guideline you should use in evaluating your deductive reasoning process concerns the minor premise. Make sure the item mentioned in the minor premise is a member of the category stated in the major premise. For example, if you say "All students at Northwoods College were vaccinated against measles," and then go on to say, "Mary is a secretary at Northwoods College," you cannot conclude that Mary was vaccinated also. In this case Mary is not a part of the category (a student at Northwoods College) mentioned in the major premise. We cannot conclude that all the secretaries at Northwoods College were also vaccinated just because the students were.

The third guideline you should follow when reasoning deductively is to make sure your syllogism is based on a truth. That means your major premise must make a statement generally accepted as truth. If the major premise is inaccurate, your conclusion will also be inaccurate even though you followed the correct reasoning pattern. Consider the following example:

All salesmen get loud at parties.
Jack is a salesman.
He gets loud at parties.

First let's check the validity of the syllogism. Ask yourself: Is the category in the major premise all-inclusive? The answer is yes. We are talking about *all* salesmen.

Next ask yourself if the person mentioned in the minor premise is part of the category mentioned in the major premise. Again, your answer will be yes. Jack is a salesman.

Therefore, if Jack is part of the category, it follows that he will do what everyone else in the category does. The syllogism is valid.

"Wait a minute," you are probably saying. "I know a salesman who hardly says a word at parties. That syllogism can't be valid. It's not true."

You are right, the syllogism isn't true—but it is valid.

Validity refers to the accuracy of the relationship between the major and minor premise. *Truth* refers to the accuracy of the major premise on which the conclusion is based. If the category stated in the major premise is all-inclusive and the item mentioned in the minor premise is a member of the category, there is a demonstrable relationship between the major and minor premise and the syllogism is valid.

In the case of our syllogism about the salesman, the major premise is all-inclusive (all salesmen) and the minor premise makes a statement about a member of that category (Jack is a salesman); therefore, the syllogism is valid. However, the major premise, "All salesmen get loud at parties," is not true. It is a stereotype—an oversimplified generalization—based on a few noticeably loud salesmen. A stereotype is a statement that makes a judgment about an entire group of people on the basis of the action of a few people within that group. "All politicians accept bribes" or "All blondes are dumb" are examples of stereotypes. When you base your syllogism on a stereotype, the relationship established in the minor premise cannot be supported; therefore you cannot depend on the conclusion to be true.

Perhaps we can understand the difference between "valid" and "true" as they relate to syllogisms by comparing deductive reasoning to baking a cake. You can follow the recipe accurately but the end result will fail if you have used stale baking powder, wormy flour, or rotten eggs. In the same way your syllogism may be valid (you have followed the recipe carefully) but your conclusion may be untrue because your major premise (the ingredients of your recipe) was unsound.

If you remember these guidelines, you should be able to use the categorical syllogism effectively: (1) the category of your major premise is all-inclusive, (2) the item mentioned in the minor premise is part of the category, and (3) the syllogism is based on a generally accepted truth rather than a stereotype.

STATEMENTS OF REPORT AND OPINION

When we talk or write, we usually use two kinds of statement: report statements and opinion statements.

Report Statement

A *report statement* can be verified. For instance, the statement:

When I use an electronic typewriter instead of an electric typewriter, I reduce my typing time by 50 percent.

is a report statement because you can time the typist to determine whether the statement is accurate.

Opinion Statement

Opinion statements cannot be verified. They express emotions, attitudes, or beliefs and provoke different responses from different readers. Unlike a report statement, which can be proven true or false, an opinion statement can be discussed from various viewpoints and requires the reader to make a judgment. The statement:

We should purchase an electronic typewriter for our office.

is an opinion statement. It can be supported (electronic typewriters are more efficient) and refuted (electronic typewriters are too expensive). The reader's final decision about purchasing the electronic typewriter will depend on which case is presented more successfully.

Assertions

Opinion statements are also called *assertions*. In an essay, assertions are usually made in the purpose statement and the topic sentences. Report statements then support the assertions and form the discussion in the paragraph. Each time you make an assertion, you must support it with report statements. Because assertions must be supported, be sure you express opinions that can be backed up with verifiable statements.

Some statements that can be classified as opinions are too general to be supported adequately. For example, "Computers will bring about the collapse of society" is an opinion statement, but it cannot be adequately supported because it is too general. Some people may say it is a wild statement, meaning that it lacks a clear focus.

Remember it is usually difficult to support an all-inclusive statement. Therefore, when making an assertion, avoid words like *never, always,* and *all.* Statements like, "Computers will *never* replace factory workers" or "*All* workers should jog during their noon hour" are difficult to support. In the first statement, the word *never* requires that you prove that for as long as society exists people will work in factories. In the second statement you must prove that everyone, even those people who may have a history of heart disease or high blood pressure, should jog during the noon hour. You can see that proving either of these statements is an impossible task: you cannot look into the future indefinitely, and you cannot say what is best for everyone.

Beginning writers often think that the more emphatically they state their assertions, the more convincing they are. Usually the opposite is true. All-inclusive wording signals emotionalism. The reader thinks, "This is a stereotype."

Your assertions will have more impact if you limit them to something you can adequately support.

In the next ten years, computers will take over many of the *routine tasks* currently being done by factory workers, but we will still need people to supervise the machines.
Many people in our company would feel better if they jogged during the noon hour.

"In the next ten years" limits the discussion to a predictable time span.
"Many people should jog" takes into account that some people should not jog.

Learn to qualify your assertions. If you do not, you will at times find yourself trying to support a statement that cannot be covered adequately.

FAULTY REASONING

Pitfalls in logical reasoning are called *fallacies.* Fallacies in reasoning can result from: (1) lack of information, (2) unclear relationships between items compared, or (3) opinions stated as facts. As you study these pitfalls to logical reasoning, think of Theresa's research techniques and completed report. How many examples of the pitfalls discussed here can you identify in the scenario? As a start, a few are mentioned for you in the discussion.

Lack of Information

First let's consider those fallacies that result from lack of information. One of these fallacies is the *Hasty Generalization*. This is a general statement based on insufficient data. We have already discussed this problem in connection with inductive reasoning. We said that sufficient items of information must be present to support a generalization. If the data are insufficient, the generalization cannot be trusted to be accurate. In our opening scenario, for example, Theresa uses a hasty generalization when she says that *numerous* personnel favor decentralization. She has talked to only five people. In a large company five people cannot be called *numerous.*

The second fallacy resulting from insufficient data is called *Begging the Question.* When you beg the question, you assume something to be true without actually proving it is true; then you use that assumption as the proof for your argument. For example, you might say, "We should change the unfair parking regulations on campus." You assume that everyone will agree with you that the parking regulations are unfair, and because they are unfair, they should be changed. You use your assumption as proof, but you do not attempt to prove the assumption (that the parking regulations are unfair) first. Begging the question confuses the issues because you are actually using what you are trying to prove (the rules are unfair; therefore they need changing) as proof (these *unfair* rules need changing).

Unclear Relationships

Fallacies can also result from unclear relationships. One of these fallacies is the *False Analogy.* An analogy is a comparison of objects with similar qualities. A false analogy compares two things that are alike in some ways but significantly different in other ways. The false analogy ignores those significant differences and bases its conclusion on the similarities. For example, when you say, "Tom will make a great supervisor; he works so hard as a salesman," you are comparing the dedication Tom has for his present job with the amount of time you know it takes to be a supervisor. A good supervisor, however, has many qualities other than dedication to the job. A good supervisor must know how to help people work together and how to evaluate other workers' progress. These qualities are not mentioned in the comparison. Tom's success as a salesman is not conclusive evidence that he will also succeed as a supervisor. When Theresa, in the opening scenario, compares Pillar Insurance to Maynard Implements, she is also using a false analogy. Two businesses must be alike in staff and the product they sell to qualify for an accurate comparison.

Another relationship fallacy results from *Errors in Cause–Effect Reasoning.* When you reason with a cause–effect relationship, you say that something (the effect) is the direct result of something else (the cause). The confusion occurs when there is no clear relationship between the stimulus and the result. The following statement illustrates an error in cause–effect reasoning. One student says to the other, "Of course, there will be more rapes in the next few years; our president is against the Equal Rights Amendment." The student has reasoned fallaciously. There is no clear relationship between the increase of reported rapes and the President's stand on ERA.

A third fallacy that results from unclear relationships is called *Ignoring the Question*. When you ignore the question, you shift the basis of the argument away from the current issue. For example, an employee caught using the computerized payroll system to add $100 to his check each week might say to his supervisor, "What's wrong with padding my paycheck? Haven't you ever failed to report extra income on your income tax?"

You can imagine the supervisor's response. Most likely, she forgets all about her employee's embezzlement and starts to defend her income-reporting practices. The real issue is ignored. The neutral observer would realize that the relationship between the employee's proved embezzlement and the supervisor's unproven failure to report extra income is minimal at best.

A fourth fallacy based on an unclear relationship is the *Either/Or Fallacy*. When you use either/or reasoning, you conclude that there are only two alternatives to a problem when there are actually more than two. For example, you could say:

Either Congress budgets for make-work jobs or our unemployment rate will remain at 10 percent.

When you reason this way, you do not consider other alternatives to the problem such as retraining programs for unemployed or lowered interest rates to encourage industrial expansion. In these complex times, few issues can be successfully resolved by one's considering just two alternatives.

Opinion Stated as Fact

The third cause of fallacial reasoning is stating an opinion as though it were a fact and then using that opinion as the basis for your argument.

The *Fallacy Against the Man* is an example of this kind of faulty reasoning. When you reason this way, you attack people personally (hence the term *against the man*) rather than the issues they stand for. For example, you could say:

Even if he hadn't been divorced three times, I couldn't go along with the way Jones has restructured our department.

You are implying that Jones's failure at marriage also makes him a failure as a manager. You are using an opinion about his personal life in place of facts about the way the restructured department is operating as a basis for your argument against Jones's reorganization of your office.

Another reasoning of this kind is called the *Appeal to Numbers*. The basis for this reasoning is the idea that what appeals to many people is good for everyone. If 50 percent of the people you work with favor working ten hours a day for four days a week, you cannot conclude that your company should implement this work schedule for everyone. There are many other factors such as cost efficiency and job efficiency which need to be evaluated before a change is made. The number of people in favor of the change is only one factor to consider. We often hear the phrase, "Everyone is doing it," as a basis for making major decisions. When we hear that, we should remember that it is an example of a faulty reasoning process.

You will remember that we started this group of chapters with a discussion of Theresa's research and writing techniques. One of her problems resulted from the logic she used to reason through the problem. Her statement, "I've talked to five people, that should be enough," indicates that she did not understand the inductive reasoning process. We might also suspect that fallacies occur in her reasoning. "Everyone wants the word processing department decentralized" is not an accurate basis for deciding to decentralize the department. The reasoning or lack of reasoning, Theresa uses to develop her report, therefore, is one of the problems she must face. In the next chapter we will discuss another problem with Theresa's report: word choice.

SUMMARY

When you have a goal in mind but don't know how to reach that goal, you have a problem. Problems may be either convergent or divergent. A convergent problem has one correct solution; a divergent problem may have numerous appropriate solutions. All problems have three parts: givens, operations, and goals. Knowing the givens, being skilled in the operations, and identifying the goals are all important to the problem-solving process. Other helpful techniques are breaking the main problem into smaller problems and diagraming the problem. As you solve problems, remember to keep an open mind and look for unique approaches to difficult problems.

Logical reasoning will help us in the problem-solving process. We reason logically by two different methods: inductive reasoning and deductive reasoning. To reason inductively, you draw a conclusion from many individual examples. To reason deductively, you use a general rule as the basis for your conclusion about one specific incident.

inductive—specific to general
deductive—general to specific

Follow these guidelines to make sure your inductive reasoning is accurate:

1. Take an adequate sampling
2. Use verifiable information
3. Make sure your examples relate directly to the problem you are trying to solve
4. Consider major factors that deviate from the data you are collecting

The thought pattern used in deductive reasoning is called a syllogism. A syllogism includes a major premise, minor premise, and conclusion. The major premise of the categorical syllogism makes a statement about a category.

If the thought pattern is followed correctly, the syllogism is valid. A valid syllogism is not necessarily true, however. Sometimes the basis of a syllogism is false.

When that happens, the conclusion drawn is also false. As a result, you can reach a false conclusion by following the deductive reasoning process correctly.

Other errors in reasoning are called fallacies. These fallacies include: hasty generalization, begging the question, false analogy, errors in cause–effect reasoning, ignoring the question, either/or fallacy, fallacy against the man, and appeal to numbers. A detailed explanation of these fallacies is given in the chapter. Understanding the pitfalls of logical reasoning will help you avoid them in your writing.

REVIEW QUESTIONS

1. Explain the difference between convergent and divergent problems.
2. What are the three parts of a problem?
3. Explain the difference between inductive and deductive reasoning.
4. What is a syllogism?
5. When is a syllogism valid?
6. When is a syllogism true?
7. What is the difference between a report statement and an opinion statement? Give an example of each.
8. Why is qualifying assertions an important part of writing? Use an example to illustrate your answer.
9. Give an example of an error in cause–effect reasoning. What is the cause in your example? What is the effect?

ACTIVITIES

1. Use what you have learned about problem solving to solve the following problems:
   a. You are an architect who has been asked to design an office for a newly formed advertising agency. The only space the four partners can afford is a strange L-shaped section on the fiftieth floor of an old building in Chicago's Loop district. The space looks like this:[3]

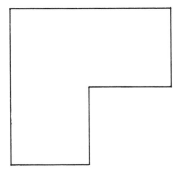

The partners want this space divided into four offices of equal size and shape. They intend to furnish the offices identically with standard office furniture, so

[3]David Lewis and James Green, diagrams from *Thinking Better.* Copyright © 1982. David Lewis, Ph.D. and James Green, M.A. Used by permission of Rawson Wade Publishers.

the rooms cannot be shaped oddly. The partners must sign a lease within the hour and they are eager to see if you can divide this space into four equal offices. You do not have any measuring tools such as a ruler to help you. How can you solve this problem?

    b. Two vice-presidents of a small manufacturing firm want to obtain the position of president when the current president retires. The current president cannot decide which person should get the job. Finally he decides on a contest to help him make his choice. He assigns each of the men a report and says the man whose report reaches the president's office *last* is the new president. Each man works very slowly, but eventually, they do finish the report. Then they start walking very slowly to the president's office. They might have spent days getting across the hall except for the expert advice of the mailroom attendant. What do you think he told them?

2. Now apply your problem-solving techniques to the problem Theresa encounters in our opening scenario. Answer the following questions as you work toward a solution:

    Is Theresa's problem convergent or divergent?

    What are the givens and the goals?

    What operations would you use to solve it?

    Can you break the problem into smaller problems?

    How would you diagram it?

    Can you identify any mind sets that prevent Theresa from solving the problem?

    Does this problem require any unique approaches?

3. Read the editorials in your school and community newspaper. Find examples of inductive and deductive reasoning. How many of the examples are true?

4. Read three newspapers (one with local distribution, one with statewide distribution, and one with national distribution). Write down the fallacies you discover in these newspapers. Share your list with your class. In which newspaper did you find the most fallacies?

5. Which of the following are opinion statements? Which are report statements? Label opinions *O* and reports *R*.

    _____ a. Gene splicing should be used to prevent birth defects.

    _____ b. You should take vitamins to maintain good health.

    _____ c. We just installed five word processors.

    _____ d. We will never find a cure for diabetes.

    _____ e. Mechanical hearts are unchristian.

    _____ f. Mount St. Helens erupted twice.

    _____ g. Food stamps should be abolished.

    _____ h. Two years of math is required of everyone graduating from our school.

    _____ i. Warren Beatty won Best Actor for his portrayal of Jack Reed.

    _____ j. Meryl Streep is the best actress of all the women in movies today.

6. Which of the opinion statements listed above are adequately qualified? Which are not?

7. Following are examples of fallacious reasoning. What fallacy is illustrated by each statement? Rephrase the statements to avoid the fallacy.

    a. I don't know why I should brush my teeth when I go camping. No one else does.

    b. I wouldn't trust Smith to build my house. He used to have a drinking problem, you know.

    c. Sue is my choice for this teaching job. Her own children are so well behaved.

    d. Either we ban all foreign cars from our highways or our economy will never improve.

    e. Why can't I smoke at this table? You're eating onions.

4

EFFECTIVE WORD CHOICE

All words are pegs to hang ideas on.

Henry Ward Beecher

After studying this chapter, you should understand:
1. How to choose effective wording
2. How to focus on the audience
3. How connotations influence response
4. How to improve spelling through the use of basic spelling aids

In Chapters 2 and 3 we discussed problems in research and logical thinking that Theresa, the employee in the opening scenario, had with her report. Mrs. Wilson's comments also indicate that Theresa had a problem choosing words that communicated clearly. An important basis for effective communication is word choice.

In this chapter we will discuss the guidelines for effective word choice. We will also discuss ways of focusing on your audience and show how your audience's emotional reaction to words can hinder or improve communication. All of the tips on word choice pertain to both speaking and writing, but when we write, we must also be aware of the mechanics of putting the words on paper. For that reason, a section on spelling concludes this chapter.

CHOOSING EFFECTIVE WORDS

We can look at four main guidelines for effective word choice:

> Choose simple, familiar words
> Use concise wording
> Speak and write in the active voice
> Avoid unnecessary jargon and vague words

Choose Simple, Familiar Words

When you are selecting words to express your ideas, you should always keep your audience in mind. Choose words that the members of your audience will understand easily. Simple, familiar words convey meaning more readily than complicated, unfamiliar words. For example, you should select words like *did* and *get* rather than *accomplish* and *obtain*, even though *did* and *get* sound ordinary next to the other two longer and more showy words.

Look at the following sentences. Which sentence conveys meaning more quickly? Which sentence do you have to think about before you understand it completely?

If we implement this modification of our billing procedure, the maximum interest rate we can charge is 10% per annum.

If we make this change in our billing procedure, the highest interest rate we can charge is 10% a year.

Although you probably chose the second sentence as easier to understand, you may also have decided that the first sentence "sounds better."

Because most people must go to school to learn to write, we tend to think of writing as a special skill of educated people. In order to keep it special, we use showy, elaborate language. Similarly, when we are talking in front of a group, we tend to use elaborate language to establish our credibility as a speaker and impress our listener with our knowledge. You must remember, however, that the purpose of writing and speaking is to communicate ideas effectively. Since the second sentence of our example communicates more effectively than the first sentence, it is the better choice.

Use Concise Wording

Using as few words as possible to convey meaning is called *conciseness*. Frequently, when we try to make our communication showy, we also tend to be wordy.

For example, one of the ways we make our writing more elaborate is to duplicate ideas. We think stating the same idea in two different ways gives it more emphasis. This duplication of ideas is called *redundancy*. "Let's assemble together at the school," is an example of a redundancy. If you assemble, you come together. If you come together, you assemble. Since both *assemble* and *come together* mean the same thing, one of the words conveys the meaning clearly, so you do not need to use the other word.

Another way we make our communication more elaborate is by using lengthy phrases when we could say the same thing in fewer words. For example, you might write or say:

It is our considered opinion that the word processing department should be decentralized.

However,

The word processing department should be decentralized.

says the same thing in fewer words.

One way you can be concise is to eliminate the habit of starting sentences with *It* and *There.*

It is my pleasure to be here.
There are many reasons for a shorter work week.

Instead, say,

I am pleased to be here.
A shorter work week is a good idea for many reasons.

Another way you can be concise is to eliminate meaningless phrases. Think of each word as costing you money and be as economical as possible in your wording. For example:

Wordy: Due to the fact that expenditures for oil exploration declined 1.8% or $4.7 million in 1983, our company was able to lower the cost of its crude oil by $2 a barrel.

could be written:

Concise: Because we spent 1.8% or $4.7 million less for oil exploration in 1983, we lowered our price of crude oil by $2 a barrel.

Although conciseness is important to effective writing, you should not confuse conciseness with brevity. Don't eliminate important facts or ideas just to keep your sentences short. Look at the sentence about the declining oil prices again. In rewriting the sentence we changed *due to the fact that* to *because* and *our company* to *we.* We also made the clause "that expenditures for oil exploration declined by 1.8 percent or 4.7 million in 1983" more direct by using a verb, "spent," rather than the noun, "expenditures." Then we could say "We *spent* 1.8 percent or 4.7 million *less* . . ." These changes made the wording more concise, but they did not eliminate any important information.

A Language Guide to Outplacement

Between jobs. Same as "unemployed," with one distinction: someone who says he is between jobs generally has been unemployed before.

Black Friday. Any day of the week you get the ax.

Blindsided. A football expression referring to the quarterback who gets sacked because his helmet restricts peripheral vision. An employee sometimes has a similar problem when he is so absorbed in his work that he can't see the signs that he's about to be sacked.

Body shop. A disreputable employment agency that fills jobs with warm bodies. Frequently, body shops do not even interview a candidate before referring him to an employer.

Boneyard. Also called the "leper colony," the boneyard is an office or office area within a company used by departing executives to conduct their job searches. These exiles generally arrive at the boneyard at 10 A.M., read the want ads, and dictate a few letters to search firms, enclosing their resumés. After a two-hour lunch, they return to check messages, which are seldom there. They head home at about 4:30 P.M., after sharing additional gossip with their former colleagues, who seldom help lepers but feel superior to them because they still have a job.

Broadcast letter. A letter announcing that a person is considering changing jobs. It is generally sent with an accompanying resumé to 300 executive search firms and 500 company presidents. The search firms seldom acknowledge it. The company president's secretary sends it to the personnel director, whose secretary sends form letter number 4. A broadcast letter most often receives a response of 1% to 3%; 95% of the responses are negative.

Deadwood. People who, in the mind of management, have no productive value and cannot contribute to profitability. Deadwood is a burden to be carried until it quietly retires, quits, or gets hit by a beer truck.

Dehiring. Same as firing.

Encouraged to leave. Fired.

Fired. Encouraged to leave.

Headhunter. Also called a "pirate." The term is another word for an executive search consultant.

Leisure time. A question in a competitive employment interview about leisure time is designed to confirm certain opinions of the interviewer. A man being asked what he does during leisure time seldom refers to avocations of flower arranging, sewing, watching TV, or ballet dancing. A woman seldom volunteers that she enjoys watching prizefighting, likes to protest, or plays football. Both, however, may state that they enjoy tennis, golf, swimming (athletic, healthy, competitive, and good for the body) or reading, theater, charity work (intellectually stimulating and good for society). Neither of them would say sex, daydreaming, sleeping, drinking, or gambling.

Mutual agreement. Canned.

Overqualified. An excuse usually given to an employment applicant who is too old or too expensive in the mind of the interviewer.

Rifle approach. As opposed to *shotgun*—identifying clearly a job objective; understanding the market for such a job; contacting individuals within that market; obtaining the exact offer and accepting it.[1]

---

[1] This material is part of "A Language Guide to Outplacement," by Thomas M. Camden, 501 West Ogden, Hinsdale, Illinois 60521. Camden is a Human Resources Consultant specializing in corporate outplacement and individual counsel.

If, on the other hand, we had said:

Because we spent less for oil exploration in 1983 we lowered our price of crude.

we would have eliminated important information. This sentence is too brief to convey meaning accurately. When you are rewriting your sentences for conciseness, eliminate unnecessary words only. Do not cross out important information just to shorten the sentence.

Choose Active Verbs

A third way to achieve effective wording is to choose active rather than passive verbs. An *active verb* shows the subject doing something.

Ron gave his report to the secretary on Tuesday.

A *passive verb* shows something being done to the subject.

The report was put on Ron's desk Wednesday morning.

In the case of writing on the job it is often easier to write:

A complaint was made about our shipping department.

than to pinpoint the problem and say:

The shipping department is a week behind in filling orders.

Nevertheless, the directness accomplished by writing or speaking in the active voice is usually appreciated.

If indirectness is necessary, you can probably accomplish that with a statement like, "I am concerned about the backlog of orders in the shipping department." The verb is active and the wording is concise, but the tone is conciliating rather than accusing.

Avoid Jargon and Vague Words

We sometimes attempt to impress our audience with *jargon,* a term used to describe technical terminology. Every occupation has its own vocabulary of technical terms. In the box is a list of terms used in the employment field. When outsiders listen to such jargon they may feel as though they are listening to a foreign language. When you are speaking or writing about your field, you must consider your audience carefully. Will all your readers and listeners understand the jargon of your occupation?

For example, if you say, "I'm going up today," your message may be interpreted a variety of ways. An airplane pilot will think of "going up" as flying, while an accountant may think of "going up" as working on the computer. If you mention flooring to a contractor and a car salesman, they will think of different things. Flooring is floor covering (carpet, tile, wood) to a contractor; to a car salesman flooring is a display of models in the showroom.

Indiscriminate use of jargon can frustrate the receiver of your message and block communication. If you think your audience will not understand jargon familiar to you, you should substitute more commonly used words for the jargon or define your technical terminology in the context of your message. The following example shows how you can define technical jargon within the context of the writing. The words "pre-trial discovery" in the excerpt may be unclear to most readers except those who are lawyers; therefore the term is defined in the text.

> These actions are still in pre-trial discovery, a legal term meaning that the plaintiffs and defendants are exchanging information, documents and so forth, to bolster their cases, and await trial in the U.S. District Court for the Southern District of New York.[2]

When writing, remember to choose specific words that convey meaning clearly to your reader. Words like *nice, good, high,* and *low* are general terms which do not convey specific meaning. What exactly does, "This applicant has good grades in writing" mean? Are good grades C's or A's? "This applicant earned an A and a B in writing" states without a doubt what kind of grades an applicant had.

Consider the following statements and their interpretation. How many interpretations of your own can you add?

Statement	Interpretation
This is a nice office.	This is a light, airy office.
	This is a large office.
	I like the color of the walls in this office.
	I like the carpet in this office.
	This is a quiet office.
Mary types fast.	Mary types 60 words per minute.
	Mary types 100 words per minute.
	Mary doesn't make mistakes when she types.
We lost a lot of money this quarter.	We lost $5,000 this quarter.
	We lost $2 million this quarter.
The Bahamas were hot this spring.	It was 60° in the Bahamas in March.
	It was 101° in the Bahamas in March.

You can see that a wide variety of interpretations is possible when you choose general words. Try to select the most precise word to express your idea. This approach will help prevent misunderstanding between you and your audience.

[2]Copyright © 1980 by the American Institute of Certified Public Accountants.

RELATING TO YOUR AUDIENCE

Familiar, concise language is an important consideration when you choose words to convey your message effectively, but you should also relate your message to your specific audience. You can do this by phrasing the message so it focuses on your audience and by being aware of the emotional response your audience may have to the words you choose. Your audience will understand and accept your message more easily when you relate it directly to them.

Focus on the Audience

The phrasing of your message can include or exclude your audience. For example you might say:

You can help us process your insurance claim promptly by returning these forms to us by 12/2/86.

or you could say

We need these forms by 12/2/86 so we can pay the contractor who repaired your roof.

The first sentence relates directly to the reader. Choosing the pronoun *you* helps involve the reader in the message. We say the sentence is "you-focused." This you-focus gives the reader an immediate reason for returning the forms.

The second sentence states the same idea from the company's viewpoint: we need the forms so we can settle with the contractor. This sentence presents the company's reason for wanting the forms filled out and has less impact on the audience.

Compare this use of concise, familiar word choice focused on the audience, with the following excerpt from the first policy ever issued by the Sentry Insurance Company in 1898:

> Against loss by reason of the liability imposed by law upon the Assured for damages on account of bodily injuries, including death at any time resulting therefrom, accidentally suffered by any person or persons by reason of the maintenance of use of any of the automobiles enumerated and described in Item 3 of said Declarations, while in charge of the Assured or his employees; limited, however, to the sum of FIVE THOUSAND DOLLARS on account of an accident resulting in such injuries to one person, and, subject to that limit, to the sum of TEN THOUSAND DOLLARS for an accident resulting in such injuries to more than one person.[3]

In 1974 Sentry sponsored a study to learn what their policyholders thought about their insurance. Findings of the study emphasized that consumers wanted a policy that was easy to read. More than 1,500 work hours were spent revising the

[3] Donald E. Reutershan and Germain E. Kunze, "Who Wants a New Insurance Policy?" *Drake Law Review*, December 1975, p. 768.

auto insurance policy but the revision reduced the policy from 12,000 words to 6,500. It also made the policy significantly easier to read. Here is an excerpt from that policy:

> We promise to pay Damages for bodily injury or property damage for which the law holds You responsible because of a Car Accident involving a Car we insure.
> We also promise to pay additional benefits as long as we haven't paid our entire limit of liability for Damages.[4]

You can see that familiar, concise language and a you-focus considerably improved the readability of Sentry's policy.

Connotations and Denotations

Another important aspect of word choice is the emotions the words you choose arouse in your readers. Most words in our language convey two meanings simultaneously, a descriptive meaning and an emotional meaning. For example, you may say "spinach" to two people. Both people understand that spinach is an edible, green, leafy plant, but one person also thinks "yum" while the other person thinks "yuk." The word *spinach* conveys two meanings simultaneously to each person: a *descriptive* meaning (edible, green, leafy plant), and an *emotional* meaning (I like it or I don't like it). We call the descriptive meaning a *denotation*. This is the meaning you will find in a dictionary, and it is the same meaning for every person in every situation. We call the emotional meaning a *connotation*. This meaning varies from person to person.

Too often we pay attention to the denotation of a word and forget to consider the emotions the word will arouse in our readers. Consider the word *home*, for example. You may attach a pleasant, restful feeling to the word *home*. Your friend, on the other hand, may think of home as a place filled with noise and contention. If you tell your friend to "Go home and get some rest," you may be surprised by the response. Your friend may label you as a noncaring person who does not understand. You, on the other hand, may never understand your friend's reaction because you are unaware of the different connotation attached to the word *home*.

Connotations also contribute to subtle differences between two words that have similar dictionary meanings. Consider, for example, the words *work* and *job*. *Webster's New World Dictionary* defines *job* as a "piece of work" and lists *job* as a synonym under *work*. Although the denotations are similar, the feelings we attach to the words influence the way we use them. For most people *work* has a slightly negative connotation. Work is the opposite of play. It is unpleasant, difficult, and tension-causing while play is fun, easy, and relaxing. A *job*, on the other hand, has a positive connotation for most people. We associate money, independence, self-fulfillment, and prestige with having a job. This difference in connotation explains

---

[4]Reutershan and Germain, p. 754.

why one day someone might say happily, "I have a job," but the next day that person might say reluctantly, "I wish I didn't have to go to work."

When you are writing letters and reports, consider the connotation as well as the denotation of the words you select.

The following scenario illustrates the importance of word connotation in delivering messages. In this dialogue the words with negative connotations are in italics.

MAX: Tom, when can we discuss the engineering supervisor's job?

TOM: Right now's fine with me. What do you have in mind?

MAX: As you know Howard Mikkleson is in that position now, but I want to *move* Bud Timken, a new man from Cal State, *in over* Howard.

TOM: What about Howard?

MAX: I want to *replace him* with Bud.

TOM: That would mean *demoting* Howard.

MAX: That's right.

TOM: Why do you want to bring someone new *in over Howard's head?*

MAX: Howard *hasn't been keeping up.* His skills are *outdated* and he hasn't taken any refresher courses in years. He *doesn't speak up* in our quality circle meetings and computers seem to *confuse* him. He *doesn't work well* with our newer employees either. In fact, I think he's *afraid* of their ambition and innovation.

TOM: I think you are right about Howard. He *is used to the old days when things were slower paced.* We should probably *demote* him to some nonsupervisory position where he *won't have much decision-making responsibility.* But how do you think he'll react to this. He's been with the company twenty years.

MAX: I don't think he'll accept it easily. He'll probably think of it as a *slap in the face.*

TOM: How you word it will make a difference. Approach the subject in a human e what happens.

e letter Max wrote to Howard explaining why he was being way the connotation has changed from the dialogue above. ness of the way connotation influences the message, word- to the dialogue but positive in connotation has been ital- ou read the letter, compare the tone of the letter with that of

ιw from your twenty years of service here that you r business and concerned about the progress of our ιe your dedication to Benson & Johnson and think of ιmployee. are someone who has watched this company grow ness to an international company, *we are sure you realize how important it is that we keep informed of new markets and continue to expand our contacts.*

For that reason we are hiring a recent graduate from Cal State. He has the most current knowledge in computer design and experience in international sales. He will *take over* your job of Supervisor of Sales on January 30, 1985.

We know he will need knowledge about *the background of our business* and a *sound basis* in sales technique. We think *you are the best person* to *help him* in these areas. For that reason, we hope you will accept the position of *Advisor to the Supervisor of Sales. Although it involves a reduction in salary*, it will *also relieve you of involvement in high-powered meetings and the need to continually update your skills.* This job will be slower paced and *give you the opportunity to enjoy the more relaxed schedule you have earned.*

SPELLING

In order to convey your meaning accurately, you must not only make effective word choices, you must also follow the standards or convention set for written communication. A *convention* is a custom or a way of doing things agreed upon by most people. Driving on the right side of the road is a convention in the United States. It is a "rule of the road" we observe to prevent confusion and help us get from one place to another easily.

Certain "rules of writing" also help us take the reader from one idea to another quickly and easily. Just as we willingly drive on the right side of the road to prevent confusion on the highway, we should also attempt to prevent confusion in our written messages by following the conventions of good writing. Some of these conventions are writing in complete sentences and paragraphs and using correct spelling and punctuation.

Just as the United States is a "melting pot" for people from different countries and cultures, our language is also a combination of different languages and dialects. Using English as a base, we borrowed from German, French, Spanish, and American Indian dialects to meet our needs for expression in this vast country. As immigrants from Ireland, Mexico, Japan, and other countries arrived, words and idioms from their dialects were assimilated into "American English." As the country expanded, we also coined new words to fit new situations. Today our language continues to change as our culture changes. This tendency to borrow and change is the sign of a healthy, living language, but borrowing from so many sources has caused confusion in spelling. Sometimes we think there is no rhyme or reason to the way words in American-Engish are spelled.

How Words Are Formed

Although English spelling will always be difficult for most people, it can be made easier by your understanding of how words are formed. Many words are made up of three parts: prefixes, suffixes, and roots. As you might imagine, the *root* is the base word.

A *prefix* is one or more letters attached to the front of the base word. Each prefix has a meaning of its own, so when it appears before the root word it modifies the meaning of the root. For example, *re* is a prefix meaning "again." When *re* (*again*) occurs with *unite* (*come together*), it modifies the meaning of *unite*. *Reunite* means "to come together *again*."

In the following list some common prefixes and their meanings are given in the first column. Add them to the words in the second column and note the change of meaning that has occurred in the resulting words, shown in the third column.

Prefix		Word	New Word
ab (away from)		normal (ordinary)	abnormal (away from the ordinary)
dis (apart or away)	+	appear (come into sight)	disappear (vanish from sight)
il (not)	+	legal (lawful)	illegal (not lawful)
mis (wrong)	+	spell (put letters of a word in order)	misspell (put letters of a word in the wrong place)
non (not)	+	functional (useful)	nonfunctional (not useful)
pre (before)	+	natal (birth)	prenatal (before birth)
re (again)	+	establish (to install)	reestablish (to install again)
un (not)	+	aware (informed)	unaware (not informed)

Not all prefixes are added to whole words that we recognize, but their meanings help us define a word nonetheless.

at (toward)	+	tract	attract
com (with)	+	bine	combine
ex (out of)	+	tract	extract
ob (against)	+	ject	object

A *suffix* is one or more letters added to the end of a root word. Suffixes may change the tense of the word or they may change the word to another part of speech. For example, the following sentence is written in the present tense.

Tom and Mary laugh.

When you add the suffix *-ed* to *laugh,* you change the word to past tense:

Tom and Mary laughed.

You can also change the root word to another part of speech. For example, in the sentence

The impressive graduation ceremony was enjoyable.

impressive is an adjective describing *ceremony.*

When we add *-ly* to *impressive,* it can no longer function as an adjective

The impressively graduation ceremony was enjoyable.

is incorrect.

Impressively is an adverb and should be used to modify a verb as in this sentence.

The president conducted the graduation ceremony impressively.

Following is a list of suffixes. Add them to the words in the second column and note whether the tense or the part of speech of the resulting words changes.

-ful	use	useful
-able	think	thinkable
-ment	agree	agreement
-ant	propel	propellant
-ent	repel	repellent
-ous	courage	courageous
-ed	joke	joked
-ing	cry	crying
-ty	subtle	subtlety

Pronunciation

Knowing how words are formed can help you spell correctly. Another aid to correct spelling is pronunciation. Often we spell words incorrectly because we pronounce them incorrectly. For example we might say:

acciden*tly* for accidentally
boun*dry* for boundary
disas*terous* for disas*trous*

Following is a list of words that may be spelled incorrectly because they are mispronounced. The italicized letters indicate the pronunciation problem.

asp*i*rin	February
a*th*letic	grievous
attemp*t*	heigh*t*
authen*t*ic	lib*r*ary
chocolate	min*i*ature
different	scenery
enviro*n*ment	temperature
exercise	

Pay close attention to the proper pronunciation of a word. It is often a clue to spelling.

Basic Rules

The third aid to spelling correctly is understanding the basic rules of spelling. Below, some of the most frequently used rules are listed. Learning to apply these rules should increase your spelling proficiency.

When you add a suffix to a word that ends in a vowel-consonant combination, you double the final consonant of the root word if the accent is on the last syllable of the root word. Examples:

refer	+	ed	referred
control	+	ed	controlled
occur	+	ence	occurrence

If the last syllable of the root is not accented or if the suffix does not begin with a vowel, do not double the final consonant when you add a suffix.

benefit	+	ed	benefited
offer	+	ed	offered
regret	+	ful	regretful

If the accent changes from last syllable to another syllable when you add the suffix, do not double the final consonant.

refér	réference
prefér	préference

When you add a suffix beginning with a vowel to a word ending in a silent *e*, you usually drop the *e*.

care	+	ing	caring
lose	+	ing	losing
live	+	able	livable

If the word ends in *ce* or *ge*, however, you often keep the *e* when adding suffixes that begin with -*a*, -*o*, or -*u*. Ask yourself, "Does the *c* sound like an *s*; does the *g* sound like a *j*? If you answer yes, then retain the *e*.

notice	+	able (the *c* sounds like *s*)	noticeable
marriage	+	able (the *g* sounds like *j*)	marriageable

When you are adding a suffix that begins with a consonant to a word that ends in a silent *e*, you usually keep the *e*.

use	+	ful	useful
improve	+	ment	improvement
sure	+	ly	surely
nine	+	ty	ninety

However, when the root word ends in *ue,* drop the *e.*

true	+	ly	truly
argue	+	ment	argument

When you add a prefix whose last letter is the same as the first letter of the root, keep all letters of both words.

mis	+	spell	misspell
pre	+	empt	preempt
re	+	echo	reecho

The same rule applies when you are adding a suffix.

drunken	+	ness	drunkenness
inter	+	racial	interracial
final	+	ly	finally

Many words in our language use the *ie* or *ei* combination. A nursery rhyme should help you remember how to use these combinations:

i before *e*
   piece
   brief
   believe
except after *c*
   receive
   receipt
   ceiling
and when sounding like *ay*
   neighbor
   eight
   weigh

Although this rule is generally true, a number of exceptions exist. Following are a few of the more common ones.

leisure
ancient
their
seize
foreign

Even when you know how words are formed, pay attention to pronunciations, and apply the standard rules, spelling can still be a problem. Many words simply do not conform to rules or offer a hint through pronunciation. For example, is it:

irresist*a*ble	or	irresist*i*ble
collect*a*ble	or	collect*i*ble
prevel*a*nt	or	preval*e*nt

Because we don't accent the endings to these words, it is often impossible to hear a distinction between *able* and *ible* or *ant* and *ent*. In these cases the word probably has to be memorized to ensure correct spelling. Following is a list of words that you may want to memorize.

accept*a*ble	indispens*a*ble
accid*e*nt	irresist*i*ble
appar*e*nt	persist*e*nt
calend*a*r	privil*e*ge
cemet*e*ry	proced*u*re
consist*e*nt	relev*a*nt
defin*i*te	respect*a*ble
incred*i*ble	

Showing Ownership

Knowing the correct way to indicate ownership is another spelling problem. Showing possession is often confusing for many writers, but it can be made easier by applying the following set of conventions.

Two symbols in our language are used to show ownership. They are: the apostrophe (') and the apostrophe plus *s* ('s). Whenever a word ends in *s*, show ownership by adding this symbol: (').

Charles(') boat
boys' game

Whenever the word does *not* end in *s*, show ownership by adding this symbol: ('s).

men('s) ideas
children('s) toys
Mary('s) dress

Notice that you do not consider whether the word is singular or plural when choosing the correct symbol to show ownership. *Men* is plural, but because it does not end in *s*, you use this symbol: ('s). *Boys* is plural also, but because it does end in *s*, you use this symbol: ('). Showing possession is easy when you look only at the last letter of the word: add (') if the word ends in *s* and ('s) if it does not end in *s*.

Personal pronouns are the only words that do not use ' or 's to show possession. Personal pronouns like *her, it, your,* and *our* form the possessive by adding *s:*

hers
its
yours
ours

Personal pronouns should not be confused with indefinite pronouns like *anyone* and *everyone.* Indefinite pronouns form the possessive according to the basic rule:

anyone('s) guess
everyone('s) problems

When showing joint ownership, add the symbol of possession to the last name in the list of owners:

Bob and Mary('s) house
Katie, Jack, and Charles(') boat

When making a hyphenated word possessive, put the symbol at the end of the entire hyphenated group:

brother-in-law('s) car
passer-by('s) reaction

Don't confuse this form with the plural form of hyphenated words. Hyphenated words are made plural by making the base word plural:

brothers-in-law
passers-by

If you have two brothers-in-law and they own one cottage, you would write:

my brothers-in-law's cottage

If you remember these conventions, you should find showing possession through writing easier.

Checking the Dictionary

Your final aid to becoming a good speller is to develop the habit of checking the dictionary regularly. When a word does not somehow look right to you, use a dictionary. Especially if you have the first few letters, you can check for spelling. Look under your best guess of the spelling and then any alternatives you can think of. Note the difference between your spelling and the spelling in the dictionary. Write the word several times during the next couple of days until you can recall the correct spelling easily.

Few people are naturally perfect spellers, but those who understand how words are formed, who pronounce words accurately, who apply a few basic rules of correct spelling, and who take time to consult a dictionary when in doubt can improve their spelling noticeably.

SUMMARY

Word choice is important to effective writing. Select familiar words that convey specific meaning. Learn to eliminate redundancies and other unnecessary words and phrases. Use active verbs and focus on the reader. Remember that most words have two kinds of meanings: a connotation and a denotation. Although both you and your reader may agree on the dictionary meaning of the word, the emotional meaning you attach to it may be significantly different. As a writer, you must be aware that differences in connotation may be a barrier to understanding between you and your reader.

Certain conventions or standards govern written communication, and we must observe them in order to communicate effectively. One of these conventions is correct spelling. Knowing how words are formed, paying attention to pronunciation, and applying basic rules of spelling will help you improve your spelling. Even then some words can be problems. Consult the dictionary when in doubt.

REVIEW QUESTIONS

1. Explain the difference between a word's connotation and its denotation. Why is it important to know both meanings of a word?
2. What is the difference between conciseness and brevity? What guidelines should you follow when revising your sentences for conciseness?
3. What are the three aids to improved spelling mentioned in this chapter?
4. "If you learn all the spelling rules, you will spell correctly 100 percent of the time." Is this statement accurate? Explain your answer.
5. What guidelines can you use to make showing ownership through writing easier? What group of words are an exception to this rule?

ACTIVITIES

1. Write synonyms with negative connotations for the following words.
   concern
   doctor
   odor
   large group
   average
2. Choose a picture of an animal from a book or magazine, write a paragraph describing the animal positively and a paragraph describing the animal negatively. Be prepared to show the picture and read your paragraphs to the class.
3. Rewrite the following sentences to make them more concise. Be sure to use simple, familiar words.

a. Reference is made to your December 15 memo where you advised us of your intention to purchase a word processor for the secretarial pool.

b. It is our intention to advise you that you may engage in leisure activities during the month of August as you requested.

c. This is to inform you that you should be cognizant of our proposed policy change.

d. At the present time we do not anticipate a modification in our compensation schedule.

e. Ascertaining the optimum performance level of our typewriter is the responsibility of our research and design department.

4. Find the misspelled words among those listed below and spell them correctly.

offerred	ninty
occurred	judgment
recieve	Charles' boat
leisure	brother's-in-law house
yours	privelige
chief	incredable
thier	apparant
transfered	ilegal
courageous	calender
careful	prefered

PART II   Listening

Andy Perkins is a sales representative for Perfect Printing, Inc. Every Tuesday afternoon he and the company's production manager, Milt Kostroski, play golf with Bud Kramer, an editor for Holiday Books, Ltd.

One Tuesday afternoon Bud and Andy hover nearby as Milt gets into position for a long drive. The ball sings through the air and the two friends shake their heads at Milt's golfing skills. As they walk to the next hole, Bud says: "By the way, we're looking for a printer for our new book on Australia. It'll be a big job. Lots of color photos. We don't get many jobs like that these days. If Perfect Printing wants to bid on it, estimates are due on Friday."

"Sounds interesting," Andy says as he watches Milt select a putter.

Milt's ball rolls effortlessly across the green and drops smoothly into the hole. "Good one," Bud congratulates Milt. Then he adds, as they walk back to the club, "Don't forget the City Tournament next week, Friday. I want a chance to get even."

When Milt and Andy return to their office, Milt says, "Don't forget that bid for the Holiday Book. It's due Friday. That doesn't give you much time."

"Friday," Andy repeats, surprised. "I thought Bud said it was due next week, Friday."

Milt frowns, struggling to recall the conversation. "I'm sure he meant this Friday," he tells Andy. "But then I was only half listening. Too busy sinking it, you know," he adds laughing. "I have to get to work," he says, starting down the hall toward his office. "Good game today. Hope you're in the same form for the tournament next week. Perfect Printing will walk away with all the trophies."

"Tournament," Andy mumbles as he sits down at his desk. "Maybe that's what was next week. I wish I could remember."

Idly, he shuffles the messages on his desk. "There's always so much to do," he thinks. "I really don't have time to do that estimate this week. I'm sure Bud said it was due next week, anyway. Maybe I should call him just to make sure. But I hate to take the time. I have too much to do before I go home."

DISCUSSION OF SCENARIO

Andy ponders his dilemma. He could make one of three decisions:

1. Andy could call Bud immediately and clarify the dates.
2. He could think about the situation a little longer. He could walk down the hall to discuss it again with Milt. Finally, about 45 minutes later he could call Bud to find out for sure when the estimate is due.

Or he could . . .

3. Assure himself that he heard correctly and submit the bid in time for the "next week, Friday" deadline.

Whichever choice he makes, Andy's impaired listening skills have cost his company money. If he calls Bud, he has used both his and Bud's time asking for a repeat of information he has just heard. In the second alternative he has wasted nearly an hour of the company's time trying to decide what to do; therefore, he has cost the company his hour's wages. In the third situation he has submitted the bid a week late and lost a contract worth thousands of dollars to his company.

Incidents similar to the first situation happen every day. In fact, Dr. Steil, a listening expert from the University of Minnesota, estimates that these small errors cost businesses $10 billion each year. Dr. Steil came to his conclusion by figuring that each worker in America makes $10 worth of errors each year. Since there are 100 million workers in America, their errors total $10 million annually.[1] Telephone messages incorrectly repeated, letters incorrectly transcribed, and directions incorrectly followed are all examples of those small errors that take time and cost money to correct.

Andy's third alternative, turning the bid in a week late, may happen less often, but when it does occur, it is a very costly listening error.

Andy was not listening to Bud, but the reason for Andy's predicament is not all his fault. Bud and Milt also did not understand the listening process. Bud talked business when Andy was not prepared to listen. Milt had just made a superb drive and Andy was thinking about golf. Milt received the information correctly, but in his excitement to follow his ball, he did not bother to repeat it to Bud. If Milt had repeated the important information that Bud gave him, there would have been no doubt in his mind that he had the facts straight. By repeating the date, Milt would have also drawn Andy's attention to the conversation.

HOW WELL DO YOU LISTEN?

Does Andy's problem remind you of a time when you could have listened better? Perhaps you would have applied for a job, avoided an argument with your spouse, or received an A on a test if you had listened more efficiently. How would you rate yourself as a listener? Take a minute now to give yourself the test on page 75.[2]

After thinking about your score, you may decide that you need to learn to listen better. Yes, "learn to listen." Although many people think listening is as natural as breathing, it is actually a skill we must learn. Unlike hearing, which is a physical process, listening is a mental skill. Most of us are born with the ability to hear, but we must develop the technique of listening.

---

[1] Charles R. Day, Jr., "How Do You Rate as a Listener?" *Industry Week,* April 28, 1980, p. 32.
[2] *Your Personal Listening Profile* (New York: Sperry Corporation, 1980), p. 7.

How Well Do You Listen?

As a listener, how often do you find yourself engaging in these ten bad listening habits? First, check the appropriate columns. Then tabulate your score using the key below.

LISTENING HABIT	FREQUENCY					SCORE
	Almost always	Usually	Sometimes	Seldom	Almost never	
1. Calling the subject uninteresting						
2. Criticizing the speaker's delivery or mannerisms						
3. Getting over-stimulated by something the speaker says						
4. Listening primarily for facts						
5. Trying to outline everything						
6. Faking attention to the speaker						
7. Allowing interfering distractions						
8. Avoiding difficult material						
9. Letting emotion-laden words arouse personal antagonism						
10. Wasting the advantage of thought speed (daydreaming)						

TOTAL SCORE _____

KEY
"Almost always" score 2   "Sometimes" score 6
"Usually" score 4   "Seldom" score 8
"Almost never" score 10

PROFILE ANALYSIS: The average score is 62. On a scale of 0 to 100, most test takers rate themselves at 55.

This material was prepared by Dr. Lyman K. Steil, President of Communication Development, Inc., St. Paul, Minnesota, for the Sperry Corporation. Reprinted by permission of Dr. Steil and the Sperry Corporation.

5

THE LISTENING PROCESS

I know you think you heard what you thought I said, but are you aware that what you thought I said is not what I meant?

After studying this chapter you should understand:
1. The difference between hearing and listening
2. The importance of listening efficiently on the job and in your personal life
3. The listening process
4. How our level of involvement affects our listening
5. Poor listening habits and the reasons for them
6. Barriers that prevent us from listening efficiently

MRS. JONES: Frank, you're not listening to me.
FRANK: I heard you.
MRS. JONES: What did I say?
FRANK: I forgot.
MRS. JONES: You weren't listening.

THE DIFFERENCE BETWEEN HEARING AND LISTENING

This familiar dialogue points out the difference between hearing and listening. *Hearing* is a physical process. When sound waves vibrate against the eardrum and the brain registers these vibrations or sounds, we hear. *Listening,* on the other hand, is a developed skill. It occurs when the impulses sent to the brain are interpreted and understood. Frank had evidently heard Mrs. Jones, but he had not interpreted and understood her message. As she points out, he was not listening to her.

THE IMPORTANCE OF LISTENING EFFICIENTLY

Sometimes the tendency to confuse listening and hearing is only irritating, as in the case of Mrs. Jones and Frank. Other times it can be more serious. A listening error reportedly cost one Wisconsin company $54,000. Evidently the foreman was not listening as his supervisor explained a change in production line operation. By the time the supervisor finally realized the foreman had not made the change, the company had lost $54,000. The foreman had *heard* the message, but he had not *listened* to it.[1]

Why Listening Is Important

Listening is important to us for many reasons. First, listening is one of the primary means of *obtaining information.* To learn about world affairs, we listen to news on radio and television. We learn new skills by listening to directions from our supervisors and teachers. Listening to politicians, co-workers, and friends helps us develop ideas and make decisions.

Second, listening is an important way to *conduct business.* For example, most business is done on the telephone. We schedule appointments, order products, and exchange information on the phone with only our listening skills to help us. We cannot see the person to whom we are talking and we cannot reread the information as we would a written message.

Third, listening carefully helps us *interpret people's responses* more accurately. Contrasting emotions such as friendliness and anger or concern and sarcasm are all revealed by tone of voice and rate of speaking. For example, slow, even speech often indicates confidence, whereas raising the voice and talking loudly or rapidly may show defensiveness. Listening carefully for these emotions can make your work life and personal life easier. Let's say you and your supervisor are discussing the work load assigned to your department. As long as your supervisor talks calmly, you can press for a lighter work load; however, as soon as you notice the supervisor talking rapidly, loudly or in a higher pitch than normal, you will want to "rest your case." Awareness of the way voice reveals emotions helps you realize that your supervisor is defensive and that you will not benefit from continuing to insist on a lighter work load.

We also depend on listening for *entertainment.* We listen to music on radio, records, and tapes. Listening helps us follow the plots of movies and television shows. Concerts, travelogues, and conversations with friends are all enhanced by good listening skills.

You will remember from the Preface that 45 percent of our waking time is spent listening. That's almost one-half of our day spent in listening to other people. Your occupation may require you to spend even more than 45 percent of your time

[1] *The Milwaukee Journal,* June 24, 1984, p. 2.

listening. Some experts estimate that executives spend about 63 percent of their time listening. Others make this estimate as high as 80 percent.[2]

When you take time to listen to people, you let them know that you think they are important. Your productive listening habits tell people that you think what they have to say is important too. The chance to give a speaker this sense of self-worth is one of the most important reasons for learning to listen effectively.

Inefficient Listening

Even though listening is so important to our work, most people do not listen well. Dr. Ralph Nichols, who began researching our listening behavior in the 1940's and who has been called the Father of Listening, estimates that people listen at 25 percent efficiency. In his research he found that people retain about one-half of what they hear immediately after they hear it. Then after a short time they lose an additional one-half of the information they originally retained. Thus, they listen at 25 percent efficiency.[3]

Some businesses report great losses due to inadequate emphasis on listening. One company, for example, found its sales dropping off considerably. When it surveyed its customers, it learned that these clients felt the salesmen were interested only in making a sale. The salesmen talked a lot about their products, but they didn't listen well to the customers' needs. The customers thought the salesmen should show more interest in them. In other words, they felt the salesmen should listen better.[4]

Sperry Corporation is one company that recognizes the importance of good listening skills. In 1979 Sperry began instructing its personnel in the listening process. "We understand how important it is to listen" became its slogan. Today the company gives classes in listening to every level of worker from executive to salesperson. It has brought its concern for listening to the public's attention through TV and ad campaigns. Sperry's interest in good listening skills emphasizes business and industry's growing concern with employing people who know how to listen efficiently. Because employers want efficient listeners working for them, we should all strive to develop our listening potential.

THE LISTENING PROCESS

To develop our listening skill we must first understand the listening process. Listening is a mental skill used to interpret, understand, and respond to the sound stimuli that reach the hearing part of the brain. It consists of four steps:

[2]Dr. T. Harre Allen, "Are You a Good Listener?" *The Canadian Banker and ICB Review,* February 1980.

[3]John T. Samaras, "Two-Way Communication Practices for Managers," *Personnel Journal,* August 1980, p. 647.

[4]Thomas Maher, "LAA Asked: 'Is Anybody Listening?' " p. 22.

1. Sensing
2. Interpreting
3. Evaluating
4. Responding

Sensing

The first step in the listening process is sensing. This is just another word for the physical process of hearing. Sound vibrations must reach the hearing part of your brain before you can complete the listening process.

Interpreting

After you have sensed the message, you must interpret it. This means you must understand the message. Understanding the message means more than attaching definitions to the words. It also means interpreting tone of voice and body language. The ways these affect listening will be discussed thoroughly in the next chapter.

Evaluating

The third step of the listening process is evaluation. When you have understood the message, you use your judgment to decide how you will respond to the message. Is what you have learned important to you? Do you believe it? Is the speaker an authority?

Responding

Finally, you respond to the message. Your response is a vital step in the listening process. It tells the speaker that you have sensed, interpreted, and evaluated the message.

Let's think about the three golfers we met at the beginning of this section. How well did they follow this four-step process? You'll notice that Milt and Andy did not go beyond step one: sensing the message. Now let's take them through the four steps of the listening process.

BUD:	By the way, we're looking for a printer for our new book on Australia. It'll be a big job. Lots of color photos. We don't get many jobs like that these days. If Perfect Printing wants to bid on it, estimates are due on Friday.	Sensing
ANDY:	Sounds interesting.	
MILT:	Do you mean this Friday?	Interpreting
BUD:	That's right.	
MILT:	That doesn't give us much time.	

ANDY: Who should we contact for more information about the   < Interpreting
        project?
BUD: Call Gene Anderson. He's handling the account.
MILT: I'll give you a hand with it, Andy. We really can't afford to < Evaluating
        miss this one.
ANDY: I guess you're right, Milt. Thanks for the tip, Bud. We'll < Responding
        have our bid in by this Friday.

As you can see, by following the listening process, Andy and Milt completed their business more successfully and saved themselves the personal embarrassment of fouling up a business transaction.

LEVELS OF LISTENING

Although we spend about 45 percent of our time listening, we do not listen in the
same way all the time. For example, you may join your friends at the lunch table and
let their conversation drift around you. You know what they are saying but you do
not react to their ideas.

Later when you return to your work area, you may discuss a work assignment with your boss. You listen to your boss' idea, then follow those suggestions as
you complete the project.

The next day you join a group discussing production problems in your company. You listen to each member's ideas, ask questions, make judgments, and express opinions of your own.

In each instance you listened, but your level of involvement varied from
minimal at lunch to maximum during the group discussion. If we rated the depth of
your involvement on a scale of passive to active, we would say you went from
passive listening at lunch to most active listening during the group discussion.
When you listen passively, you let the sounds drift around you. You do not evaluate
the ideas expressed nor react to them. As the scale shown here indicates, you move
from passive listening to ever-increasing levels of involvement. When you listen actively, you may interpret the main ideas, question them, add information of your
own, or make judgments.

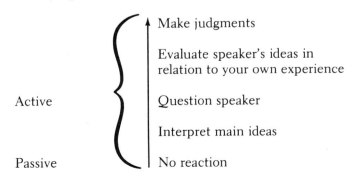

Researchers have found that efficient listeners vary the depth of their involvement to meet individual situations. Understanding how your level of involvement changes and knowing how to adapt your listening to each situation will help you listen efficiently.

Passive

Many people think all listening is passive. "You don't have to do anything. You just sit there and listen," Mary tells Allan when she wants him to attend the monthly sales meeting in her office. Although some situations lend themselves to passive listening, the listening process should usually be an active one.

When, then, might you just sit back and listen? When you relax with a favorite TV program, you might listen passively. You don't have to evaluate the main ideas in the script and the actors do not require immediate feedback from you. Another time you might listen passively is when you are not directly involved in the conversation. Sometimes we tune in and tune out conversations near us. Parents of small children, for example, may keep "an ear" on their children's activities even though they don't participate in the children's play. If the conversational level remains steady, the parents don't worry, but when they tune in to hear too much noise—or too much silence—they go to investigate. When you listen passively you do not use much energy as you listen.

Active

Active listening, on the other hand, requires more energy. You will remember at the beginning of this section, we said that the listening process should usually be active. Since so much of our time is spent listening actively, you should expect to vary the intensity with which you listen in these situations. In other words, there are several levels of active listening.

Listening for main ideas   One of these levels is listening for main ideas. When you listen for main ideas, you are interested primarily in obtaining information. Listening to a class lecture or a presentation about a new piece of office equipment are examples of active listening at this level. You do not question the information you are given; you simply absorb it. When you listen for main ideas, you probably take notes to help you recall the information later, but you do not interact with the speaker.

Interacting   When you participate in a conversation, however, you must both listen for main ideas and interact with the other speakers. Listening in this situation requires more effort than listening to a lecture. While you listen to the words of the speakers, you also pay attention to their gestures and facial expressions. This body language helps you judge their sincerity, accuracy, and interest in the subject. When they finish speaking, they will expect you to react to their ideas or to add information. To do that effectively, you should have been following the conversation closely.

Evaluating   The third level of active listening, the level that requires the most energy from the listeners, is listening to evaluate the ideas expressed. Some people call this level of listening *creative listening*. Creative listening combines the skills you use in the first two levels of active listening—absorbing information and observing body language—and adds a third skill to the listening process: questioning. When you listen at this level, you think about the speaker's ideas and you evaluate the facts used to support those ideas: Was the speaker's reasoning logical? Were the facts cited accurate and adequate proof? Did the speaker discuss all important aspects of the topic?

You may do all your questioning silently, forming opinions as you listen, or you may write down questions to ask the speaker later. Either way, you are totally involved in the listening situation. You pay close attention to the material the speaker presents; you watch for facial expressions and gestures and listen for voice inflection that will help you interpret the speaker's message; then you consider your own background and the information you already have on the subject. You use the total listening situation, which includes all of these elements, to evaluate the ideas presented.

You can see that this third level of active listening requires the most energy. The listener must be continuously alert. There is no opportunity to sit back and let your mind wander for a few minutes when you are listening creatively. You might miss important details you need in order to make an accurate evaluation.

ADAPTING YOUR LISTENING INVOLVEMENT

It's obvious that you cannot listen in this intense way in every situation. You would be exhausted after a few hours if you listened to every TV show and every friend's casual conversation with the intensity required for creative listening. You will not even want to listen to every lecture or presentation at this level. As you begin to listen, you should decide what level of listening is required for that specific situation; then apply the skills necessary to listen efficiently at that time.

You have probably known people who leave a training session drained of all energy. They seem to work so hard, but often they do not remember much about the lecture or discussion they have just heard. These people do not understand how to adapt their level of listening to the listening situation. They think the more energy they exert, the better they are listening. The most efficient listener, however, listens differently in different situations. This ability to adapt is the most important factor for efficient listening. Don't feel guilty if you relax with a half hour of passive listening to the television or radio. Think of it as a way to recharge yourself so you can listen creatively the next time your co-workers meet to discuss a production problem. Learn to identify the listening techniques needed in each situation and be continuously sensitive to the manner in which you are listening. When you can move freely from one level of listening to another as your activities change, you are a truly efficient listener.

UNPRODUCTIVE LISTENING HABITS

If effective listening is so important to success, why do most people listen ineffectively? Your first response to that question might be, "Well, people are so caught up in their own lives they don't want to take the time to listen to other people." Certainly self-interest can prevent us from listening to other people. We have all known people who seem to wait impatiently for a break in the conversation so they can begin talking about themselves.

However, interest in their own activities is probably only one of the reasons people listen inefficiently. Most of us have not been taught to listen. We have acquired our listening skills haphazardly as we went from experience to experience. In this way, some people developed useful listening skills, but most of us acquired more bad listening habits than good.

Learning on your own to listen is like learning to bowl without some instruction. Although you can throw the ball at the pins, you may not develop the special skill, like keeping your shoulders even when you release the ball, that distinguishes a good bowler from someone who throws more gutter balls than strikes. When someone points out to you that lowering one shoulder makes your ball curve and head for the gutter, you are surprised that a simple thing like straightening your shoulders will improve your bowling score.

The same is true of listening skills. Because we have picked up on our own the few things we do know about listening, many of us have acquired some bad habits. These are difficult to overcome, but if we realize that they are unproductive, we can try to correct them as we listen.

Fidgeting

The first unproductive listening habit is fidgeting. Scratching your head, pulling on your earlobe, or shuffling your feet while someone else is talking shows impatience. This behavior tells the speaker that you can't wait until you have a chance to talk. Although you don't voice it, your body language says, "I don't care about what you are saying."

Aggression

At the other extreme is the aggressive listener. When you sit absolutely still and stare intently at the speaker, you are an aggressive listener. You are probably concentrating so hard on *looking like* a good listener that you don't concentrate on *being* a good listener. If you have ever talked to someone who seemed to be "staring you down," you know how intimidating this behavior can be. The speaker becomes rattled and communication breaks down.

Passive Listening

Just as you can listen too aggressively, you can also listen too passively. Passive listeners do not contribute to the conversation. They just nod in agreement with everything that is said. When you readily agree with everything, the speaker labels you as insincere.

Pseudo-intellectualizing

The fourth type of unproductive listening habit is pseudo-intellectualizing. When you listen this way, you pay so much attention to the speaker's ideas that you forget to relate to the speaker's emotions as well. You should remember that every speaker projects two messages: the ideas that are spoken and the emotions that are conveyed through body language and tone of voice.

Inaccurate Listening

The opposite of the pseudo-intellectual listener is the inaccurate listener. Rather than ignoring emotions while listening, the inaccurate listener pays too much attention to emotional messages. If your supervisor says, "I can't discuss this project with you right now; I have another meeting," and you think, "He doesn't like my work; he's going to let me go," you have listened inaccurately. You have projected your own insecurity into the speaker's message. You have made up something that your busy supervisor did not intend.

In the next chapter we will discuss ways to correct these unproductive listening habits. First let's discuss some of the reasons we listen ineffectively.

REASONS FOR INEFFICIENT LISTENING

Many of us are unaware of poor listening habits which hamper our productivity and complicate our personal lives. Consider the following three situations. Which ones do you recognize as showing poor listening habits?

1. Chiming in with your own observations and experiences before the speaker is finished. This lets the speaker know that you are interested in the subject.
2. Closing your eyes when a person is talking so you can concentrate on the ideas the speaker is presenting.
3. Keeping "an ear open" for what is going on in the next room. A good listener is aware of outside stimuli.

Actually all three of the situations represent faulty listening. You can probably remember times when you have listened in one or more of these ways.

Why are we poor listeners? One reason mentioned earlier in this chapter is that until recently we have thought of listening as an ability we are born with. Quite the contrary is true. Listening is a highly disciplined skill. Some people call it an art. Productive listening takes time and energy. It is hard work. Before we can become good listeners, we must accept the idea that we have to practice listening as we practice public speaking or speed reading.

Another reason for faulty listening is the difference between the rate at which we speak and the rate at which we can think. We speak at about 125 words per minute, but we can think at about 400 to 500 words per minute.[5] Because we can think so much faster than a person can speak, our minds tend to wander as we listen. A word or a phrase makes us think of something else that causes us to think of another idea and soon we are "a million thought miles away" from the subject of the speaker.

You can probably think of times when you have experienced this "time gap." It may have gone something like the following episode:

MR. A: Don't forget our monthly meeting on Wednesday, Ms. J. This is an especially important meeting because Mrs. P. will be here and we will be discussing. . . .

MS. J: *Wednesday . . . I nearly forgot Wednesday is my dental appointment. I wish I could remember what time that appointment is. I know I have two cavities. I really should stop eating so many sweets. I hope I can get back in time for that monthly meeting he's talking about. How could I have forgotten Wednesday was the meeting, too.*

MR. A: . . . so bring along a list of suggestions. We'll see you on Wednesday.

MS. J: Suggestions . . .? Suggestions about what?!

This difference between our rate of speaking and our rate of thinking can cause listening problems. When you are listening to a person talk, you must discipline yourself to concentrate on main ideas even though your mind can move ahead more quickly than the speaker is talking. Use the "time lag" to put the speaker's ideas in your own words, interpret those ideas and take notes if necessary.

BARRIERS TO LISTENING

Many things in our environment distract us from listening. We call these distractions *listening barriers*. Barriers are things that prevent or block our ability to listen, just as a roadblock prevents us from traveling down a road or fallen trees made it difficult to stay on a path. They can be grouped into two categories:

1. Distractions that occur in the listening environment, such as background noises.
2. Distractions that occur within the mind of the listener, such as personal prejudices.

[5] Samaras, "Two-Way Communication Practices for Managers," p. 648.

Distractions in the Environment

Noises   Typical distractions that occur in the listening environment are background noises and nearby activities. Sometimes these noises are so loud that they actually prevent us from sensing the message, but usually they can be tuned out if we concentrate on the speaker. While you are sitting in a sales meeting, for example, someone may be air-hammering in the street below. This noise may irritate you. It may even give you a slight headache, which may cause you to wonder how anyone can operate an air hammer for a living. You may think about his stiff joints and shocked spine. This may cause you to remember your painful bout with torn ligaments after a skiing accident last winter. Finally, you tell yourself that you feel fortunate to have the job you do. By the time you are brought full circle back to the subject of sales, you find your meeting is concluding and you have missed material important to your job.

Activities   Activities nearby may also distract you. While you are discussing the idiosyncracies of a new machine with your supervisor, you may see two of your friends laughing over coffee in the next room. You may wonder what they are laughing about and wish that you could join them. Their activity has distracted you from listening to your supervisor. You may forget what you were saying or miss something important your supervisor says because you focused on your friends' laughter.

Interruptions   Interruptions are another barrier to listening. Telephone calls that interrupt person-to-person communication are an example of this kind of barrier. If you have ever been interrupted by a ringing phone during an important discussion, you can remember the irritation and frustration you felt as you tried to pick up the thread of the discussion after the call. Usually, the spirit of the conversation is lost, and the main ideas must also be repeated. Distractions caused by TV or radio programs while you are working or by people stopping at your work area to chat may also cause barriers to listening.

Ten Keys to Effective Listening

These keys are a positive guideline to better listening. In fact, they're at the heart of developing better listening habits that could last a lifetime.

Ten Keys to Effective Listening	*The Bad Listener*	*The Good Listener*
1. Find areas of interest	Tunes out dry subjects	Opportunitizes; asks, "What's in it for me?"
2. Judge content, not delivery	Tunes out if delivery is poor	Judges content, skips over delivery errors
3. Hold your fire	Tends to enter into argument	Doesn't judge until comprehension is complete

4. Listen for ideas	Listens for facts	Listens for central themes
5. Be flexible	Takes intensive notes using only one system	Takes fewer notes; uses 4–5 different systems, depending on speaker
6. Work at listening	Shows no energy output; fakes attention	Works hard; exhibits active body state
7. Resist distractions	Is easily distracted	Fights or avoids distractions, tolerates bad habits, knows how to concentrate
8. Exercise your mind	Resists difficult expository material; seeks light, recreational material	Uses heavier material as exercise for the mind
9. Keep your mind open	Reacts to emotional words	Interprets color words; does not get hung up on them
10. Capitalize on the fact that thought is faster than speech	Tends to daydream with slow speakers	Challenges, anticipates, mentally summarizes, weighs the evidence, listens between the lines to tone of voice

This material was prepared by Dr. Lyman K. Steil, President of Communication Development, Inc., St. Paul, Minnesota, for the Sperry Corporation. Reprinted by permission of Dr. Steil and the Sperry Corporation.

Surroundings   Your surroundings may also affect your ability to listen. Is your chair uncomfortable? You may be more concerned about your aching back than about the speaker's message. Is your chair too soft? You may fall asleep and not hear the speaker's message. Are you too hot or too cold? Is the room too bright or too dim? Are you unhappy where you are sitting? All these things can prevent you from listening efficiently.

Distractions in the Listener's Mind

We cannot place all the blame for our listening problems on environmental factors, however. Some of our difficulty in listening originates within ourselves. Some experts call these roadblocks to listening *internal barriers*. Others refer to them as *personal prejudices*. Whatever you call them, you should be aware that emotions and personal reactions to outside stimuli affect listening.

Emotions   Each of us brings a certain set of ideas and emotions to the listening situation, and these influence our reactions to the speaker and subject. For example, a Midwesterner might say, "I never could understand someone with a Southern drawl." The Midwesterner reacts negatively to the speech patterns of the Southerner and uses the unfamiliar inflections as an excuse to tune out the speaker's message. A male speaker with a beard may be labeled as "far left" just as a female speaker with long blond hair may be judged "dumb" by listeners who evaluate speakers on the basis of preconceived notions rather than careful listening practices.

Internal barriers are especially evident when we evaluate speakers by the position they represent rather than by what they say. Welding instructors, for example, are usually men. If students laugh when they are greeted on the first day of classes by an attractive young woman who says, "I'm your welding instructor this semester," they are stereotyping. Since she does not fit their preconceived notion of the way a welding instructor should look, they also decide that she doesn't know anything about welding. Personal prejudices may prevent them from learning welding from her.

Opinions   In a similar way, your personal opinion about a subject can cause you to tune out speakers before you have given them a chance to present their views. For example, you might hear someone say, "I hope you will attend the conference," but you do not listen to the rest of the sentence. When you hear the words "attend the conference," you think "I promised Mary I would sub in her bowling league that night." If you had allowed yourself to listen to the rest of the talk, you might have become so interested in the conference that you would have canceled your bowling date and attended the conference instead.

Although you may not actually voice them, feelings like:

I never was good in math, so I don't expect to learn anything from this math instructor either.

or

Wellness! I know everything there is to know about that subject. You can't tell me anything new!

are examples of ways the opinions we already have can prevent us from listening in new situations.

Total Acceptance   Thus far we have seen ways our personal prejudices can make us tune out a speaker, but prejudices can also make us accept, without question, anything the speaker says. Just as you think an attractive young woman doesn't know how to weld, you might also decide that everyone who goes to church is honest or that every accountant makes wise investments. Then if that accountant tells you to invest in energy options, you do so without evaluating the accountant's reasoning. You allow your respect for the position to keep you from listening to the way the idea is supported.

As you listen, be sensitive to the way your personal opinions influence your reaction to the speaker or the subject. Set aside your predetermined ideas about a speaker's appearance, style of dressing, and speech patterns. Base your decision about the subject on what the speaker says rather than on an opinion you have always had on the topic. Continually evaluate your reactions. Learn to recognize internal barriers to listening and eliminate them from your listening habits.

In the next chapter we will discuss ways to tune out distraction, overcome barriers, and listen efficiently.

SUMMARY

Although we often use the words *hearing* and *listening* interchangeably, they actually describe different processes. Hearing is the physical act of registering sounds. Listening is a mental skill of interpreting and evaluating sounds we hear.

There are four steps to the listening process: sensing, interpreting, evaluating, and responding. Following these steps is important in listening efficiently.

We must also recognize that we listen with different levels of involvement depending upon the situation. These range from passive listening, which does not require a response, to active listening, which allows us to take in information, observe body language, and form opinions about the things we see and hear. Adapting your listening behavior to the situation will help you listen efficiently.

Because few people have been taught how to listen, many of us have acquired poor listening habits. Some habits we should strive to avoid are: fidgeting, listening too aggressively or too passively, and paying too much attention to one aspect of the situation such as the listener's ideas or emotions rather than the total presentation.

Listeners must also be aware of the barriers that prevent them from listening. These can be external distractions such as noise or physical discomfort, or they can be internal roadblocks that listeners bring to the listening situation. Internal barriers include personal prejudices about the speaker's appearance, style of speaking, or subject. Recognizing our tendency to set up roadblocks when we listen can help us overcome those barriers and listen effectively.

REVIEW QUESTIONS

1. Why is training in listening important to employers?
2. What is the difference between hearing and listening?
3. Explain the listening process.
4. How does our rate of thinking affect our listening?
5. How does our level of involvement in a situation affect our listening?
6. What is a listening barrier? Give examples of barriers to listening.
7. Describe a truly efficient listener.

ACTIVITIES

1. During the next few days identify problems that occur on the job or in the classroom. How many of these problems are directly related to inefficient listening? Choose one of these problems and write a paragraph including the following:

   a. Statement of the problem
   b. Description of the events leading to the problem
   c. Discussion of the way inefficient listening contributed to the problem
   d. Suggestions about how efficient listening could have helped prevent the problem
2. Using the Listening Chart shown on p. 91, record your level of listening periodically throughout the day. How often did you find yourself listening passively? Actively? How much of your active listening was evaluating? Listening for information? Listening to conversation? Were there times when your listening level was inappropriate to the situation? Explain.
3. Choose a situation at work, in school, or at home that you think illustrates efficient listening. Be prepared to describe that situation to the class and trace the listening process from sensing to interpreting, evaluating, and responding as it occurs in your example.
4. Can you think of a time when a barrier has prevented you from listening efficiently? Write a paragraph explaining: (1) what the barrier was, (2) how it affected your listening, (3) what you could have done to reduce or eliminate the problem as you were listening.

Listening Chart

TIME	LISTENING LEVEL	TYPE OF ACTIVITY	LEVEL: APPROPRIATE/ INAPPROPRIATE
7:30			
8:00			
8:30			
9:00			
9:30			
10:00			
10:30			
11:00			
11:30			
12:00			
12:30			
1:00			
1:30			
2:00			
2:30			
3:00			
3:30			
4:00			
4:30			
5:00			
5:30			
6:00			
6:30			
7:00			
7:30			
8:00			
8:30			
9:00			
9:30			

TOTALS: Passive   _____
          Active   _____
Divide your active listening into:
          Creative   _____
          Informational _____
          Conversational _____

6

LISTENING SKILLS

I know how to listen when clever men are talking. That is the secret of what you call my influence.
Sudermann, *Es Libe das Leben* I. iv, trans. Edith Wharton

After studying this chapter you should understand the importance of:
1. Taking time to listen
2. Ignoring distractions
3. Concentrating on main ideas
4. Reinforcing the speaker with positive feedback
5. Asking questions and restating main points
6. Putting personal prejudice aside when you listen
7. Tuning into the speaker's voice inflections and body language to help you understand the message

"I'm not going to class today," Bob told Kate. "I never get anything out of Mrs. Rogers' lectures."

"I know what you mean," Kate answered. "She does talk with a funny accent. I have trouble understanding her too. Just about all I ever remember are the stories she tells about her childhood in Poland during World War II. She really tells interesting stories."

"You're right, her stories are interesting," Bob agreed. "But you can't pass her tests by listening to her stories. And every time I try to ask her a question she starts to answer before I'm finished asking the question. Half the time she doesn't even know what I want to ask her before she starts talking."

"She just wants to do a good job," Kate said. "You have to overlook it."

"No thanks," Bob said. "I'm transferring into Mr. Allan's class tomorrow. I've heard he has lots of time to answer questions."

As you read Bob and Kate's conversation, you were probably reminded of times when you or someone you know complained because the speaker "talked funny." The problem may have been an unfamiliar accent or dialect, or the speaker may have talked too fast or too slow. As a result, you tuned out the speaker's message. The strange way a person talks is only one of the reasons we often give for not listening. In our example Bob may have used the way Mrs. Rogers talked as an excuse for not attending her lectures, but if you think carefully about his conversation with Kate, you'll notice that his real reason for dropping the class is the way Mrs. Rogers *listens*. Actually, she doesn't listen. She interrupts him and does not give him time to ask his questions. So Bob goes to Mr. Allan's class because supposedly Mr. Allan listens better.

Taking time is one of the skills you must acquire so you can listen efficiently. Other efficient listening skills are: ignoring distraction and concentrating on main ideas, giving the speaker positive feedback as you listen, asking questions and restating main points, being aware of how your personal prejudices influence your ability to listen, and tuning into voice inflection and body language. We will discuss each of these effective listening techniques in this chapter. When you thoroughly understand the specific traits involved in good listening, you should be able to combine them to listen effectively in any situation.

TAKING TIME TO LISTEN

As a child you were probably told that interrupting a speaker is impolite. Yet you have probably seen a number of people whom you know to be thoughtful and considerate interrupt speakers.

Interrupting or cutting off people before they are finished expressing a thought is actually a poor listening habit. Two types of interruptions characterize inefficient listeners: the interruption that indicates impatience, and the interruption that signals boredom.

Impatient Listeners

An impatient listener may cut in to supply words or thoughts for the speaker.

In the following conversation Rodney listens impatiently. To understand this illustration better, ask someone to read the part of Rodney while you read Roberta's lines. Remember, wherever you see three dots like this . . . Rodney should cut in on Roberta's statement. Roberta does not pause at those times. She is not groping for a word; she knows what she wants to say. But Rodney anticipates her thoughts and cuts in anyway, evidently in an attempt to hurry the conversation along.

ROBERTA: Dr. Hanson wants to redecorate the patients' waiting room. He asked me to do some research to find out what colors would be best.

RODNEY: That sounds like quite a job. How did you research something like that?

ROBERTA: Well first of all I went to the library to get some decorator magazines. I looked under "color" in the . . .

RODNEY: *Reader's Guide?*

ROBERTA: Yes, *Reader's Guide.* I found about five magazines on selecting colors for an . . .

RODNEY: An office. That's quite a few sources.

ROBERTA: Yes, I thought so, too.

RODNEY: What did you find out?

ROBERTA: Well, three magazines suggested earth tones because . . .

RODNEY: They relax the patient.

ROBERTA: That's right, they are relaxing. But I don't know about that. I really think blue is more . . .

RODNEY: Peaceful?

ROBERTA: Well, peaceful, maybe. But I was thinking that blue is more cheerful.

RODNEY: Sounds good to me!

As you read Roberta's lines, how did you feel? Did you find yourself getting nervous or wanting to rush through the information? Did you become irritated with Rodney? Do you think he cared about Roberta's project or did he just want to finish the conversation?

Anticipating a speaker's thoughts has the same effect on the speaker as tailgating has on a driver. The speaker, like the driver, tends to react to the other person's impatience by speeding up or becoming irritable. As a driver, you might take the wrong turn in your haste or you might have an urge to slam on the brake and let the tailgater hit you. Neither reaction results in very effective driving practices. In the same way, if an impatient listener makes you feel confused or angry, you will probably say the wrong thing or stop talking altogether and communication will break down.

You'll notice in this example that Rodney really didn't care about the reasons Roberta chose blue; the words *peaceful* or *cheerful* both sounded fine to him even though they described quite different emotions. Completing a meaningful discussion with an impatient listener is a difficult task.

Boredom

Sometimes listeners interrupt to change the topic. "That reminds me" is a usual way of shifting conversation, but when it is inserted before the speaker has completed a thought, it inhibits productive listening.

If you have ever experienced this kind of interruption, you can remember the disjointed conversation that resulted. Meaning was lost on both sides and the conversation probably dissolved without either person feeling satisfied.

Efficient Listeners

Efficient listeners take time to listen. They don't hurry the speaker along by anticipating ideas or cutting in with reactions to the speaker's half-expressed thought.

Efficient listeners accept pauses as a natural part of conversation. They are not afraid of silence. In fact, they think of silence as a healthy activity and use the pauses in conversation to reflect on ideas and facts discussed.

Efficient listeners let the speaker lead them from one topic to another. They save ideas they want to discuss until there is a suitable break in the conversation. Efficient listeners establish a comfortable environment so the speaker will feel free to share ideas and emotions. In our heavily scheduled, clock-centered world, giving other people your time is the first step in finding out what they have to say.

IGNORING DISTRACTIONS

Many things can distract you while you are listening. A phone call, a neighborhood baseball game outside your office, or another person walking into the room are all potential distractions. If you allow your attention to shift from the speaker to these other activities as they occur, you lose track of your reason for listening.

On the job when you have important issues to discuss, you can find a quiet place where you and the speaker will not be interrupted. You can ask someone else to take your phone messages while you are listening.

Even when you are prepared to listen, you can be distracted. You will remember that the mind can think faster than people can talk, so even when you concentrate on the speaker you might find yourself with a lot of spare thinking time. Use the part of your brain that is not following the speaker's ideas to filter out those extra, potentially distracting, sounds in the environment while you continue to focus the major part of your attention on the speaker. Most sounds can be ignored and the listening activity can continue uninterrupted; some sounds are important enough to take your attention away from the speaker. Common sense will help you differentiate between the sounds you can and cannot ignore.

Efficient listeners eliminate as many distractions as possible before they begin listening. Then they try to ignore the distractions they cannot control.

CONCENTRATING ON SPEAKER'S MAIN IDEAS

Thus far we have seen that the mind can do two things while listening. It can focus on the speaker and it can filter out background noises and other distractions. A third mental activity that is important to effective listening is concentrating on the speaker's main ideas and remembering those ideas by arranging them into meaningful groups.

Understand Thought Patterns

Listening for main ideas is easier when you understand the typical structure of our thought patterns. Usually people state an opinion; then they set out to prove it.

For example, Mike might say:

We should buy word processing software for our office computer. We could cut the time needed to write letters by 50 percent. We could also make sure the letters are mechanically correct. It's also more fun to write with a word processor than with pen and paper.

Mike stated his opinion first; "We should buy word processing software." Then he supports it with three reasons: it saves time, produces a better letter, and is fun to use.

Less often, we use the reverse thinking pattern. The supporting details come first:

If we use a word processor, we could cut the time needed to write letters by 50 percent. We could also guarantee that our letters would be mechanically correct because the word processor would check for spelling and punctuation errors. But best of all our staff would write letters more willingly because it's more fun to use a word processor than pen and paper.

Then the main idea is stated last:

For these reasons, I think we should buy word processing software for our office computer.

Listeners who understand these typical thought patterns can follow the structure to pick up main ideas. Main ideas, or *assertions,* as they are sometimes called, usually precede specific facts, examples, or illustrations. If the main idea is not stated at the beginning, listen for it immediately after a series of specific details.

Remember to listen for ideas rather than unrelated details. For example, if all you remember about the preceding statement is the detail "processors are fun," you have missed the speaker's principal reason for talking.

Group Details Around Main Ideas

Learn to group the details you hear around main ideas. As you are listening, use your spare thinking time to summarize the speaker's comments. When listening to Mike you should ask yourself these questions:

What is Mike's topic? The purchase of word processing equipment.

What does Mike think? He thinks we should buy word processing software for our office computer.

What reasons does he give to support his opinion? Saves time, corrects mechanical errors, is fun to use.

As you group the supporting details around the main idea, you eliminate stories or examples that are used solely to embellish or elaborate on the details already given. For example, if Mike continued with a description of his son's fascination with computers or a story about the last time he used a word processor to write a letter, you would not include these extra things in your summary. Mike is inserting them to elaborate on a point he has already made or to liven up his presentation. Stories and examples may make the listening experience more enjoyable but they are usually not vital to your understanding of the main idea; therefore, you will not usually include them in your mental summaries.

REINFORCING THE SPEAKER

Listeners tend to think that keeping the conversation moving is entirely the speaker's responsibility. Actually, the listener contributes significantly to the success or failure of oral communication. Efficient listeners continually reinforce the speaker with positive feedback. Most of this feedback is nonverbal body language such as a nod or a smile. One of the most important things a listener can do is to look at the speaker. Eye contact encourages the speaker to continue talking. Although it seems like basic good manners to look at the person talking to you, a surprising number of people do not consistently maintain eye contact with the speaker. These people say, "I'm listening even though I'm finishing up the notes for my own talk" or "working this crossword puzzle" or "writing a letter to a friend."

The speaker, however, often is not confident that a listener can pay attention to two things at once. Much is written today about the importance of making eye contact with a baby as the infant eats or plays in your arms. As we grow, we continue to need eye contact to feel secure. An efficient listener remembers this and uses eye contact and other body language to encourage or discourage the speaker.

We must remember that listening to a person is different from listening to television. The television cannot form an opinion about your level of interest. It will say the same thing whether you sit in front of it or go to the refrigerator for a snack. It keeps talking while you read or talk to someone else. A person, however, evaluates the listener's level of interest and responds accordingly.

ASKING QUESTIONS AND RESTATING MAIN IDEAS

Another way you can encourage the speaker is to ask questions and restate main points. This shows the speaker that you are interested and also helps you make sure you understand the speaker's meaning. Often we assume we understand what the speaker is saying, but because we misinterpret a reference or have a slightly different meaning for a word, the entire message is misconstrued. The story about the village blacksmith and his apprentice illustrates how serious the wrong assumption can be.

Ask Questions

One day the village blacksmith said to his apprentice, "I'm going to take this horseshoe out of the fire and lay it here on the bench. When I nod my head, you hit it with the hammer."

The apprentice followed the directions as he interpreted them and hit the blacksmith on the head. Now the apprentice is the village blacksmith. If the apprentice had been listening efficiently, however, he would have been evaluating the blacksmith's message. He would have thought, "Does the blacksmith really mean I should hit him on the head?" How will that help shape the horseshoe?" Then the apprentice should have asked the blacksmith, "Do you really want me to hit you on the head?" This would have given the blacksmith a chance to explain more clearly what he really meant.

In the case of the blacksmith and his apprentice, misinterpreting the message earned the apprentice an instant promotion. In the real world, however, such success seldom results from poor listening skills. Instead the poor listener files important papers in the wrong place, arrives late for an appointment, or passes on a message incorrectly.

Learn to clarify the speaker's statements by asking questions; then make sure you interpret the speaker's message correctly by restating the main ideas as you hear them.

Paraphrase

Restating ideas is called *paraphrasing,* and it is a special skill. An inaccurate paraphrase can create as much misunderstanding as neglecting to paraphrase altogether.

For example if your boss says,

Sales in your department have been lower than those of the store's other departments in February.

you would paraphrase that:

My department sold less in February than other departments in the store.

You would not restate your boss' comment this way:

My salespeople are lazy.

or this way:

The boss is going to fire me.

Your boss has not said either of those things. All you can accurately say from your boss' statement is that your department had the lowest sales in the store during February.

When you paraphrase, make sure you restate the ideas and details as the speaker has expressed them. Do not include your personal opinions in the paraphrase.

Time Your Questions

Just as accuracy is important, timing is also vital. Do not interrupt the speaker with a question or paraphrase. Wait for suitable breaks in the speaker's flow of thoughts. Ask questions or summarize main points when the speaker has finished a main part of the presentation.

Introduce your questions and paraphrase with a smooth transition such as, "Let me see if I understand what you are saying," or "Then do you mean that. . . ." Smooth transitions make your questions and paraphrases a natural extension of the speaker's idea.

Asking questions and restating main points are effective listening tools because they give the listener a chance to make sure the message is understood. These skills also keep the listener involved in what the speaker is saying and provide verbal feedback to the speaker.

We have discussed several specific things you can do to get more out of each listening experience. Two other factors that influence effective listening are the listener's personal prejudices and the speaker's body language. Although these factors are less noticeable than some of the things we mentioned earlier, they can undermine a listening situation and hinder its effectiveness. Being aware of our opinions and observing the speaker's action will help us interpret messages accurately.

TUNING OUT PERSONAL PREJUDICE

Personal prejudice works against the listener in many ways. You may think the material or concepts the speaker is presenting are too difficult for you to understand. You may not like the way the speaker talks or looks, so you may stereotype the speaker with comments like: "Management never understands the worker's problems" or "All English teachers are boring." These personal prejudices cause you to tune out the speaker and miss the importance of the message.

Efficient listeners are aware of their personal prejudices and the way these prejudices may prevent them from listening. They learn to set aside their prejudices about the speaker's voice, appearance, or subject and concentrate instead on what the speaker is saying. They give the speaker a chance to express the entire idea before they disagree or show lack of interest.

You should approach each listening experience with the idea that you can learn something. As the speaker talks, ask yourself: "What can I learn?" "What are my reasons for disagreeing or agreeing?" "How can I remember this material more easily?" Questions like this will help you concentrate on the message.

Remember: efficient listeners don't always agree with the speaker. They don't always like what the speaker is saying. But they always respect the speaker's right to express an idea. Efficient listeners base their reactions on what the speaker is saying rather than on their own personal preferences.

OBSERVING VOICE INFLECTIONS AND BODY LANGUAGE

When we listen, we should tune into more than sounds. We should also be aware of what the speaker is telling us with body language and voice inflections.

Voice Inflections

Voice inflection is the different emphasis we put on words. We use word emphasis as well as word choice to convey meaning. The meaning of a sentence can change when the emphasis on the words in a sentence is changed. Let's look at the sentence, "I don't want that job." How many meanings can you give that sentence by varying the emphasis?

You might say, "*I* don't want that job." When you stress *I*, you indicate that someone else might want the job but you don't want it.

Or you might say, "I don't want *that* job." When you stress *that*, you imply that something is distasteful to you about that particular job.

Try emphasizing other words in the sentence and discuss how each change of emphasis changes the meaning.

Body Language

Efficient listeners use the speaker's body language to add to their understanding of the message. Speakers convey meaning through their posture, gestures, and facial expressions. Body language is discussed thoroughly in the section on speech, and you should review that material carefully.

As you listen, ask yourself, "What can I add to my understanding by the way the speaker stands or looks at me?" Confidence, for example, is indicated by standing straight and looking at the listener, lack of confidence by a slouch or difficulty in meeting the listener's eye.

Watch the speaker's movements. Does that frown mean the speaker is angry or thinking? Do the arms folded across the chest mean the speaker is timid, forceful, or cold? Try to relate what the speaker shows through body language with what the speaker says as a way of getting the entire message.

ADAPTING SKILLS TO THE SITUATION

As a listener, you should use all the skills discussed in this chapter, but there will be situations in which you will emphasize certain skills over others. For example, taking time to listen is important in every listening situation, but asking questions and restating main points will be emphasized when you are in a group discussion or communicating one-to-one. In the same way, reinforcing the speaker with positive feedback is emphasized when you are involved in one-to-one communication or group discussion. It is usually not a primary emphasis in lectures or public speaking situations, except during political rallies, religious revivals, and other situations where group involvement is emphasized.

SUMMARY

Efficient listening is an active process. The listener must take time to listen, must ignore distractions, and must concentrate on the speaker's main idea. The listener also must assume some responsibility for moving the listening situation along. The listener should encourage the speaker with eye contact and other body language. Asking questions and paraphrasing important ideas are other ways the listener can encourage the speaker and clarify main points.

Many factors contribute to an effective listening situation. Some of these are so subtle we must be constantly on the alert for them. Be aware of how your personal prejudices may affect your ability to listen. Learn to set aside your personal likes and dislikes and evaluate the messages on the basis of specific things a speaker says. Also when you listen, watch the speaker's gesture and facial expression and listen for voice inflection. These things will help you interpret the speaker's entire message.

Reading this chapter has probably impressed you with one thing about listening: good listeners work hard while they are "just listening."

REVIEW QUESTIONS

1. List the seven techniques of efficient listening mentioned in this chapter. Which one do you think is most important? Why?
2. If the phone rings while you are discussing an idea with someone, how should you handle it? Explain why you think your technique is best.
3. Can you think of a time when you let a personal prejudice interfere with your listening? How did this prejudice interfere? Explain.
4. If, as a speaker, you could give a listener one bit of advice, what would you say?
5. How has reading this chapter changed your understanding of the listener's role?

ACTIVITIES

1. Bring a trade magazine to class. Select a couple of paragraphs from the magazine and read them to a classmate. When you have finished, ask the classmate to write down the main idea(s) you have just read. Compare your classmate's interpretation with your own. Do they agree? Discuss your answers.
2. Prepare a short talk (one or two minutes) on a topic that is important to you. This may be a current events issue that you feel strongly about or a description of an interesting experience you have had. Sit down with a classmate and share your in-

formation with that person. While you are talking, your classmate should look around the room, doodle on paper, or interrupt with "that reminds me . . ." comments. When you are finished, record how you felt while the listener was distracted. Did you have trouble finishing your talk? Did you forget what you were saying? Were you frustrated or confused?

3. Choose a tool related to your occupation; then select a partner from the class and sit back to back with that person. Without naming the tool, describe it to your partner. While you are describing the tool, your partner should try to draw it.

Now face your partner. Repeat your description but supplement that description with gestures and other appropriate body language. When you are finished, compare the drawings. Which is more accurate?

Now reverse roles. You draw the mechanism your partner describes. When you have finished both drawings, discuss the reasons for the difference between the two drawings. How effective is body language as an aid to communication?

4. Attend a lecture by someone in your community. Use the following list to record your observations during the lecture. Be attuned to barriers present in your surroundings and to internal barriers that you bring to the situation. Pay attention to how the speaker's body language adds to your understanding or to your opinion about the speaker or the subject.

   a. Briefly describe the listening situation.
   b. List external barriers that you recognize when you begin listening.
   c. What additional external barriers do you sense during the lecture?
   d. What internal barriers are you aware of concerning (1) the speaker, (2) the place, and (3) the subject?
   e. On what level did you listen most of the time?
   f. What listening level would have been most appropriate to the situation?
   g. If you listened creatively, what questions did you ask as you listened?
   h. How did you evaluate the information you took in?

PART III   Speaking

Corrine Haskins is manager of Patient Accounts at West General Hospital. Recently her department has been behind in billing. Customers have received late and inaccurate statements. Insurance payments have not been recorded on time. Because other hospitals in the city are experiencing similar problems, Corrine's supervisor has arranged for monthly meetings to discuss ways of improving all the hospitals' billing procedures. The managers and two staff members from each hospital's accounting department are invited to attend these meetings. Corrine has been appointed group leader.

As the members of the discussion group begin to arrive for this month's meeting, Corrine shuffles the papers in front of her and thinks, "What can we talk about today?"

As if reading her thoughts, Sean, the manager of Jackson Community Hospital, asks, "What's on the agenda today, Corrine?"

"I didn't have time to make out an agenda," Corrine answers. Then she asks the group, "Any ideas about what we should talk about today?"

A couple of members shuffle their feet, one girl shakes her head and looks down at her hands, but no one answers Corrine's question. Corrine looks around the group. Finally she singles out Tony. Slumped in his chair, Tony is doodling on a piece of paper.

"Tony," Corrine says, attempting to get his attention, "What do you think we should talk about today?"

Slowly Tony looks up from his doodling. Very deliberately he says, "I think we should cancel these meetings. They never accomplish anything."

"How can you say that," Ann says. "I like the way we talk about things here."

"Tony's always negative," Sean volunteers.

"I agree with him," Peggy speaks up. "Our computer is down and we're trying to do some of the bills by hand. I could use this time to help the people in my office."

"Hey, did anyone see *The Hospital Story* last night on TV?" Jim asks. "They had the same problem we do."

"How did they solve it?" Corrine asks, attempting to get the discussion back on the subject of computerized billing problems.

"I don't know," Jim laughs, "I fell asleep. It was a good show, though."

"I'm sorry, Corrine, but I really don't have time for this today," Peggy says. "I have to get back to the office. We're up to our eyebrows in work."

Without a word Tony gets up and follows Peggy out the door. Confused, the rest of the group looks at Corrine. "Since we're all so busy this month," Corrine says, "maybe we should reschedule the meeting in two weeks."

"I'll be on vacation then," Sean says.

"Not two weeks from now," Ann says. "That's the worst time of the month for us."

"Call us in September," Sean says. "We'll all feel more like tackling this problem in the fall."

As the group moves toward the door, one young woman, who has sat quietly in the far corner of the room throughout the discussion, hands Corrine a piece of paper.

"I jotted down some possible solutions to our billing problem," she says shyly. "Maybe we can discuss them next time."

"Why didn't you bring them up today?" Corrine asks, looking at the comprehensive list.

"I don't know," the young woman says. "There just didn't seem to be time."

When everyone has left, Corrine puts the piece of paper in her notebook. "I just hate these meetings," she says to herself. "Nobody cooperates."

DISCUSSION OF SCENARIO

The members of Corrine's discussion group do seem uncooperative. Peggy and Tony have closed their minds to the group's activities. Jim doesn't take the discussion seriously, and Sean establishes hard feelings by labeling Tony as negative. Even the young woman who has compiled a list of possible solutions does not contribute to the group's success by sharing her ideas with them.

Nevertheless, as the leader, Corrine must also assume responsibility for the failure of this discussion group. First, she is unprepared to lead the group. She does not have a written agenda or any clear goal in mind for today's discussion. Second, she ignores the messages conveyed through body language when she calls on Tony, who is obviously disinterested in the group. His negative response sets the tone of the discussion. Corrine also fails to use the resources of her group. She lets the more outgoing members dominate the discussion and does not draw out the less verbal participants.

HOW WELL DO YOU COMMUNICATE ORALLY?

Although fictional, this scenario probably reminded you of times when you have been involved in similar groups. Perhaps you were the participant who couldn't get up the courage to share your ideas with the entire group, or you may have been the leader who couldn't get the members of the group to cooperate. You may even have let negative feelings about the group's activity interfere with the discussion process.

How well you communicate orally relates directly to your on-the-job success. One source estimates that 80 percent of the people who fail at work do so because they do not relate well to their fellow workers.

How well do you relate to others? The following activity will help you evaluate your oral communication skills.

Choose a partner from the members of your class. Now select an object in the room such as the pencil sharpener, tape player, or an article of clothing someone in the class is wearing. Describe that object in detail to your partner. Use gestures and facial expressions but do not point to or look at the object. When you have finished describing the object, reverse roles and let your partner describe an object to you. Were you both able to identify the objects described? What gave the best clues: words, tone of voice, or body language? Were any elements of oral communication missing from either your or your partner's description?

Relating well to others involves a variety of communication skills. First, you must express your own opinion concisely and confidently. Be aware that your facial expression, posture, and tone of voice as well as the words you choose convey meaning. Second, pay attention to your listener. Observe facial expression and other body language for clues to how your message is being received. Last, when you have finished talking, take time to listen to those who have been your listeners.

In the preceding section of this book, we discussed listening skills. In this section we will discuss the remaining area of successful oral communications: learning to say what you mean and developing an awareness of your listener's response to your message.

7

COMMUNICATING ONE-TO-ONE

A free conversation will no more bear a dictator than a free government will.
                                                          Lord Chesterfield

After reading this chapter you should understand:
1. Purpose of one-to-one communication
2. The process of one-to-one communication
3. Styles of conversation in one-to-one communication
4. Conflict in one-to-one communication
5. One-to-one communication as it applies to three work-related situations:
    talking with your boss
    dealing with gamesmanship
    talking on the telephone

Although entrepreneurship is currently enjoying popular attention, most of us will spend the major part of our working lives in small businesses or large corporations where we will work as part of a team. Because you will likely be working closely with a boss and co-workers, you should understand how to communicate effectively with them on a daily basis.

For that reason we will begin our discussion of speaking skills by considering the most often used form of communication, talking face to face. Beginning with infancy, we communicate one-to-one throughout our lives, first with our parents and siblings, later with teachers and classmates, then with bosses and subordinates, and finally with our own children. Unlike speaking and group discussion, which usually mark special events, one-to-one communication is a basic part of our daily lives. We use it to relate to people we love as well as to strangers. Social occasions, home life, and work experience all require this two-person communication. We may observe that some people are more popular at parties or have an especially fulfilling home life; often these people also get along well with their bosses and co-workers. "Just lucky," you might say. "Some people lead charmed lives while others are always embroiled in conflict." If you watch and listen closely, however, you will probably observe that people who enjoy satisfying personal and work relationships are skilled in two-person communication. They know how to use verbal and nonverbal signals to convey messages and they are perceptive readers of the signals other people send. In this chapter we will discuss the process of one-to-one communication and see how it applies especially to situations you will encounter on the job.

PURPOSES OF ONE-TO-ONE COMMUNICATION

There are two main purposes of one-to-one communication: (1) for immediate pleasure, and (2) to accomplish a goal or to solve a specific problem. The first purpose is usually evident in social conversation. We tell jokes and stories, talk about movies we have seen or vacations we plan, simply to entertain our listeners and share pleasant experiences with them. We look forward to our coffee breaks, special lunches, and chatty phone calls as pleasant breaks in the day. Their main purpose is to relax us, lift our spirits, or provide a change from our work routines. The effects of social conversation are immediate and short-term.

The second purpose of one-to-one communication—to solve a problem or accomplish a specific goal—has a more long-range effect. We use this communication to discuss problems at home or at work. We have specific goals in mind, reach definite conclusions, and live with the results of the decisions made during these two-person talks.

Both types of one-to-one communication are necessary to well-rounded lives; however, because the main purpose of this book is to prepare you to communicate on the job, we will focus on the two-person communication you will use to solve problems and achieve goals at work.

PROCESS OF ONE-TO-ONE COMMUNICATION

Like other forms of verbal and written communication, two-person talks have a beginning, a middle, and an ending.

Beginning

During the first stage the participants get to know each other and define the reason for the talk. This is the time for a neutral exchange of basic information while both parties search for common ground. Usually participants begin with demographic information such as: "Where are you from?" "Where did you go to school?" or "How long have you worked for _____?" This information is used to reduce the uncertainty each party initially has for the other and is a way to find similarities they share. You can probably remember a feeling of relief when during your first few hours on a new job you discovered that one of your co-workers shared your interest in a particular football team or had a cottage near your favorite fishing lake. Research shows that other types of information exchanged during this time may be: attitudes and opinions, future plans, personality characteristics, past behavior, other people you may have in common, and hobbies and interests. During the first stage participants also use appearance and body language as clues to "read" the other person. We are all aware of how definite and lasting these first impressions given by the dress, posture, or greeting of the other person can be.

Middle

If both parties find the first stage satisfactory, they will move into the second stage, during which the relationship established in stage 1 is maintained. In order for a satisfactory relationship to be maintained, certain factors must be present. Three factors that are especially important are affection, control, and appropriate response.

To maintain a satisfactory relationship, both parties must agree on how close they want to become during the relationship. If one person seeks more intimacy than the other, the relationship is off balance and the two-person communication is jeopardized.

In the same way both parties must also agree on who will control the discussion. You have probably noticed in most conversations one person talks more, initiates compromises, and makes the final decision. If both parties agree on who will control the relationship at any given time, the communication is completed successfully. However, problems may occur when one participant resents making decisions or feels that the other party talks too much.

The third factor in maintaining a successful relationship is responsiveness. Conversation depends on appropriate responses by each listener in turn. When you ask a question, you expect an answer. We like laughter for our jokes and expressions of sympathy for our concerns.

Researchers have defined a number of other factors that are usually present in successful two-person communication, but an awareness of these three will help you communicate successfully on the job.

Observe the nonverbal feedback you receive from your boss and co-workers; then relate these messages to your understanding of the two-person communication process. Bosses who enjoy informal camaraderie with their subordinates can be approached differently than bosses who want a formal employer–employee relationship. Sensitivity to the needs of the person sharing your conversation will help you "tone down" your approach or "take charge" as the situation demands. Giving appropriate feedback and understanding your own need for appropriate responses from others will help you maintain satisfactory working relationships.

End

Both verbal and nonverbal signals are used to conclude a conversation. Nonverbally you may break eye contact or lean forward to indicate that you want to end the conversation. Verbally you reinforce the ideas or emotions you and your partner have expressed. As you end the conversation, you show support for what has happened during the communication and indicate a willingness to talk again.

STYLES OF COMMUNICATION

The process of two-person communication we have just described is evident in various styles of conversation. Understanding these styles and knowing when to use each will help you communicate effectively one-to-one.

Dr. Sherod Miller, Dr. Daniel Wackman, Dr. Elan Nunnally, and Carol Taline, the authors of *Straight Talk,*[1] identify four main styles of conversation: small talk, control talk, search talk, and straight talk. Matching the style with the content and situation is the key to effective communication.

Small Talk

Small talk is a noncommittal, chatty conversation suited to casual subjects. Its purpose is to maintain a friendly, relaxed atmosphere. We use it to give information:

I'm going over the Wilson account now.

to tell a joke:

Have you heard the one about. . . .

or to ask a routine question:

Are you going to the beach for Labor Day weekend?

Small talk is not used to express emotions or give directions. We all enjoy small talk at parties, in our car pool, or with our neighbor across the backyard fence. It also has a purpose on the job. Small talk helps maintain a pleasant relationship with other people in your work area. It is a nonthreatening way of keeping in touch and therefore the most commonly used conversation style.

[1] Sherod Miller et al., *Straight Talk: How to Improve Your Relationships Through Better Communication* (New York: Rawson Wade, 1980), p. 26.

Although small talk is an important part of on-the-job communication, it can also create problems. Because it is benign, we tend to retreat to small talk when we are faced with resolving conflict or making an important decision. People who feel uncomfortable with emotion or are reluctant to discuss unfamiliar subjects often resort to small talk to divert the conversation. Although it can lighten a tense mood, small talk is inappropriate when your co-worker wants to discuss an issue seriously. At those times it causes frustration, hinders communication, and can lead to tension in the work place.

Control Talk

Unlike small talk, which is used to keep things as they are, control talk is used to direct actions. Through control talk you take charge of a situation. Bosses use it to direct their employees' work habits:

Please update the Wilson account for me by Thursday.

salesmen use it to persuade buyers:

This ten-speed bike will help you lose those extra pounds.

and co-workers advise new employees with control talk:

If I were you, I'd concentrate on the Wilson account. The boss puts a high priority on it.

Control talk serves an important function in the work place. It lets people know what is expected of them and helps the workday move along efficiently.

Control talk too can create problems on the job. A boss or co-worker who is interested only in compliance and uses control talk to assert indisputable authority creates tension and negative feelings. Using control talk to get your own way at all costs or to attack another person verbally establishes a threatening, nonproductive atmosphere. The authors of *Straight Talk* call this "heavy" control talk. Some of their examples of this kind of talk are:

Labeling: "That's a totally irresponsible statement."
Name Calling: "You're a coward."
Ordering: "Don't leave until you're finished."
Ridiculing: "That's your idea of dressing for success?"
Evaluating: "You're wrong again."[2]

Avoiding heavy control talk and using other kinds of directive talk effectively are important requirements of efficient on-the-job communication.

---

[2] *Ibid.*, p. 26.

Search Talk

Search talk combines some important aspects of both small talk and control talk. Like small talk, search talk is nonthreatening; like control talk, it can be used to accomplish tasks. Through search talk, we analyze problems and think about possible solutions, but we do not feel any pressure to make decisions or do anything about the ideas we express. We use search talk to discover, explore, and reflect. It is an intellectual process used to concentrate on issues. You can use search talk to ask someone's advice:

My boss expects me to work every Saturday morning without extra pay. What should I tell him?

to offer solutions to a problem:

Well, you might tell your boss you visit your parents every weekend so you can't work on Saturdays. Or you could work a few Saturdays, complete a project, then ask for a raise to reflect the extra effort you've made for the company.

or to get information:

You seem tired this morning, Mary. Did anything unusual happen last night?

Brainstorming is another example of search talk. Participants feel free to offer any ideas that come to mind because they know that those ideas will be welcomed rather than censored by the other people involved. According to the authors of *Straight Talk*, search talk can be used to:

Check out uncertainties
Share impressions and hunt for explanations
Examine possible causes
Pose tentative solutions[3]

Search talk eliminates the blaming or accusing attitude often evident in control talk and the superficial meandering of small talk; it establishes a non-threatening atmosphere in which issues can be meaningfully discussed. It is therefore an effective way of conversing about concerns both on the job and in your personal life.

Straight Talk

The fourth conversational style described by Miller and colleagues is straight talk. Its purpose is to handle conflict in a constructive manner. Unlike the other three styles, straight talk makes you examine your own feelings about an issue

[3] *Ibid.,* p. 26.

and face the feelings of others. It deals with a situation in the present rather than speculating on the future as does search talk or discussing the past as small talk often does.

You might use straight talk when you must disagree with your boss, want to ask for a raise, or hope a co-worker will assume some of your job responsibilities. Its goal is to decide on an action as a result of shared thoughts and feelings.

Because straight talk is used to make decisions, it requires more concentration than the other three styles. Understanding the process developed by Miller, Wackman, Nunnally, and Taline will help you see straight talk effectively.

The first step in straight talk is to *acknowledge*. Here you realize how you feel about the issue and how the other people involved feel. During this stage you are aware of your inner feelings and sensitive to the feelings of others.

From acknowledgement you move into *acceptance*. During this second stage you accept the reality of your feelings and the feelings of the others involved. You may find this difficult because we often associate acceptance with giving in. Acceptance should not be looked at this way, however. The acceptance we are discussing allows you to consider possible alternatives and choices. It helps you understand rather than control the situation.

The final step in straight talk is *action*. Because you understand the situation, you can work with your partner to achieve a solution to the problem. Unlike control talk, where the decision is handed down, straight talk emphasizes a decision reached from the sharing of ideas. The following dialogue shows how straight talk can be used in the work place.

WORKER:	I'm very interested in this special project you have asked me to do, but I cannot take it on in addition to my regular work load. I know the project is very important to you, but when I think about it I feel panicky. I do not think I can do a good job when I feel this way.
SUPERVISOR:	This project is especially important to me and I think you are the only one who can do it effectively. But I can understand what you are saying. The project will require a lot of time and energy.
WORKER:	Can we work out a schedule so I will have time within my normal workday to spend on this project?
SUPERVISOR:	I think I can call in Kelly to take over three of your accounts. She has just been part-time but she will be graduating from college in January and could take on full-time work after that.
WORKER:	Do you think the project can wait until January?
SUPERVISOR:	Yes, I think we can work this out.

(Acknowledgement and acceptance)

(Action)

Although we have emphasized straight talk as requiring the most awareness and skill, it is not the only conversational style you should use on the job. Each style has a place in your work life. As with the various listening skills, you will want to adapt your conversation style to the situation at hand. Learn when and how to use them as one way of communicating successfully on the job.

CONFLICT

Regardless of how skilled you become in face-to-face communication, you will not always be able to avoid conflict on the job or at home, nor would you want to end all controversy. Conflict can be a constructive force that challenges you to clearer thinking and improves your relationship with the other people involved.

An understanding of conflict and some ways of handling it will help you use what you have already learned to talk through your conflicts with other people and improve your two-person communication.

Sometimes you may be involved in a conflict in which one side must win and the other must lose. A war is an example of this kind of conflict. "Battles" over controlling interest in a corporation may be another example of a win–lose conflict. However, most controversies can be resolved so the people involved share a satisfactory outcome.

Three techniques can be used to achieve this sharing process. They are compromise, mediation, and arbitration.

Compromise

Through compromise each party wins some important points by giving up others. When you compromise, you willingly "settle for less" to reach a decision or decide on a plan of action. You may use compromise when you and your boss discuss your annual raise or when your co-workers must approve your marketing plan.

Mediation

When you cannot reach a satisfactory agreement with the others involved in the conflict, you may decide to use mediation or arbitration to resolve the conflict. In mediation you ask a third party to help you negotiate until you can reach a satisfactory conclusion. That person hears both parties talk reasonably about the conflict. Marriage counselors are often mediators in conflicts between spouses. You can call in other co-workers when you and your team partner are having a problem deciding on an advertising plan. The mediator listens, questions, and helps draw the people in conflict toward a compromise.

Arbitration

Sometimes the conflict is so intense or the factors dividing the two are so diverse that a compromise cannot be reached even with the help of a mediator. Then you and the others involved may have to give up your right to influence the decision. You may have to ask an arbitrator to make a decision for you. An arbitrator listens to both sides, considers the reasoning presented, and makes a decision about the issue. The people involved in the conflict agree to go along with the decision the arbitrator makes. This is the most formal way of handling conflict and is usually used to resolve major problems such as contracts and other conflicts involving workers and management. A form of arbitration also occurs in our courts, where judges and juries hear both sides and make a decision that is honored by everyone involved.

If you recognize the worthwhile aspects of controversy and approach conflict reasonably, you should be able to handle it constructively on the job and at home.

COMMUNICATING WITH YOUR BOSS

Understanding two-person communication will be as helpful in communicating with your boss as with your co-workers, your friends, and members of your family, but talking to your boss also requires awareness of some additional factors involved in upward communication.

First you should be aware of the difference in viewpoints with which you and your boss approach a problem. Remember that your boss' responsibility is to consider the well-being of the entire company. You, on the other hand, may be considering the problem from a more personal or departmental viewpoint. An awareness of this difference in outlook will help you and your boss communicate more effectively.

Although bosses try to be objective and may even appear impersonal, you should remember that your boss has strengths and weaknesses like any other employee in the company. Make an effort to understand your supervisor. Does your boss work best in the morning or afternoon? Does your supervisor understand information best when it's written or spoken? When you know these things, you will know how and when to approach your boss with important concerns.

When you must disagree with your boss, choose the timing and the wording carefully. Rather than blurting out, "You're wrong about that" or "Why do we have to do it this way?" during a meeting, wait until afterwards when your boss is alone to discuss your disagreements. Even then, try to avoid negative language. A statement beginning, "Your proposal is basically sound, but I wonder if we could consider a few alternatives," will help encourage your boss to listen to you.

Your keeping your boss informed, presenting your ideas in a nonthreatening manner, and reading nonverbal signals correctly will help your boss know that the two of you share common work-related goals.

AVOIDING GAMESMANSHIP ON THE JOB

Another problem you may experience when communicating at work is gamesmanship. Gaming is an attempt by one person to manipulate another person by indirect methods. It indicates a lack of trust between communicators. Because it garbles the messages being sent, it places barriers between the sender and receiver rather than allowing them to share ideas.

Some examples of gamesmanship are:

1. Answering a question with a question.
2. Discussing what other people think, feel, or do rather than one's self.
3. Sending incomplete, cryptic messages that seem to suggest rather than state.
4. Providing superficial or emotional information about an important issue.
5. Use of *we* or *they* rather than *I* or *you*.
6. Asking questions that limit or suggest a response (for example, "This is a good proposal, isn't it").
7. Withholding important information because "no one asked."
8. Sending nonverbal negative messages but refusing to verbally discuss an issue.[4]

An awareness of the techniques of gamesmanship and the problems it causes will help you recognize it in the work place. When you realize that a co-worker is indulging in gaming, rather than thinking "I don't understand why Mary and I can never discuss a problem," you can say to the person directly, "You seem to be saying . . ." or "Do I understand this correctly?" In this way you will overcome some of the barriers the other person is placing in the way of communication and reduce the gaming problems.

TELEPHONING

Until now we have discussed one-to-one communication as being face to face, but the same factors are evident when you talk on the phone. Telephoning, however, is a unique form of two-person communication and therefore requires additional discussion.

In 1980 Americans made more than 700 million phone calls.[5] This figure emphasizes the importance of the telephone in our lives. Because we use the phone so much, a particular code or style has evolved as correct telephone usage. In this

[4]Sally Bulkey Pancrazio and James J. Pancrazio, "Better Communication for Managers," *Supervisory Management* (New York: AMACOM, a division of American Management Associations, June 1981), p. 35.
[5]Statistical Abstract, 1981.

section we will discuss the effective verbal and nonverbal techniques for using the telephone.

Like any other two-person conversation, talking on the phone has a beginning, a middle, and an ending and uses the four styles of conversation.

Beginning

Open your phone conversation with a friendly statement. During business hours, when you are answering the phone, you should greet the caller, identify your company and indicate, either with a specific question, a pause, or a voice inflection, that you are willing to help the caller. If you are the caller, wait to be greeted, then state your name and the main reason for calling.

OPERATOR: Mayer & Gordon Company. This is Ann Johnson. May I help you?
CALLER: Hello, I'm Ron Smith. I'd like to talk with you about my bill, please.

Middle

As the conversation moves into the second stage, remember the four styles of conversation we discussed earlier and use the style appropriate for the situation. Recognize the purpose of small talk, avoid heavy control talk, and use search talk and straight talk to solve problems as they occur. When explaining procedures or policies to someone outside your business, use language the caller will understand rather than in-house jargon. When you are the caller, state your areas of concern specifically and listen to the other person's explanation.

End

Ending a phone conversation is difficult for many people. Sometimes you will hear silence on the line followed by an almost whispered "Goodbye." End a telephone talk in the same way you would end any two-person conversation. Repeat important points, indicate that you appreciate the chance to talk, and reinforce that thought with a statement like:

Let's talk again.

or

I'll look forward to hearing from you later.

Give Clear Verbal Signals

Many business calls you receive will be requests for information from or referral to another department. Handle these calls as though the callers were in your office and you were directing them in person.

OPERATOR: Hello. Mayer & Gordon Company. May I help you?

CALLER: Yes, this is Ron Smith. I'd like to talk with someone about my bill.

OPERATOR: If you'll stay on the line, I'll connect you with Ann Johnson in client accounts. In case we're cut off, her extension is 406.

In this case you have given specific directions to the caller. If Ron Smith is cut off, he knows who to call and how to reach her efficiently. Although it takes more time than a brief "Hold please," it is more effective communication.

Be Aware of Nonverbal Signals

You have probably heard the statement: "Thank goodness we don't have telephones with visual screens. I don't want anyone to see how I look when I talk on the phone." We tend to think that we can ignore nonverbal signals during our phone conversations. But you can also probably remember a time when you felt rejected or angry because you could hear the person on the other end of the line shuffling papers, drinking coffee, or munching a cookie, behavior that would be inappropriate if you had been there in person.

Nonverbal signals are as important during a telephone conversation as they are in other forms of two-person talks. The first nonverbal signal you give the caller is how soon you answer the phone. Most businesses will ask you to answer the phone by the third ring. After that, the caller begins to wonder if anyone is in the office. When people come to your desk, you do not let them stand silently in front of you while you finish your paperwork. In the same way, answering the phone promptly shows the caller you are interested.

Although you cannot make eye contact with the person on the other end of the line, you can give the same effect as eye contact by keeping the phone's mouthpiece near your mouth and looking in one direction. When you drop the mouthpiece or continually turn to look at people coming in and out of your office, the effect is the same on the phone as glancing around the room or doing paperwork while someone is talking to you. Pay attention on the phone as you would in person.

Your facial expressions are also important to effective phone communication. When you smile, your voice will sound happy and in effect "send the smile over the phone." In the same way, frowns are also heard on the phone. Use facial expressions to convey meaning on the phone just as you would if you were talking face to face.

Although the same verbal and nonverbal elements are apparent in all kinds of two-person talks, the barrier of distance is a factor in phone conversation. Voice inflection can help overcome this obstacle to effective phone conversation. Be especially aware of voice variety to offset the fact that a machine is aiding this conversation. Use voice variety to show enthusiasm and friendliness and to emphasize important parts of the conversation.

Be aware of nonverbal signals even as your phone conversation ends.

Often, without thinking, we set down the receiver as we say goodbye. A hurriedly placed receiver is a nonverbal signal which can be interpreted, "I'm glad the conversation is over." Just as you would not turn away from a person standing in front of you before the conversation is finished, don't cut off a caller abruptly. Keep your voice pleasant and be sure the person on the line is finished talking. Let a second or two elapse then set the receiver down politely rather than letting it drop unceremoniously into the phone cradle. Paying attention to these nonverbal signals will leave a positive impression at the end of the talk.

SUMMARY

One-to-one communication is often intended to accomplish a particular goal or solve a problem. Like other forms of verbal and written communication, it has a beginning (when the relationship is established), a middle (when the issue is discussed), and an ending (when appreciation and an intention to talk again are usually expressed).

Four styles of conversation are used in two-person talks. They are small talk, control talk, search talk, and straight talk. We use small talk to give information or ask a routine question. Control talk may be used to give directions or persuade someone to do something. Control talk can create problems when the speaker uses it to assert indisputable authority. When we want to analyze problems in a non-threatening way we use search talk, and when we want to handle a conflict in a constructive manner we turn to straight talk. Examples of each are given in the chapter.

Even people who understand the aspects of two-person communication and use these conversation styles appropriately can be involved in conflict. Conflict, often considered a negative factor, can be a constructive force in a relationship. Conflicts can be handled effectively in a variety of ways depending upon the situation and intensity of the conflict.

Two-person communication can be used to communicate in many situations including discussions with your boss, avoidance of gamesmanship, and telephone conversations. In this chapter the process and technique of two-person communications are applied to these areas in detail.

REVIEW QUESTIONS

1. Think of the last two-person talk in which you were involved. Did it have a beginning, a middle, and an end? Was it more difficult to start the conversation, keep it going, or end it? Explain your answer.
2. What do you find most difficult about communicating one to one? Explain your answer.
3. When was the last time you used control talk? How did your listener respond? If the response was negative, what type of conversation do you think would have

been more appropriate? If the response was positive, why do you think that was effective?

4. Where do you think you could use straight talk? Why would it be effective in that situation?

5. What do you think is the most effective way to solve conflict? Is there any one of the techniques mentioned in this chapter that you think would not be appropriate? Explain.

6. Have you ever experienced gamesmanship? If so, how did you react?

ACTIVITIES

1. Think of the last time you discussed a problem or assignment with a boss or an instructor. Write a paragraph describing that conversation. How did the conversation begin and end? What style of conversation was used?

   Now write another paragraph evaluating the conversation. Consider the following questions:
   a. Did you respond appropriately to your boss' comments?
   b. What style of conversation did you use?
   c. Did your boss accept that style or want to use another style?
   d. Was the style you used appropriate to the topic?
   e. What was the strongest plus about this encounter?
   f. What one thing would you change about it?

2. The next time you have an opportunity to discuss a problem or assignment with a superior, pay close attention to the way your two-person talk proceeds. Remember the one thing you wanted to change in activity 1. Attempt to change it in this encounter. Write a paragraph describing your modified approach and indicating whether or not you were successful in improving one-to-one communication with your boss.

3. Choose a problem related to your major area. Your problem may concern:
   a. Labor–management issues such as work load, benefit package or employee safety
   b. Personal issues such as time off for personal emergency, personality conflict with co-worker, change in the time you start and end work
   c. Other work-related concerns such as the most efficient use of a word processing system, suggestion for making billing procedures more efficient, or arrangement of the grocery store's produce department
   Discuss this problem briefly with a classmate. Each of you should support a different side of the issue. Then decide who will be the boss and who will be the employee and discuss the issue in front of the class. Your goal is to reach a conclusion about the issue. When you are finished, ask the class to evaluate the effectiveness of your communication on the basis of the information given in this chapter.

4. Plan a telephone conversation concerning a problem in your field. Decide whether you will send positive or negative nonverbal signals. Choose a partner and make your call in front of the class. When you have finished the call, ask your partner to interpret the signal you sent. Then ask the class for their comments. How do their interpretations agree with your original intention?

5. The next time you call a business, evaluate the conversation according to the following questions:
   a. What positive verbal and nonverbal signals did you send? What positive verbal and nonverbal signals did the receiver send?

b. What negative verbal and nonverbal signals did you send? What negative verbal and nonverbal signals did the receiver send?

c. Where was the conversation the weakest—beginning, middle, or ending? Why?

d. What is the one most positive thing about the conversation?

e. What is the one area that most needs improving?

8

TALKING IN FRONT
OF A GROUP

No glass renders a man's form or likeness so true as his speech.

Ben Johnson

After studying this chapter you should understand:
1. What public speaking is
2. How to get started preparing your talk
3. How to organize your talk
4. Applying speaking techniques to informative, demonstrative, and persuasive talks
5. How to talk effectively in front of a group

You may be wondering, "Why should I learn to talk in front of a group?" Politicians, clergy, and public relations personnel are not the only people who talk to groups of people. The information age provides an opportunity and an obligation for many people to speak in front of groups. In fact, according to one estimate, more than 500,000 public talks are given each year.[1] Managers use closed-circuit TV's to present their idea to co-workers. Supervisors train new employees and retrain older ones in an attempt to keep their staff up-to-date. We form our opinions about government and social problems from the speeches we hear on TV and in our communities. These are only some of the ways we use public speaking skills on the job and in our personal lives.

The following story taken from an editorial by Herbert E. Markley, chair-

---

[1] William D. Brooks, Speech Communication (Dubuque, Iowa: Wm. C. Brown Company Publishers, 1981), p. 223.

man of the Executive Committee for the Timken Company, shows how one person's career in business benefited from knowing how to talk in front of a group.

> A true story about a friend of mine will make my point about the value of speechmaking as a tool. This friend, a city fireman, concluded there would be more available to him in life if he could only speak in public. The trouble was he could not stand in front of a group and say his own name. Then he heard about Toastmasters International. He joined and developed the ability to talk better. That got him a salesman's job, from which he was promoted to a sales manager.
> Later, he became president of a small enterprise that, in turn, was acquired by a well-known national group, which promptly made him president of a large division. From this lofty perch he spotted an opportunity to acquire a small business of his own. Not only has that business grown, but along with new companies he has formed and owns in the Orient, it has also become a small conglomerate worth millions. And all because he learned how to give a speech.[2]

This person's experience shows you a good reason to develop your public speaking skills. Although you may avoid talking to groups when you hold entry-level jobs, you will most likely need public speaking skills to be considered for management or supervisory positions. In this chapter we will discuss ways you can learn to talk effectively in front of a group.

WHAT IS PUBLIC SPEAKING

When you talk in front of a group, you send one continuous message intended to make the group respond in a certain way. This continuous message is what makes public speaking different from other spoken communication. Conversation and group discussion are a give and take of individual thoughts. Your ideas follow the flow of the discussion and are often responses to the ideas of other people involved. When you talk in front of a group, however, you are solely responsible for the message; therefore, you must prepare carefully.

GETTING STARTED

"What will I say?" is the first thought most people have when they are asked to talk in front of a group. Although we tend to think first about what we will say, we should think instead about our reasons for talking and the people who will be listening to us. Before you begin planning the content, you should establish groundwork that will help you prepare an effective talk.

Determining the Purpose of Your Talk

The first thing you should do to prepare is to decide the purpose of your talk. Most talks have one of three purposes: to inform, to persuade, or to entertain.

---

[2]Herbert E. Markley, "Speaking Ability Is a Valuable Asset," *Industry Week*, January 10, 1983, p. 102.

Inform   When your purpose is to inform, you increase your audience's awareness of the subject. A class lecture, club report, and CPR demonstration are examples of this purpose. Statistics, definitions, descriptive details, and demonstrations are used to present new ideas or clarify concepts. Your goal is to add to your audience's knowledge with the information you present.

Persuade   You may also want to *persuade* your audience. Sales pitches and political speeches are examples of this purpose. Logical reasoning and emotional appeals are used to influence your audience's opinion. When your purpose is to persuade, you want to convince your audience to share your beliefs or follow your lead. You may simply want to reinforce beliefs they already have. Sermons and pep rallies are examples of persuasion talks given to reinforce beliefs held mutually by the speaker and audience.

Entertain   The third purpose you may have in talking in front of a group is to entertain them. A comedy routine is an example of this purpose. Humorous stories and illustrations are used to make the audience laugh and relax. When your purpose is to entertain, your main goal is to increase your audience's feeling of enjoyment. You want your listeners to have a good time rather than learn something or change their attitudes toward a controversial issue.

Combining Purposes   Although you will usually decide on one of these purposes as the main goal for your talk, you may also combine them. For example, in order to persuade your audience to do something, you will probably have to give them information first. Although you may decide to leave the entertainment talks to your favorite comedian, you will probably find that an audience is more interested in what you say when you add some entertaining details to it.

Once you have decided on your main purpose, you should keep it clearly in mind as you prepare the rest of the talk.

Audience Analysis

The next step is to gather some information about your audience. This information will help you decide on a topic and slant that topic to your listeners. When analyzing your audience, consider three factors: characteristics of the group, psychological makeup of your listeners, and the place in which you will be talking.

Characteristics   Characteristics of your audience, often referred to as demographics, include age, sex, and educational background. Try to find out as much as you can about your audience's racial heritage, age, and work experience as well as the churches, clubs, and political groups they have joined. This information will help you choose examples and illustrations that will be relevant to them.

Psychological Makeup   Information about the attitude and beliefs of your audience will also help you plan your talk. Does your audience have any strong religious or political convictions? What cultural and social values can you expect from your listeners? How will they react to certain topics, and how will they react to you as the speaker? Why are they coming together to listen to you? The answers to these questions will help you choose an interesting topic and slant it toward your listeners. They will also help you anticipate positive and negative reactions and prepare for them. An awareness of your audience's attitude and beliefs will help you make wise word choices in presenting your ideas.

Setting You should also find out some things about the place where you will be talking. The setting can influence your audience's reaction and affect your presentation. Find out how large the audience will be and whether you will be talking inside or outside. Will you have a podium, microphone, or other speaking aids to help you deliver your talk?

Can you foresee any problems with the setting such as a room that is too hot or too noisy? If you can predict these problems ahead of time, you can sometimes correct them before you begin talking.

SELECTING A TOPIC

Considering your audience's background, likes and dislikes, and physical comfort is important, but this emphasis on audience analysis does not mean that you should talk only about topics that already interest your audience. It does mean, however, that you should be prepared for your audience's reaction. If you can predict that your audience will be bored or angry with your topic, you know you will have to work harder to win them to your side. If you can't make the room cooler, you can let your audience know that you recognize and share their discomfort. Often a joke will relieve tension.

When you have decided on a purpose and learned some things about your audience and the place where you will be giving your talk, you should select a topic. First take an inventory of your hobbies, skills, and special interests. Ask yourself what beliefs and values are especially important to you. List whatever comes to mind; remember you do not have to talk about every topic you list.

When you have five or six—or maybe fifty or sixty—topics listed, review them. Ask yourself which of the topics interest you most. Then consider which would appeal to your audience or which you could adapt to the group. For which topic do you have the most background, and which one will you be able to research thoroughly? These questions will help you select a topic you can develop into an effective talk.

ORGANIZING YOUR TALK

After you have selected a topic, you should research it using the skills discussed in Chapter 2. When you have enough information to talk knowledgeably about your topic, organize the material into a logical pattern of development. Effective talks have three main parts—introduction, body, and conclusion—and each of these parts has a distinct purpose.

Introduction

The first impression your audience forms of you and your topic is established by your opening comments. Therefore, although the introduction is a small percentage of your complete talk, it is vital to your speaking success. Plan your introduction carefully and polish it so you can begin your talk smoothly.

Because of its importance, a lot is expected of an introduction. In it you will try to accomplish three things: get the audience's attention, establish rapport, and state the purpose of your talk.

Get Attention   You can get your audience's attention in several ways. You might begin your talk with a story. It may be humorous or dramatic, true or fiction, but it must catch the audience's attention and relate to your topic.

A question is another effective opener. Remember that an opening question is usually rhetorical, meaning that you don't expect everyone in your audience to answer directly. You just want to start them thinking about the subject. Be sure the question you ask is thought provoking. If you are giving a talk on bicycle repair and you ask the question, "How many of you own bicycles?" you may find the question works against you rather than for you. Your audience's response to this general question may be, "Doesn't everyone own a bicycle?"

Startling facts and impressive quotes are also effective ways to begin a talk. Again the key to their success is impact. Remember you are using these openers to gain your audience's attention.

Establish Rapport   Next you try to establish rapport with your audience. You can create a friendly feeling by showing them that you understand and share their interests and concerns. One or two sentences following the attention getter should set a friendly tone and establish goodwill between you and your audience.

State Purpose   The attention getter relates generally to the topic but does not reveal your specific purpose. The introduction should conclude with a sentence that clearly states your purpose. This last sentence should sum up the introduction and pave the way for the rest of your talk.

The following excerpt by Val Olson, president of Creative Management Alternative, Inc., illustrates the three goals of an introduction.

> By way of background, Sentry is a large insurance company, having assets of more than $2.5 billion dollars. We are dealing with a substantially white collar work force of 10,000 employees.
>
> I'm going to make an admission I think each one of us makes simply by attending this program. Sentry has had productivity problems. However, Sentry is not alone. The entire insurance industry is wallowing in a productivity dilemma.

Builds rapport

Attention getter

Let me give you some facts. Some of the worst labor productivity records, reported in the Gross National Product, since World War II are the insurance and finance sector. Between 1948 and 1965, while many sectors of the GNP were having average annual productivity improvements rates of +2 to +5 percent, the insurance and finance industry was "zipping" along at an average annual improvement rate of +1.3 percent. And as deplorable as that sounds, that was its productivity heyday. From 1965 to 1973 its average annual productivity rate declined slightly to +1.2. Between 1973 and 1979, the average annual labor productivity indicator for the insurance and finance sector was –.1 percent. Today, it is at the deplorable rate of –.2 percent.

It is probably safe to assume that today the productivity level in the insurance and finance sector is not much better than in 1948. (The actual improvement rate 1948–81 is only an average annual rate of +.9 percent). Well, during the 1970s, Sentry did make some attempts at efficiency improvements.

In 1975, Sentry's property and casualty company hired a consulting firm to install work measurement in its personal lines division. At the same time, Sentry's life insurance company hired another consulting firm to install work measurement and a gain sharing plan in its operation. The work measurement programs that were purchased produced limited results. In 1976 I was directed to solve a productivity problem that had developed in Sentry's largest subsidiary.

The system we designed and put into the subsidiary was an exciting success. It is the nucleus around which we built Sentry's productivity department and productivity enhancement techniques.

Purpose statement

Obviously, white collar productivity is heavily involved with people. Therefore, my discussion is going to center around people. I firmly believe that people, not machines, are the key to solving the white collar productivity problem.[3]

Another example, a talk given by Frank J. Farrell, president of Grolier Electronic Publishing, Inc., illustrates another approach to introducing a topic.

Attention getter

The title of my speech, "The New Wealth of Nations: Information," finds its origins in Adam Smith's master-work published in 1776—An Inquiry into the Nature and Causes of the Wealth of Nations. Adam Smith considered the primary wealth of nations to include capital, manufactured goods, natural resources, and labor. But if Smith were alive today, I am convinced that he would place very near the top of his list, information—timely, relevant, accessible information—information for those decisions that give direction and value to natural resources, capital formation, and virtually every area of contemporary living. This, I'm suggesting, may well constitute the new critical wealth of enlightened nations today.

If we think of information as a resource—somewhat akin to one of our most basic natural resources, say water—we will begin to see and understand the fascinating parallels between this rather abstract, man-made resource—information—and that fundamental natural resource—water.

Attention getter

—Both seem to flow continuously from numerous, all but invisible tributaries.

—Both are very useful while under control but overwhelming when they flow too fast to be properly harnessed.

—And both have value only when they are present in the right place, in the right form, and at the right time.

[3] Val Olson, "Gaining the Productivity Edge—A Case Study," *Source APC, Multiple Input Productivity Indexes,* September 1982, p. 9.

Establish rapport

In fact, there seems to be a rising flood of data and information that all of us must face daily and attempt to control. I think most of you have had the same experience I have, now and then, of looking at the deluge of magazines, reports, memos, and letters and saying, "How am I going to read all that, let alone digest it?" And I might add, that is only the visible surface of the information flood—the portion we see day-to-day. The flood is actually very deep, as we see when we seek a particular fact and find dozens of options for information sources.

On the other hand, and as a commentary on our ability to survive, technologists have developed and are developing an increasingly complex system of electronic tools to assist us in our attempts to harness that rising flood of information into useful reservoirs that can ultimately be directed into streams of helpful, knowledge-enhancing, and, if you will, profit-making aids to learning and decision making.

But let's not stretch the analogy too far. And let's not lose sight of these two very important issues—namely, the exponential rate at which people are generating and gathering information, and the equally astounding rate at which we are developing new technological means of dealing with this vast and ever-expanding store of information. These two phenomena are intimately linked. The increasingly sophisticated technology we use to control information also contributes to the rapid increase in the speed of its creation and dissemination.

Purpose statement

Now within all of this is an enormous risk—an enormous risk for you, and I would suggest, an enormous risk for all of us. *If we don't learn to apply the newly available electronic tools, if we don't begin to harness the power of the information flood, in a relatively short period of time, we could literally become obsolete.* That may sound like a bit of hyperbole, a bit too life-threatening, but I would suggest to you that it is in fact a very real threat! Let me see if I can develop a sensitivity and concern on your part for my point of view.[4]

Body

In the body of your talk you will discuss the ideas mentioned in your introduction. Its purpose is to answer questions or explain ideas that have already been introduced. To be effective, this part of your talk must be organized into a thought pattern that your audience can follow easily. You must remember that your audience has only one chance to understand your ideas. Unlike written material, which can be read several times until the meaning is clear, spoken material must be thoroughly understood the first time. Careful organization helps your listeners grasp your main ideas and understand your point of view.

Three organizational patterns—sequential, logical, and topical—are especially helpful in arranging your information. You should be familiar with all three patterns so you can choose the one that best fits your purpose.

Sequential   When you use the sequential pattern, you arrange things in a sequence such as first to last (time order) or east to west (space order). Sequential organization is one of the most familiar patterns, since our lives are often organized by time or direction.

[4]Frank J. Farrell, "The New Wealth of Nations," *Vital Speeches of the Day,* July 1, 1983, pp. 562–63.

Logical   Although all organizational patterns are logical, the type specifically called *logical* emphasizes reasoning processes in its development. When you use this pattern, you arrange your details to show how one thing affects another.

There are two types of logical organization: cause–effect and problem–solution. The cause–effect pattern is usually used in information talks. You should use this order when you want to emphasize what will happen as a result of a certain event or idea.

The problem–solution pattern is especially effective for persuasive talks. With this pattern you take a cause–effect pattern one step further and offer a solution to the result (effect) of the problem (cause).

Topical   When you use the topical pattern of organization, you divide a topic into related parts and organize your information by categories.

Think carefully about the organization of your talk; then choose a pattern that helps you arrange your ideas clearly and follow that pattern faithfully. The examples included in this discussion should help you outline your own ideas and organize your information so your listeners can easily understand your main points.

Conclusion

As you near the end of your talk, you may be tempted to say: "That's it. I've told you all I know," and sit down. Many speakers seem to run down near the end of their talks. Although you may indeed feel weary at that point, you should remember that a conclusion is your last chance to impress your listeners. Therefore, it deserves your careful attention.

A conclusion has three purposes: to summarize the main points of your body, to tie the entire talk together, and to leave a lasting impression with your audience.

First, restate the main ideas you used to develop your purpose statement. Reword them to give variety to your talk and help keep your audience's attention.

Second, relate your conclusion to your introduction, in order to tie all your ideas together. Choose one or two key words that appeared in your introduction or purpose statement and that you developed throughout the body of your talk, and use those words near the end of your talk.

Third, leave your audience with a final impression. Usually, you will emphasize an emotional appeal to impress your audience with the importance of your purpose. A quote, fact, or other startling information that sums up your attitude on the subject is usually an effective close.

When we discussed introductions, we used Frank J. Farrell's beginning to "The New Wealth of Nations" as a model. His conclusion is also a good illustration of an effective way to end a talk. It is reprinted here with marginal notes to point out the three purposes of a conclusion.

In short, I am saying that you should become *aware,* become *literate,* become *functionally conversant* with all of these new technologies, and *as soon as possible.* Because no matter who you are or what you do (whether you are a dentist, or a stockbroker, a corporate officer, or whatever), you are going to be directly affected by the new information technologies. They won't change the substance of what you do; you will still be making the same kinds of decisions, dealing with the same kinds of problems. But you will be facing greater challenges as your competitors and your colleagues begin to use the technologies to their advantage. And you will be increasingly faced, unarmed, with that flood of new information that I described early on, unless you take advantage of the tools available to you.

In the final analysis, it really isn't elective. The new information delivery systems are here, and they are already in the process of making the changes I have been describing. You may elect not to get involved. But if you do that, I suggest that you are electing to become informationally obsolete.

Now perhaps you are thinking that the changes I have described are some ways down the road, say the year 2000—which used to sound so distant but is now just 17 very short years away. But I think it is coming sooner. Forecasts indicate that within just three to four years, there will be over 50 million microcomputers humming away throughout the U.S. Several of the major consumer-oriented online services are doubling their customer base each year. Analysts predict that within five years up to 50 million American homes could be receiving some kind of videotex or teletex service. And with such corporate giants as AT&T, Time Inc., IBM, CBS, and Times Mirror involved, one can easily predict that teletex and videotex will be major presences in the consumer market in the very short term.

I have been talking about a series of issues of critical importance to every executive, manager, professional, laborer, housewife, and student. And the crux of the matter is an old valediction: *We have to learn not to work harder but to work smarter.* The new information technologies offer a vast array of methods for us to increase our productivity. A recent *Business Week* article noted that the use of new information technologies has more than doubled the productivity of the account executives of a major Wall Street broker.

Our objective should be to maximize our understanding of and the creative applications of the new information technologies, so that we can profit in full measure from this *new wealth of nations: information.*[5]

(margin notes: Summary of main points; Quote for lasting impression; Tie in to introduction)

APPLYING SPEAKING TECHNIQUES TO SPECIFIC PURPOSES

The basic organization of introduction, body, and conclusion and the various thought patterns—sequential, logical, and topical—can be used to develop any of the purposes discussed at the beginning of this chapter. Nevertheless, each purpose has some unique features, and special techniques are used to develop each. In the next sections we will talk about the typical information talk, the demonstration talk, and the persuasion talk, the most common purposes for most speakers.

[5] *Ibid.,* pp. 565–66.

INFORMATIVE TALK

Since the purpose of an informative talk is to increase your audience's knowledge, specific examples, quotations, and statistics should be used to support your main ideas. Without support information, your ideas lack substance and are easily forgotten. On the following pages we will discuss the kinds of information you can use to develop your main ideas and show the importance of support details to the content of your information talk.

Statistics

Dates, monetary figures, percentages, and other statistics can be used effectively to support your main points. When using statistics remember to: (1) choose only significant data that will impress your reader with the validity of your ideas, and (2) use only a few statistics to support only one point; too many details will make it difficult for your audience to absorb the information.

Below is an example of a paragraph developed with statistics. Notice how the data prove the main idea.

> Women college students made up a tiny fraction of the age group in 1870, but what is also very important, men college students also made up a very small fraction of the age group then. In 1860 about one percent of the age group was in college, and the proportion of these who were women was very small indeed. A decade later, the one that included the Civil War, the proportion of the 18–21 year olds who were in college was half again as much, 1.68 percent. What is most striking about that increase, however, is that already 21 percent of the undergraduates were women. A decade later, 1880, almost three percent of the age group were in college, and 32 percent were women. Undergraduates of whom 32 percent were female is the same proportion that was true for the U.S. in the early 1950's. The great difference was that in 1880, roughly one hundred years ago, slightly under three percent of the age group was in college. In the 1950's nearly thirty percent of the age group was in college. Thus, the late nineteenth century students who attended college were a tiny fraction of the population, and by virtue of being such a small group they became exempt from many of the strictures of the society. They enjoyed some of the benefits of an elite, of a group who somehow did not have to play by the same rules as the rest of America.[6]

Examples

You can also use specific examples, such as an event or the actions of another person, to explain an idea. Usually your audience will relate to this kind of support and remember it easily. Examples, illustrations, and stories add human interest as well as support to your talk.

[6]Patricia Albjerg Graham, "The Cult of True Womanhood," *Vital Speeches of the Day,* April 15, 1983, p. 401.

The following paragraph illustrates the use of examples to develop an informative talk.

> In its simplest form "information" is an organized collection of data. For example, a random list of names and telephone numbers would be considered data, whereas a telephone directory turns that data into useful information. On a different level, what does the U.S. Census Bureau do? It collects vast amounts of data, data that only become useful when they are analyzed and organized into tables and graphs that inform the reader about trends and relationships in population shifts or market demographics. And these kinds of information are very valuable tools for marketing and business planning. Information, as I am using the word, is the link between raw data and knowledge that leads to effective action.[7]

Quotations

Another effective method of proof is a quotation. The exact words of an authority on the subject create impact and help establish the validity of your own ideas: if an authority agrees with you, you can't be too far off the mark. When choosing a quotation for support, be sure it is easily understood. Give credit to the original speaker or writer and explain that person's job title, experience with the topic, or any other information that will help your audience accept the idea presented in the quote.

Following is an example of a quote used to support an idea.

> Now let's look at other, perhaps less abstract, qualities that can affect the value of information. Those are the accessibility, the accuracy, the appropriateness, the timeliness of information. I think it was Samuel Johnson who said, "Knowledge keeps no better than fish." And for certain kinds of information, he was right. Stock brokers, for example, make thousands of buy-and-sell decisions on the basis of an almost constant stream of timely information. Within hours that same information is virtually worthless, except as history—tomorrow's *Wall Street Journal*.[8]

Importance of Support Details

By this time you have probably noticed that a talk is developed with two kinds of information. First, you state a main idea, then you support your idea with details. Typically, an idea is an abstract thought—a feeling or concept used to start discussion of a topic. That concept must be related specifically to your audience with the second kind of information necessary: concrete details. The following paragraphs illustrate the importance of both kinds of information. The first paragraph lacks a main idea. Notice how the support details lack direction. You're unsure what the speaker intended to illustrate.

[7] Farrell, "The New Wealth of Nations," p. 563.
[8] *Ibid.*, p. 563.

Today, people protest the cost of public education, child care or child-health programs, or food stamps. Some object to children's shelters being located in their neighborhoods, where they might lower property values. Public accommodations ignore the existence of children and their needs. Many transit systems, stores, and museums prohibit baby strollers. Some shops, restaurants, and moviehouses prohibit children altogether. Curbstones, public benches, toilets, telephones, and door handles are too high for little ones. (Ironically, lowering these facilities for wheelchair access has made life easier for children.) While the pornographic display of women's breasts is undeterred on newsstands and movie marquees, official and unofficial prohibition of breastfeeding in public places forces nursing mothers and babies into unsanitary bathroom stalls.[9]

The second example presents an idea but does not support it. Notice that the idea lacks significance and is easily dismissed.

Collectively, we are heirs to a strong legacy of pedophobia from the past, including such practices as infanticide, inhumane child labor, and indentured servitude. In our own era, pedophobia is more subtle. It is also more pernicious because it exists within the lie that Americans are a child-loving people. Public accommodations ignore the existence of children and their needs.[10]

The third paragraph shows how main ideas and supporting details work together. The general concepts make us want to think, and the details give us something concrete to think about. Ideally you will include both abstract concepts and supporting details in your talks.

Collectively, we are heirs to a strong legacy of pedophobia from the past, including such practices as infanticide, inhumane child labor, and indentured servitude. In our own era, pedophobia is more subtle. It is also more pernicious because it exists within the lie that Americans are a child-loving people. Today, people protest the cost of public education, child care or child health programs, or food stamps. Some object to children's shelters being located in their neighborhoods, where they might lower property values. Public accommodations ignore the existence of children and their needs. Many transit systems, stores, and museums prohibit baby strollers. Some shops, restaurants, and moviehouses prohibit children altogether. Curbstones, public benches, toilets, telephones, and door handles are too high for little ones. (Ironically, lowering these facilities for wheelchair access has made life easier for children.) While the pornographic display of women's breasts is undeterred on newsstands and movie marquees, official and unofficial prohibition of breastfeeding in public places forces nursing mothers and babies into unsanitary bathroom stalls.[11]

[9]Adapted from Letty Cottin Pogrebin, "Do Americans Secretly Hate Children?" *MS*, November 1983, p. 48.

[10]*Ibid.*, p. 48.

[11]From Letty Cottin Pogrebin, "Do Americans Secretly Hate Children?" *MS*, November 1983, p. 48.

DEMONSTRATIVE TALKS

Sometimes your main purpose is merely to *tell* your audience *about* something. In that case you relate facts and ideas that help them understand your subject. At other times, however, you want your audience to use that information to do something. When your purpose is to *show* your audience *how to do* something, you will demonstrate how to use the information you give them.

A demonstrative talk is a variation of an informative talk. It takes the information one step further and puts it into practice. Like other informative talks, it includes an introduction, body, and conclusion which satisfy the goals established earlier in this chapter. In addition, though, a demonstrative talk includes a few special techniques which set it apart from other information talks.

Use of Props

One of the most important aspects of a demonstrative talk is use of props. Immediately after your introduction and as the first step in the body of your talk you should list and explain all the tools, ingredients, and equipment your audience will need to repeat whatever process you are demonstrating.

Efficient handling of your props will contribute to the success of your demonstration. Be sure to arrange all of the props before you begin talking. If you have to dig through a grocery bag to find a spatula or a piece of string, you may distract your audience and hinder communication.

You should also make sure your audience can see all your props and how you use them. Several techniques will help you make any process clearer to your audience. First, you may ask your audience to gather around so they can see the demonstration better. This method is especially helpful if you are demonstrating a detailed process such as the tying of fishing flies.

You may also use drawings to help illustrate a process. For example, if you are showing your audience how to tie a square knot you might use line drawings to illustrate the steps. You could project your drawings on an overhead projector or prepare charts ahead of time or draw on a chalkboard as you talk.

A third way to make sure your audience follows each step of your demonstration is to walk around the room as you demonstrate. For example, if you are showing your audience how to tie a necktie, you can walk between the rows stopping at groups of three or four people as you demonstrate. In this way members of your audience can see the process close up.

A fourth way to make your demonstration clear is to involve the audience in the demonstration. If you are showing them how to sew on a button, give each of them a button, needle and thread, and a piece of fabric and ask them to follow along with you.

Another way to involve your audience is to ask several of them to help you.

If you are demonstrating how to braid hair, ask someone with long hair to be a model for you. If you are demonstrating dance steps, choose a few people from your audience to dance with you or with each other.

Whatever props you decide to use, keep your audience's safety in mind. Don't ask them to gather around when you are showing how to fry doughnuts, for example, with hot oil that could splatter. Be careful when you handle knives and other sharp tools and think twice before you use props such as weapons, blow torches, grinders, and other hazardous equipment.

Without props you can only *tell about* a process; you cannot *show* the process. But efficient use of props is not the only requirement for an effective demonstration. You must *tell* your audience what you are doing while you *show* them the process. Choose descriptive language to explain the process you are demonstrating. For example, if you are showing your audience how to do Japanese paper folding, do not tell them:

Fold the paper this way.

Tell them instead:

Fold the upper right-hand corner forward to the center of the page one-third of the way down from the top.

In that way your verbal description is as clear as your actions.

Remember to talk all the while you are demonstrating. Long silences while you work away in front of the room will cause your audience to lose interest and their attention may wander. You should not expect your audience to be engrossed while you shred a head of lettuce or beat frosting in silence. Talk to them about what you are doing. Offer them tips for completing the process efficiently or add interesting information related to the topic.

Organization

Most demonstrative talks are organized chronologically (time sequence). A step-by-step explanation from the first to the last thing you do is vital to an effective demonstrative talk. List all the steps in order, then see if you can complete the activity by following your own directions. Be sure to include even minor points; don't assume that your audience will know them. Each step, no matter how simple, is important in learning how to complete the activity. Also be sure to include special caution or safety tips.

To conclude your talk, review the main points. Don't just hold up the finished product with the comment, "Here it is." Your audience may still wonder about the sequence of the steps. A quick repeat of the steps as they look at the finished product will help your audience clarify any confusion they may still have about the process.

Your main purpose in a demonstrative talk should be to teach your audience a skill. Although the group may not be able to tie fishing flies or fold paper birds as well as you can, they should be able to complete the process correctly. Clear use of props, descriptive language, and a complete summary at the end of the talk will help you satisfy this purpose.

The following demonstrative talk illustrates the techniques discussed in this section.

OUTDOOR COOKING EQUIPMENT

Outdoor cooking is growing in popularity and there are several reasons for it. It's a fun way to prepare meals. But also the tips and ideas I'm going to share with you today can come in handy because summertime often means storm time, too, which can leave a family without the cooking equipment—their stoves, electric fry pans and such—so they might have to resort to cooking outdoors. Some of the reasons it's growing in popularity are:

First, it is convenient. It's very easy to prepare the foods in this manner and a lot of times there's less mess than there is cooking in your kitchen.

Second, it is also good energy conservation. As I mentioned before, if your stove is not working for some reason, build your charcoal, wood, or other energy-saving equipment on which you can create a fire and heat for preparing your meal.

Next, for those who are diet conscious, nutritionists recommend that they bake or broil their food and these are the two methods that are used in preparing outdoor cooking meals.

Another reason is the better taste of food when it is prepared outside. There are some people who claim you just can't beat the taste of food when it is cooked in the outdoors, and I tend to agree with that.

The last reason that outdoor cooking is so popular these days is the improved equipment that is on the market. We have our covered kettles, hibachis, gas grills and they all help us in preparing virtually anything that you can make in your kitchen. However, today I'm going to take a different angle or view on the equipment used in outdoor cooking.

In my backpack today I have some ideas on how you can create some simple and easy cooking equipment. When you are cooking outdoors there are basically two things you need to find in your equipment. The two items you need to look for are: one, a container on which to hold your fire and, secondly, a device to hold the food. And you see those items listed on the screen right now.

Equipment needed
Container to hold fire
Device to hold food

As I mentioned, one of the key ingredients that you need for your equipment is something in which to hold the fire. And what I have here is what we call a buddy burner. The items needed to make this quick, easy heating method are items that you have easy access to around the home. The materials needed include: a tuna fish can, corrugated cardboard, and paraffin wax. The process for making this buddy burner are just as easy as the items that are necessary.

Our first step is to take our corrugated cardboard and cut it into strips, and we want to make these the width and the height of the tuna fish can. In cutting them,

(margin notes)

Introduction Gives audience reasons to listen

Purpose statement

Takes off backpack

Visual

Slide

Tuna can
Corrugated cardboard
Paraffin wax

Shows props

Chronological listing of steps

Cuts strips and
shows how they fit
around can

Specific direction

Coils and places it in
the can

Puts wick in center

we want to cut them so the holes run vertically up and down, so as you look through the cardboard you can see from the top to the bottom. We then want to take the cardboard and you will coil it up, placing it inside of our can. I might add at this moment you do not have to use tuna fish cans. Pet food cans such as dog food cans work just as well. **Next,** we are going to have to create a wick so we can begin to start our fire. Now this wick can be composed of either cord or string or you can take that same cardboard and cut a strip, placing it in the center, and there we have our wick.

Gives audience uses

Now the last procedure for this is when we take some paraffin wax which has been melted and pour that over our cardboard to cover the entire surface—such as has been done here. The paraffin is what is going to help you keep the fire going and it's going to help get the flame started. And there we have one of our first heating sources I'm going to talk about—the buddy burner.

Shows slides
of burner in use

And how can you use the buddy burner? Well, we have a slide that shows the buddy burner being ignited. As you see here, you get quite a flame and that is a good source of heat for cooking. One way you can also use the buddy burner is to place it under a tin can stove. You can see that on the screen now also.

[The speaker continues to demonstrate other outdoor cooking equipment such as egg carton starters, tin can stoves, and aluminum foil pans.]

Conclusion

I would just like to review then. Perhaps we could scan what some of the items were and help you go through the process. The two fire starters that we had were our buddy burners and our egg carton starters. Over here in the corner our two tin can stoves were: number 1 that had vents made entirely with a can opener (the punch style) or our stove number 2 made with a door. You can make your own aluminum foil pans with clothes hangers. And you can also use aluminum foil and tin cans to make a tin can barbeque. And last but not least we'll want to be safe; we'll put out our fires so we have our damper, also, which incorporates our clothes hanger and our tuna can lid. So with that I would like to add that you do not have to go out and spend a lot of money this summer in order to cook in the outdoors. This helps prove that there are inexpensive ways to prepare outdoor cooking equipment.[12]

PERSUASIVE TALKS

Another way you may decide to use the information you have gathered is to persuade your audience: you use logical reasoning to change the minds of the people (convince them) or inspire them to do something (persuade to act). Like an informative talk, a persuasive talk follows a certain pattern of development, with an introduction, body, and conclusion. The introduction and conclusion have the same goals and follow the same pattern as the introduction and conclusion of an informative talk, but the body for a persuasive talk may vary somewhat from the pattern we have discussed. In this section we will discuss the special features of a persuasive talk.

When you talk to persuade, you should use main ideas to start your audience thinking and support those ideas with concrete facts, just as you did in your

[12] Billie Jean Harrison, "Outdoor Cooking Equipment," Knowledge for Living, University of Wisconsin Extension/Cooperative Extension Service, Wisconsin, June 3, 1983.

informative talk. The introduction makes the audience want to listen and the conclusion sends them away thinking about your subject, but the organization of the body of a persuasive talk varies somewhat from that of other types of talks.

Goals

A persuasive talk has two main goals: to establish a need or describe a problem, and to show how that need can be met or the problem solved.

The following outline for a persuasive talk shows you how these goals are accomplished.

I. Attention getter: begin your talk with material that satisfies the three purposes of a good introduction (gets attention, establishes specific rapport, and states the purpose of the talk).
II. Establish the need or describe the problem: In this section you will use statistics, examples, quotations, and other proof to convince people that a need exists. This is a very important part of your talk because you must prove there is a problem before your audience will be interested in solving it.
III. Satisfy the need: In this step you give your solutions to the problem. If you want the audience to do something, tell them in this section exactly what you want them to do. Make sure your action step is concrete and within your audience's power. For example, you should not ask a church group to abolish hunger from the world, but you can ask them to contribute money to be used to buy food.
IV. Visualize what will happen if they share your beliefs or do what you ask them to do. You may find it is more effective to show them what will happen if they do *not* follow your request.
V. Conclude with a summary and an emotional appeal. Impressing your audience emotionally as well as intellectually is especially important in a persuasion talk.

Purposes

The three purposes of persuasive talks—to convince, actuate, and reinforce—are developed differently. When your purpose is to *convince,* you want the audience to share your beliefs. This talk omits the action step. When your purpose is to *act,* you first convince the audience, then you tell them what you want them to do about their belief. This type of persuasive talk includes an action step as the final part of Step III. A talk to *reinforce* may or may not include an action step. Since your audience already agrees with you and wants to follow your lead, you use facts and emotional appeals to keep them on your side.

The following talk illustrates the five steps to a persuasive talk.

Retooling the Workforce
The Need for a National Employment Policy

If, as the late Philip Graham suggested, news is the first rough draft of history, I'm not anxious to hear how future historians will view the 1970's and 1980's. Reading the chapters on unemployment will be rough going, for there is disenchantment in the land of plenty.

Attention getter

Today, one tenth of the labor force is out of work. Youth unemployment stands at 25 percent; among minorities it is 36 percent. Unemployment among black teenagers is a staggering 50 percent. All this in a country built on the principles of hope and opportunity.

When the 20th century began, the American workforce was very different than it is today. Nearly half of America's workers earned their living on farms; today only 4 percent do. The steel industry was in its infancy; the automobile industry did not exist. Computer technology lay two generations away, in the minds of scientists yet to be born. The transformation of our jobs, the movement of our people, the improvements in our skills over the first eighty years of this century have been stunning. But it is entirely likely that the changes recorded in those eighty years will be matched and surpassed by the changes of the final twenty years of this century.

The significance of that projection is overwhelming. It means that all the displacement, all the adjustments, all the technological advances of eighty years will be collapsed into twenty years. While it may be hard to believe that our economic society is going to change that quickly in two decades, consider what has happened already—during just the first two years of that period.

There are one-third fewer autoworkers today than when this decade first began. For the first time in our history more than half the workforce is female. The last black and white television set was produced in America—probably ever—while home computers passed one billion dollars in sales. The same year that an artificial heart is implanted in Barney Clark, the *Washington Star* dies, in part because it could not move papers efficiently from Capitol Hill to Silver Spring at 4 P.M. Yet Ganett begins a newspaper that is designed for national simultaneous distribution. With all of these changes in just two years, the next eighteen are likely to be exciting, challenging, but also damn tough on all of us.

Everywhere we look there is change, but nowhere is it greater than in the technological progress that is reshaping the very fundamentals of the American economy. The national issue of 1983 is whether we are ready to deal with that change. Will we despair in the face of it? Will we resist and deny it, or will we use that change to better the employment opportunities for the people of our nation? The answers may lie in the way we define the problem.

Statement of problem

Too often we see the villain as recession. We believe that the recession causes unemployment. We believe the recession is caused by the government. If Washington would just make the recession go away, unemployment would go away too. So our national employment policy is really an economic policy geared entirely to the question of growth.

But if the final fifth of the 20th century will see as much change as the first four-fifths, then growth is only one part of the employment puzzle. Indeed, Martin Feldstein, Chairman of the President's Council of Economic Advisors, pointed out from this very podium that perhaps half our current unemployment is structural, not growth related. Of course, sustained, adequate growth is essential to expanding employment opportunities, for sound economic policies do create jobs. But what America needs in addition to an economic policy to stimulate real growth is an employment policy to insure that our people can do the jobs that are created by that growth. After all, a job unfilled is no job at all.

Historically, the focal point for reacting to changes in skill needs in the workplace has been our education system. Each new generation was sent into the marketplace with a set of skills that would serve it usefully for a lifetime of productive employment. But now the skills required for continued employment are changing so rapidly that "one-skill-per-generation" is no longer sufficient.

Consider the plight of the unemployed steelworker in Youngstown. He's forty-two years old. He and his wife have a sixteen-year-old daughter who is having trouble finding a summer job. Their eighteen-year-old son is proud of his family and wants only to follow in his father's footsteps. But the steelworker's job is unlikely ever to return. Their daughter has not taken enough math or science courses to understand computer technology. Their son has watched the steel mills shut, one by one, losing his motivation to do much of anything. Do our current unemployment programs respond to the needs of this American family? Sadly, the answer is no.

While Americans and Washington have periodically focused on the plight of the family in Youngstown, we are only recently recognizing its solution. It is not just ending the recession. It is not just extending unemployment benefits. The key to solving the problem is training. In the last month, President Reagan and Dan Rather, Henry Kaufman and Lane Kirkland, have all spoken of the need for improved training and retraining programs.

When the Speaker of the House took office two weeks ago he too made the theme of his opening remarks to the 98th Congress the need for jobs—and jobs now. Yet, I fear the Speaker was referring to the jobs of 1933, not the jobs of 1983. If 1933 comes back I know Tip O'Neill will be ready. But his answers, the answers of the Congress, are not the answers for the 80's and 90's. The jobs of tomorrow require new skills and different education than the jobs of yesterday. Traditional depression-age employment programs will do little to impart technical skills to space age workers.

Some estimates indicate that as many as twenty million Americans will need to be entirely retrained in the next ten years as their current skills become almost obsolete. The American Society of Engineers estimates that by 1990 more than half of the workforce on the industrial plant floor will be white collar technicians who are there to maintain the computer and robot systems that are manufacturing our durable products.

Given these immense changes taking place in the American workforce one would expect to see a host of innovative and creative ideas presented to policymakers in the Congress and in the Administration. But the few that are offered up are tired retreads: the old public works jobs programs that have proven costly, inefficient, and ineffective in providing skills usable in our new labor market; and the building of protectionist walls around our industries that will cost the American consumer more dollars and more jobs and protect industries from the competition that would stimulate investment and innovation.

With the national unemployment rate approaching 11 percent, the past Congress managed to enact an extension of the already extended Unemployment Insurance Benefits, and a 5 cent gasoline tax on Americans whose average wage is $7.80 per hour, to pay highway repair workers an average wage of $11.80 per hour. Now, that may be a good way to repair roads, but it's clearly not a jobs program.

Neither Congress' attempts to throw money at the problems, or simply waiting for an economic recovery that seems always to be just around the corner is enough. It is

Satisfy need

time to focus on the development of a single, national employment—as opposed to unemployment—policy that emphasizes training people for permanent employment, instead of only attempting to cushion the severe blow of unemployment.

It's time to focus on prevention as well as remediation. We need a plan that challenges the traditional principles of our patchwork federal unemployment policy. We need a plan that offers both an immediate response for today and a comprehensive strategy for tomorrow; a flexible system that creates job skills to match job opportunities. It is time to change both the context and the content of the unemployment debate.

To begin with, a comprehensive national employment policy must reach the same level of priority in the eyes of government as national defense, the maintenance of a sound currency and support of a healthy economy. The following four-point program would produce an immediate, double-barreled assault at both ends of the unemployment line. It would establish training as the centerpiece of governmental action to deal with unemployment, and reorganize government to manage effectively this new national employment policy.

First, for those people currently drawing unemployment benefits and whose jobs will not come back, we should create a *National Employment Assistance Program* that would offer a single package of unemployment benefits, training vouchers and immediate job search and location assistance. For perhaps a million and a half individuals who are now displaced, and many more who will be displaced in the next decade, such a package of employment assistance would be standardized for an equal deal for everyone. But it would be up to the individual to use the opportunities provided to get back to work.

Using some of the funds now allocated to benefit payments beyond thirty-nine weeks (Federal Supplemental Compensation benefits), plus additional funding through Title III of the new Job Training Partnership Act, this program would provide a package of opportunity to displaced workers: unemployment insurance to bridge the transition from job to job; retraining to improve personal skills; counseling, job seeking and relocation assistance to move the individual from a lost job to a new job. In 1982, while 10 million people were unemployed there were over one million skilled jobs that were vacant in this nation. We can substantially reduce the number of current and future unemployed if we can begin to retrain people to fill the jobs that are, even today, available.

What would our unemployed steelworker from Youngstown like to do: continue standing in the unemployment line waiting for a recall notice that will never come, or get some training so he can enter a training program leading to employment as a machinist, for example, a skill in which there are 150,000 job openings today? You know the answer as well as I.

Second, a program of immediate relief is clearly needed for those who are on extended benefits, or who have exhausted their benefits, and so would not qualify for the regular program. I would propose a two year, $2 billion emergency program that would provide equivalent assistance on a one-time basis to a million individuals in the most dire circumstances.

Third, we must launch a new assault on the front end loading of the unemployment lines that occurs when young people graduate from high school and cannot find or do not have the skills to get a job. An additional $1 billion school-to-work transition program could assist nearly one fourth of the estimated graduating class of 1985—perhaps 650,000 youth—who might otherwise become unemployed. I am particularly excited about this approach since as Chairman of such a program—*Jobs for America's Graduates,* already functioning in eight states—I have personally seen the success of a school-to-work transition program. It is both inexpensive and highly effective. These funds could be made available to local public-private partnerships, or to school districts to extend the reach, capacity and responsibilty of our educational system. Such a program might have prevented the 40 percent of our unemployed who are under twenty-four years of age from becoming unemployed in the first place.

The Youngstown steelworker's son provides a good example. For years he has planned to join his father at the steel mill after graduation. But there will be no job waiting there; unless we help him, he will join the army of unemployed youth. We need a program to counsel him, motivate him, and help him find a job in an industry that will be looking for willing and capable young people.

To further help local educational agencies, we must redirect the existing $700 million in federal vocational education funds, supplemented with the existing $300 million in federal economic development assistance funds, to improve the training facilities and programs of our vocational education system. In order to accom-

Visualization

modate the massive retraining effort needed over the next decade, the vocational education system must be expanded and strengthened.

The fourth part of the program is the most difficult—yet the most necessary. That is to create a new governmental system at the federal, state and local level that can help organize government programs around the principle of employment.

The matter of reorganizing government to manage an effective employment policy is not simply one of reshuffling bureaucracies. Of course, we could restructure the Department of Labor to manage the new employment policy: bring into the department vocational programs from Education, EDA programs from Commerce, and so forth. But the new economic reality and the need to focus our energies on a national employment policy calls for more.

What is needed is a new management mechanism built on the joint public-private partnership concept born in the Job Training Partnership Act of 1982. The management of the new program would be entrusted to a relatively independent board of private and public sector people able to respond swiftly and effectively to the problems and challenges of unemployment without months of debate and the paralyzing influence of special interests.

Such a *National Employment Investment Board* would be vested with broad authority over employment and training programs. Its members would serve independent, staggered terms and be drawn from the most senior levels of government and private sector experience in the fields of economics, business, labor, education and training. The Secretary of Labor would serve as the Chairman of the Board.

Similarly, Congress—where eight committees alone must deal with even minor changes in our Unemployment Insurance system, not to mention dozens more involved in employment and training matters generally—must adapt itself to the new realities of the 1980's. A single *Joint Committee on Employment Policy* of both Houses should oversee the work of the Board, recommending budget allocations, programmatic changes and related actions to the two Houses and the President.

These two structural changes would permit the federal government to streamline its operational mechanisms and play its crucial role in a new employment policy.

Finally, the federal government must provide small partnership grants to help state and local governments prepare their own employment strategies. Many localities have created effective development strategies—North Carolina's Research Triangle, Louisiana's offshore oil industry and Delaware's financial services development are examples. Job creation is often more a local than a national issue, because education, taxation, zoning and transportation policies are frequently decisive in changing stagnation into economic growth. Our unemployed and our jobs are not on Capitol Hill; federal encouragement of state employment programs is, therefore, an important part of a national employment policy.

The case for the approach I have outlined is compelling on several levels. First, it shapes an employment and training role for the federal government marshalling the nation's resources to assist the unemployed by preparing them for new jobs in a changing marketplace. Second, it puts the responsibility to obtain the skills necessary to find a job on the individual, thereby helping people help themselves. Third, it seeks to foster a new relationship between the federal government and the education community by making funds available for school-to-work transition programs and the strengthening of vocational education. Fourth, it acknowledges that the federal government must work in concert with state and local governments to foster effective community economic development programs. Finally, the plan is characterized by an affordable cost—perhaps $3 billion in net new funds in the first year, and less in the future as retrained Americans rejoin the workforce.

But most important, the plan brings a new measure of hope and opportunity to three million Americans in its first year of operation—Americans who desperately need our assistance. It gives the unemployed steelworker from Youngstown retraining and a chance at a new job. It gives his daughter and son the help they will need to compete for jobs in a changing marketplace. It gives that American family the opportunity to make tomorrow better than today.

Conclusion

Simply put, America can no longer afford its current policy of billions for income maintenance and pennies for employment training. Our national employment policy must strive to help individual Americans take full advantage of the opportunities of the 1980's. It demands a new partnership between government, education, labor and business to create in the classroom, on the shop floor, and in the living rooms of Youngstown's steelworkers an employment program to make America's workers employable in tomorrow's marketplace.[13]

GIVING YOUR TALK

When your talk is thoroughly prepared, you are ready to share your ideas with an audience. Giving a talk can be a stressful experience. You may worry about forgetting ideas or saying the wrong thing. You may think your voice will crack or squeak, your vision will blur, or your mind will go blank. This fear of embarrassment, better known as stage fright, may be keeping you from talking to groups of people. You should remember that every speaker experiences some stage fright. In fact, in the *Book of Lists,* fear of public speaking was listed as the greatest fear people have.[14]

A certain amount of tension before you begin talking can be productive. Like any feeling of fear, it can heighten your awareness and give you more energy which, in turn, will help you relate effectively to your audience and talk more enthusiastically. Accepting some nervousness as natural is the first step in giving an effective talk. Instead of using your fear as an excuse to avoid talking to groups, welcome it as a tool you can use to increase your speaking effectiveness.

Voice

When we give a speech, take part in a group discussion, or even chat informally with friends, we pay a lot of attention to selecting the right words to get our message across, but oral communication is much more than words. In fact, researcher Albert Mehrabian believes that only 7 percent of an oral message is conveyed by words.[15] Because we tend to emphasize the words of our message, it is difficult to believe that such a small portion of a message is conveyed that way.

The importance of voice tone was emphasized by Mehrabian's research. He determined that 38 percent of a message is conveyed through tone of voice.[16]

[13]Pierre J. Dupont, IV, "Retooling the Workforce," *Vital Speeches of the Day,* February 15, 1983, pp. 268–71.

[14]David Wallechinsky, Irving Wallace, and Amy Wallace, *The New Book of Lists* (New York: William Morrow & Company, Inc., 1977), p. 469.

[15]William G. Neal, "Focusing on Nonverbal Communication in Business," *Journal of Business Education,* November 1982, p. 78.

[16]Neal, "Focusing on Nonverbal Communication in Business," p. 78.

Each word can carry several different meanings. In fact, studies show that each English word has an average of 28 different meanings. The tone of voice with which the word is said helps to distinguish one meaning from another. For example, "You're right" can mean "I agree with you" or "I give up" depending upon the tone of voice. "Super" can convey enthusiasm or sarcasm by how it is said.

Talking clearly and loudly enough so everyone can hear is a basic requirement of spoken communication. Remember, too, that your audience has only one chance to understand your message. Readers set their own pace, rereading passages, stopping to think about unfamiliar ideas. In oral communication the speaker sets the pace. For that reason you must be sure to talk slowly enough so your listeners can follow your thought patterns and understand your message the first time they hear it.

Correct pronunciation will also help your audience understand your message. Be sure you learn to pronounce names and terms used in your talk, and practice them so you can say the words smoothly and naturally as you talk. Also watch standard enunciation. Say your *th*'s and *ing* endings clearly. *Dat* and *goin'* are not generally accepted and will lower your credibility with most audiences.

When you are competent in the basics of volume, rate, and pronunciation, learn to use your voice for emphasis. Vary pitch and rate to stress important ideas. This variety will add interest to your talk and show enthusiasm for your subject. Using your voice effectively will help maintain your audience's interest.

Body Language

Understanding how body language contributes to your message will also increase your success as a speaker. An awareness of the messages you send through nonverbal means will help you understand why people react to you in certain ways, and you will know how to modify those signals to send the message you intend. Three factors—facial expression, gestures, and appearance—help relate meaning to your audience.

Facial Expression   The greatest portion of a message is conveyed through facial expression. Mehrabian's research showed that we pick up 55 percent of a message's meaning from body movements such as gestures and from facial expression.[17] Ray Birdwhistell, a pioneer researcher in nonverbal communication, supports Mehrabian's observation. According to Birdwhistell, the face can form 250,000 different expressions.[18] That may be difficult to believe until you remember how carefully you watch your opponent during cards or chess. The slightest flexing of the facial muscles can tell you a lot about your opponent's thoughts; on the basis of a slight smile or grimace you may decide to play cautiously or to go all out for a win.

[17]*Ibid.*, p. 78.
[18]J. Burgoon and T. Saine, *The Unspoken Dialogue: An Introduction to Nonverbal Communication* (Boston: Houghton Mifflin, 1978).

When we watch people's faces for expression, we often concentrate most on their eyes. If the person looks away from us, we sense boredom, guilt, or dislike. If the person looks directly at us, we usually feel liked and appreciated. Direct eye contact can also signal defensiveness or aggression, though. Remember also that shy people tend to avoid eye contact. This should not be interpreted as hostility or boredom but may merely indicate the uncomfortable feeling characteristic of shy people. Regardless of our feelings, we tend to look more steadily at people when we listen to them and look away more when we talk.

Lack of eye contact may be interpreted as nervousness or insincerity and cause the audience to question your interest in them. They may then question the validity of your information and your concern for the subject. If you can't meet their eyes, how interested can you be in sending a message to them? Learn to look directly at specific people in your audience. Although in the beginning you may find one or two friendly faces and concentrate on them, as you become more accustomed to talking in front of a group try to look at each one (or at least in all areas of larger groups) at some point during the talk.

Avoid breaking eye contact with your audience to look at the clock or out the window. Your audience will focus attention whenever you do. If you look at them, they will think about what you are saying. If you glance nervously at your watch, they will use your distraction as an excuse to pursue distractions of their own.

Most of the nonverbal clues we pick up from people come from their facial expression and the amount of eye contact we have with them. An effective communicator learns to use these signs to help send and receive messages accurately.

Gestures   Gestures are another form of body language you can use to send and receive messages. The old Chinese proverb, "Watch out for the man whose stomach doesn't move when he laughs," shows that people have observed gestures as a form of communication for a long time.

Today we receive messages from how people wear their suit coats, what they do with their eye glasses, when they light up a cigarette, or how they sit, stand, and walk. Gestures can indicate an openness to discussion or a closed mind. They show eagerness to get a job done or defensiveness in certain situations. Gestures can even be used to express territorial rights in much the same way animals mark territories.

Studies show that when businessmen unbutton their suit coats or take them off altogether, they are ready to make concessions and "get down to business." On the other hand, buttoning up the suit coat indicates a reluctance to negotiate.[19]

The quick removal of glasses also signals displeasure.[20] When you are discussing a problem with co-workers and one or two of them remove their glasses

---

[19]Gerard I. Nierenberg and Henry H. Calero, *How to Read a Person Like a Book* (New York: Hawthorn Books, Inc., 1971), pp. 38, 78.
[20]*Ibid.*, p. 58.

quickly, you should change your approach until they put their glasses on again. Only then are they ready to discuss the problem reasonably.

Other gestures that may indicate a closed mind are arms or legs tightly crossed. These movements say, "Don't come near me" or "I don't want to talk about it." On the other hand, palms extended upward or arms held open indicate an acceptance of the person talking or the ideas expressed.

We have usually associated smoking with nervousness, but studies show that letting a cigarette burn in the ashtray or putting it out altogether are the real signs of tension. Women may also indicate anxiety by toying with necklaces or reaching for their necks. This gesture indicates the need for reassurance.[21]

Can you recall the last time you sat on the edge of your chair? Were you eager to discuss an idea or looking for an excuse to escape from the room? Leaning forward can indicate either of these attitudes. Salespeople have found customers will lean forward in their chair both when they want to sign a contract and when they want to end the conversation. The accompanying facial expressions (a smile for acceptance, avoidance of eye contact for rejection) clarify the gesture.

Gestures can also be used to mark territories. When supervisors put their feet on their desks, for example, they are saying: "This is my territory. I'm in control here." Territories are also often "staked out" with objects. A picture of your family distinguishes your work area from your co-worker's space. We "save" seats at the theater or restaurant by placing books, coats, or other personal belongings on them. All these things are nonverbal ways of saying, "This space belongs to me."

When you are talking, a straight, confident posture gives you credibility. It tells your audience that you care about your subject and think it is worth their time to listen.

Purposeful walking can also contribute to the effectiveness of your talk. Move away from the podium and walk toward the audience to emphasize an idea. If you think you are losing the audience's attention, move physically closer to them either by standing at the edge of the stage (for larger groups) or walking among the audience (in smaller groups). The closer you are to your audience, the less easily they are usually distracted.

Your audience may also be distracted by your gestures. When we are nervous, we show tension in a variety of ways. Some people fold their arms across their chests. Others show nervousness by shoving their hands deep inside their pockets and jingling their keys or change. You might grasp the podium until your knuckles turn white or punctuate important points by waving your arms wildly. You will find your audience watching these unusual gestures instead of concentrating on what you are saying. Use gestures that will call attention to your ideas rather than to the gestures themselves.

Appearance   The way you dress is another nonverbal signal. People form opinions about your self-confidence and your competence on the basis of the clothes you wear. Certain styles of clothing are acceptable for each work situation.

[21]*Ibid.*, p. 75.

For example, a suit is often appropriate for men and women in business; uniforms are the expected dress for police officers and other people whose occupations must be quickly identified. Polished shoes, pressed clothes, and groomed hair and nails all say, "I feel good about myself."

Each of us wears certain symbols to tell people specific things about ourselves. The high school athlete reveals an identity through a letter jacket. In much the same way, businesspeople wear lapel pins symbolizing their companies and perhaps even their position in those companies. Wedding and engagement rings are other traditional symbols by which we identify ourselves to others.

Visuals

Using visuals to illustrate your ideas will increase the effectiveness of your talk because people will remember facts and ideas better with these aids. One study showed that three days after listening to a talk people will remember 65 percent of the speaker's content if that information was illustrated with visuals. They will remember only 10 percent if visuals were not used. Increasing your listener's recall by 55 percent is an excellent reason to use visuals when you talk.[22]

Visual aids may include charts and graphs, pictures, or props. You may make your own or use illustrations you find while researching for your talk. Whatever visuals you choose, they should meet certain requirements. First, make sure your visual aids are clear and can be easily seen by your audience. Contrasting colors for charts, careful printing for transparencies, and selections of large photos and pictures will help your audience see the visual easily.

Second, use the visual effectively. Make sure it illustrates the points you intend it to represent and refer to it as you discuss those ideas. Point to specific things in the visual as you talk about the subject. Don't just hold the visual up briefly or tape it to a board and forget it.

Handouts may also be used, but they may cause problems as you talk. One problem is that you lose control of the material as soon as you hand it out. Many people will read the entire handout on their own rather than follow along with you as you discuss each point. Handing out material is also noisy and distracting. You must be confident of your ability to bring the audience's attention back to you before you consider using handouts.

On the positive side, handouts relate directly to each member of your audience. You know that everyone can see the illustration and will be able to take this visual material along when they leave.

Figures 8–1 through 8–4 show a variety of visual materials. Whichever kind you choose, remember that its purpose is to focus the audience's attention on important parts of your talk. If your visual does that, it will add to the effectiveness of your talk.

[22]Bobby R. Patton, Kim Griffin, and W. I. A. Linkugel, *Responsible Public Speaking* (Chicago: Scott, Foresman & Company, 1982), p. 137.

Figure 8-1   This line graph shows the comparison of jobs in agriculture, industry and information from 1860–1980. Source: Joseph F. Coates, ''The Changing Nature of Work,'' *Voc Ed*, Jan/Feb. 1982, p. 27.

SUMMARY

Because you are responsible for a continuous message when you talk in front of a group, you must prepare carefully before you give your talk. Decide on the purpose of your talk (information, persuasion, entertainment). Analyze your audience and adapt your topic to the audience. When you have chosen a specific topic, plan an introduction that will get attention and establish rapport with the group. Then state your purpose clearly and organize the content following sequential, logical, or topical order. Finally, sum up your main points and leave your audience with one main thought. This concludes your talk.

Giving the prepared talk to a group also requires special skills. Voice, body language and visuals are important parts of your delivery. Talk enthusiastically, focus your attention on the audience and use gestures and visuals that will emphasize rather than detract from your main points.

Careful organization and a practiced delivery will help you talk effectively in front of a group.

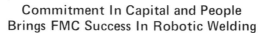

Commitment In Capital and People Brings FMC Success In Robotic Welding

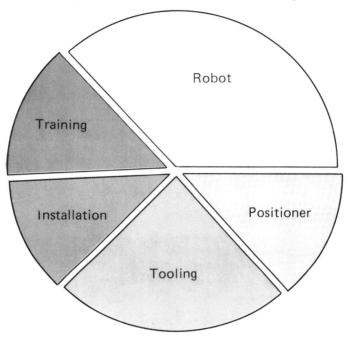

Money and manpower are necessary for successful welding with a robot. At FMC, 37 percent of the total cost paid for the robot, 23.5 percent for tooling. The next largest slice was 14 percent for training of the cell team. The positioner share was 13.5 percent, 12 percent paid for installation, seam tracker, and accessories.

Selection of people is as critical as selection of the robot. The people must be dedicated to a methodical approach and clever enough to correct bugs. And management must support those people completely and openly. FMC found that the best personalities for the team is a mix of analytical and hard-driver types — they complement each other and produce good results in the shortest time.

Figure 8-2   This pie chart shows the relative cost of expenses for a robot installation. Because the percentages are not included on the graph, an explanation of the chart is included. When you use a chart like this in an oral presentation, you should discuss it thoroughly so your audience understands the percentages it represents. Source: Robert N. Williams, "Robot Welding Cell Lifts Crane roduction," *Welding Design & Fabrication,* November 1983, p. 41.

Neuro-Linguistic Programmers believe that eye movements are linked to sensory processing and reveal thinking and feeling. The charts below are for a righthanded person.

Eyes up and to the viewer's right: Trying to envision an event that has never been seen.	Eyes up and to the left: Recalling an event that has been seen.
Unfocused eyes looking fixedly into space: Visualizing an event, real or imagined.	Eyes central, but glancing right or left: Processing actual, remembered or imagined sounds.
Eyes down and to the right: Sorting out sensations of the body.	Eyes down and to the left: Carrying on an internal conversation.

Figure 8-3   This is an example of how you can use a drawing to illustrate a talk. The picture of the eyes helps your audience visualize the positioning of the pupils as you discuss them. Source: Diagram by Joe Lertola. Copyright 1983 Time Inc. All rights reserved. Reprinted by permission from *Time*.

REVIEW QUESTIONS

1. How is public speaking different from other kinds of spoken communication?
2. What are the specific purposes of an introduction and conclusion?
3. What would be the best organizational pattern for a talk on:
   a. The history of computers
   b. Uses of computer graphics
   c. Robots eliminating jobs
   Explain why you chose each organizational pattern.
4. Show how a demonstrative talk and a persuasive talk "build on" an informative talk. How are they similar? How are they different?
5. How does an awareness of body language help us communicate?
6. What specific gestures or facial expressions have you noticed among your classmates or co-workers that signal:
   a. defensiveness   d. unhappiness
   b. acceptance   e. enthusiasm
   c. displeasure
7. How can you use your voice to emphasize a point? How can your voice expression change the meaning of a message? Give examples from your experience.
8. Which part of giving a talk is the most difficult for you? Why do you think you have difficulty in this area? What are you doing to improve this part of your delivery?

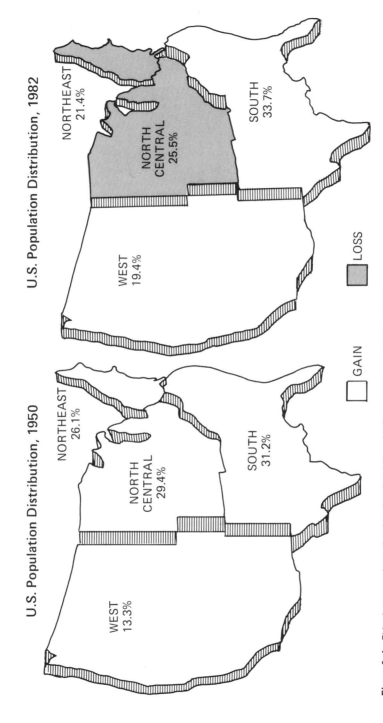

U.S. Population Distribution, 1950

NORTHEAST
26.1%

NORTH
CENTRAL
29.4%

WEST
13.3%

SOUTH
31.2%

U.S. Population Distribution, 1982

NORTHEAST
21.4%

NORTH
CENTRAL
25.5%

WEST
19.4%

SOUTH
33.7%

LOSS

GAIN

Figure 8-4 This pictogram shows the changing distribution of U.S. population from 1950–1982. Source: Carl Haub, "Demographies: What Lies Ahead? Shifts, Growth and Change," *Voc Ed*, May 1984, p. 29.

ACTIVITIES

1. Choose one of the following situations:
   a. You have just received a layoff notice in your office mailbox.
   b. You have been offered a job you can live with, but it is not the one you wanted.
   c. You have just been offered a long-hoped-for promotion.
   d. The doctor tells you, "It's a girl" or "It's a boy" (whichever you hoped it would be).
   e. Your best friend just won a swimming championship.
   f. Your favorite team lost a game and you lost a $100 bet.

   First communicate your feelings to the class nonverbally. Ask them to write down what they think your message is. Then add words to your message. Ask the class to compare the message they picked up from your nonverbal cues with the message you sent verbally.

2. Choose a partner from your class and start telling that person a story that is very important to you. It may be an account of the time you caught a trophy fish or saw the Statue of Liberty for the first time or any other event that was meaningful to you. While you are talking your partner should:
   a. Withdraw eye contact
   b. Show boredom
   c. Become interested in someone else's conversation
   d. Show approval

   When you have finished talking, write down your reactions to each nonverbal cue from your partner, and have your partner write down observations about how you changed in reaction to each signal. Compare your observations with those of your partner and discuss the ways nonverbal cues influenced your message.

3. Observe a public speaking situation and analyze the nonverbal cues from the speaker and listener. How well do they interact? Trace the communication process. Is it completed? If it is, what aids communication? If it is not, where does communication break down and why?

4. This section will help you develop a talk following the discussion in this chapter. By means of the charts and forms, it will take you step by step through the organization and delivery of the talk.

   Using the column headings on the Audience Description chart as questions, (see end of chapter, p. 152) interview a member of your class and then tell the group about that person. Each person will be introduced to the group in this way. As each is introduced, record the demographics on the Audience Description chart.

   After everyone has been introduced, compile the information from this chart onto the Audience Analysis chart (see end of chapter, p. 153). You can use this chart and the form, Selecting a Topic (see p. 153) to choose topics for all the talks you will give this semester. We will use it here specifically to plan the informative talk.

5. Using the form, Selecting a Topic (see p. 153), choose an appropriate topic for your informative talk. Using the planning sheet for informative talks on p. 155, prepare a 5-minute talk on the subject of your choice.

6. Select a process related to your major area and demonstrate that process to your class. The planning sheet on p. 154 will help you organize your demonstration talk.

7. Decide on a problem related to the job you are preparing for. Describe that problem and show how it can be solved. Persuade your audience to help you solve the problem by following the plan you propose. Use the planning sheet on p. 154 to help you organize your talk.

Audience Description

Person's Name	Age	Major	M/F	Special Interests	Work Experience	Long-Range Goals	Likes/ Dislikes	Misc.

Audience Analysis

1. What is the average age of your audience? _____
2. Is the group made up mostly of men or women? _____
3. What are the major fields of study of the group? _____
4. Describe their work experience:
   Full time career/part-time jobs for extra money _____
   Entry level jobs/skilled or semiskilled positions _____
   Types of jobs (industrial, retail service) _____
5. List special interests indicated by audience. Group these interests into categories such as outdoor sports, needlecrafts, music, etc. _____
6. What are the likes and dislikes expressed by your audience?
   Likes _____
   Dislikes _____
7. Summarize the goals of the group:
   Short range _____
   Long range _____

Write a paragraph describing your audience from the data you have recorded.

Selecting a Topic

Using your audience analysis sheet, list topics you think would interest your audience.	List five topics of interest to you.
1.	1.
2.	2.
3.	3.
4.	4.
5.	5.

From these two columns select a topic for your talk: _____

Limiting Your Topic

List five areas you could talk about within your topic:
1.
2.
3.
4.
5.

Choose one of these areas: _____

List three things you could talk about within the area you have chosen above:
1.
2.
3.

Choose one of the three areas you have listed above for your talk.

The topic for my talk is: _____

Planning Sheet: Demonstrative Talk

General purpose: To demonstrate a process

General topic:

Restricted topic:

Specific purpose:

List the sources you used to gather information:
   1.
   2.
   3.

Write out the introduction, labeling the attention getter, rapport statement, and specific purpose.

List the props you will need:

List the steps to your process in the order in which you will discuss them:

How will you conclude the talk?

Planning Sheet: Persuasive Talk

General purpose: To persuade to actuate

General topic:

Restricted topic:

Specific purpose:

List the sources you used to gather information:
   1.
   2.
   3.

Write out your introduction, labeling the attention getter, rapport statement, and specific purpose.

State the need and outline the main ideas and supporting details you will use to prove that need.

How will you satisfy that need? Outline your main points.

Write out your action step.

Outline your visualization step.

List the main points you will summarize in the conclusion. What will you use to impress your listeners with the importance of your subject?

Planning Sheet: Informative Talk

General purpose: To inform

General topic:

Restricted topic:

Specific purpose:

List the sources you used to gather information:

   1.

   2.

   3.

Write out your introduction, labeling the attention getter, rapport statement, and specific purpose.

Outline the main ideas and supporting details you will use to develop the specific purpose. Use the skeletal outline below as a beginning and add to it as needed.

   I.

     A.

     B.

     C.

   II.

     A.

     B.

     C.

   III.

     A.

     B.

     C.

Reword the main points as a summary for your talk and underline the one main idea you want your audience to remember.

9

GROUP DISCUSSION

Some people mistake weakness for tact. If they are silent when they ought to speak and so feign an agreement they do not feel, they call it being tactful. Cowardice would be a much better name.

Sir Frank Midlicott

After studying this chapter you should understand:

1. What group discussion is
2. How members of a group interact
3. Organizing the discussion
4. Brainstorming as it relates to group discussion technique
5. A member's responsibility to the group
6. A leader's responsibility to the group
7. How a group reaches a decision
8. Advantages and disadvantages of working in a group

A retail store asks a group of employees to discuss ways to handle shoplifting. Result—a 44 percent decrease in the store's shoplifting.[1]

An insurance company asks its employees to discuss solutions to work-related problems. Result—a 72 percent increase in productivity.[2]

A bank sets up teams to discuss more cost-effective procedures. Result—the bank's net costs are cut by more than $100,000 in one year.[3]

[1] "Rites of the Round Table," *Chain Store Age Executive,* October 1982, p. 22.

[2] "Quality Circles Program Reaps a $350,000 Harvest," *Modern Office Procedures,* August 1982, p. 54.

[3] Louis E. Tasliaferri, "As 'Quality Circles' Fade, a Bank Tries 'Top-Down' Teamwork," *ABA Banking Journal,* July 1982, p. 99.

These are all examples of the way group discussion can solve problems, help make decisions, add to the participants' knowledge, and relieve tension on the job. As U.S. industry struggles with economic slowdown, discussion groups modeled after the Japanese quality circles are expected to lead us to better times. Because of the importance placed on solving problems, this chapter emphasizes techniques of groups involved in decision making.

On the job and in our personal lives we are continually involved in these discussions. We meet with co-workers to discuss production problems and working conditions, we join church and civic groups to discuss social problems, and we get together with family members to make decisions about crises that occur within the family. Like quality circles, these meetings usually have purposes, but unlike some of the most successful groups that make news, many meetings fall short of their goals. You have probably heard statements like:

Dan always dominates the discussion. Let's just turn the whole thing over to him.

or:

We always go to the movie you want to see. Why bother to ask my opinion?

The process of sharing opinions or making decisions through group interaction requires a specific communication skill. The scenario that introduced this section on speaking showed what can happen to a group when the people involved do not understand the techniques of group discussion. When you have finished studying this chapter, you should be able to reconstruct the activities of that group so it accomplishes a worthwhile goal.

GROUP DISCUSSION DEFINED

A discussion involves two or more people. Although 30 to 40 people may work together successfully, most experts agree that people interact best when the group is limited to from 2 to 20 members.

Interaction of members is a vital part of the group's success. Interaction suggests give and take among participants. As a group member you should express your own opinion and react to the opinions expressed by others. This interaction is easiest when participants face each other. Face-to-face contact helps members interpret body language and tune in to positive and negative reinforcement from other participants.

A third characteristic of groups is that group members influence each other. As they work together to reach a common goal, each member adapts to beliefs expressed by other members and in turn modifies the opinions of those participants. This mutual influence helps the group accomplish its purpose.

In summary, a discussion group is made up of 2 to 20 people who influence each other through their interaction. Keeping this definition in mind, look at the following groups of people. Which of these groups can be called a discussion group?

20 students in line to rent lockers on the first day of school

4 baseball fans clustered around a television set watching the last game of the World Series

7 nurses drinking coffee and talking about ways to reduce rising hospital costs

You probably chose the group of nurses because they are interacting. But if the baseball fans start to discuss strategy or if the students talk about ways to make the first day of school move along more efficiently, they too will have formed discussion groups.

Interaction is the key difference between a gathering of people and a discussion group. Because interaction is so important to group discussion, we will discuss it in more detail in the next section.

HOW GROUPS INTERACT

Think back to the last time you participated in a group discussion. How did you feel as the discussion started? Were some members hesitant to express their opinion at first? As the discussion continued, did you and the other members warm up to the topic? If there were differences of opinion, how were they resolved? Did you feel closer to the other people in your group when the discussion was finished?

These changes in attitude characterize the normal progress of group discussion. In a study of decision-making groups, Aubrey Fisher found that during a discussion group interaction moves through four phases: orientation, conflict, emergence, and reinforcement.[4]

Orientation

During the first phase of a group discussion group members get to know each other. They are somewhat hesitant to express ideas because they are unsure about how those ideas will be accepted by the rest of the group. During the orientation phase participants are usually noncommittal. Most ideas are accepted without question. The discussion is just beginning and group members want to maintain a friendly atmosphere.

Conflict

When the members begin to feel comfortable in the group, the discussion moves into the conflict phase. During this phase the issues are clearly defined and members begin to take sides. Positive and negative feelings are expressed as members try to influence each other.

[4]Adapted from Kenneth D. Benne and Paul Sheats, "Functional Roles of Group Members," Journal of Social Issues, 1948.

Emergence

Eventually members begin to agree about certain issues and the discussion enters the emergence phase. Now ideas most acceptable to the group are clarified and definite proposals are mentioned. Group members seek approval for their ideas and express approval for other members' ideas. Ideas that meet with disapproval are dropped.

Reinforcement

In the last phase of group discussion, reinforcement, the group settles on a few preferred ideas. Members express their approval of these ideas, thus reinforcing the group's decision. As the discussion concludes, the group tries to establish a feeling of unity. Participants feel that they have satisfied a common goal.

ORGANIZING GROUP DISCUSSION

Although interaction is an important part of group discussion, a group's effectiveness depends on more than that. We have all been involved in groups where members talked a lot and reacted to each other's ideas but the group did not decide anything. The interaction was disorganized, maybe even chaotic. You probably left thinking: "Just another meeting. Meetings never accomplish anything."

To be effective, group discussion must be organized. Members should be encouraged to interact within a specific structure. Groups may be organized in a variety of ways, but problem-solving groups are probably most effective when patterned after John Dewey's process of reflective thinking. Near the turn of the century this American philosopher described the way people think through problems. This process, described in his book *How We Think*, can be applied to discussion and used as a basis for organizing a group.

Identify Problem

When your group meets for discussion, the first thing you should do is identify the problem you want to discuss. Make sure everyone in your group clearly understands the group's purpose. A clear statement of the problem will help keep your group on track as the discussion progresses. You may even want to write the problem on a blackboard or project it on an overhead projector to make sure everyone keeps in mind the purpose for the discussion.

Discuss

When everyone understands the problem, you can begin to discuss it. Talk about all aspects of the problem. This is the time for members to share information about the problem's history, its causes, and repercussions. Make sure the group has the information needed to make a decision.

Set Standards

Third, a problem-solving group sets up standards by which they will evaluate possible solutions and which will form a basis for the group's final decision. They may be statements about cost or people or time needed to implement the solution. For example, if one of the group's standards is that the solution they adopt cannot cost more than $50,000 to implement, they would learn the cost of each solution and discard those that cost more than $50,000.

Present Solutions

Fourth, once these standards are set, the group can present and discuss solutions. The advantages and disadvantages of each solution are presented and each solution is weighed against the standards set. In this step the group narrows its choices to a couple of the best solutions.

In the final step the group members agree on one solution. Following Dewey's pattern on reflective thinking will help a group move smoothly from the introduction of the problem to a solution acceptable to the group.

BRAINSTORMING

You may be thinking, "Following the steps sounds easy, but how does a group think up solutions to a problem or standards by which to judge those solutions?" Several techniques can be used to generate ideas. One of the most popular is brainstorming.

Brainstorming is used to get as many ideas in front of the group as possible. Group members express ideas freely without paying attention to how other members might react to the ideas. In fact, in successful brainstorming all ideas are accepted equally. Unusual ideas are encouraged so participants feel free to offer whatever comes to mind. During brainstorming, ideas are not discussed or evaluated. They are merely put before the group for consideration later. For this reason, brainstorming is a good ice-breaker. It is a nonthreatening activity which can be used to start a group thinking.

Brainstorming helps a group generate ideas for discussion. To discuss those ideas, however, you should use the logical thinking skills described in detail in Chapter 3. Decisions should be based on inductive and deductive reasoning and participants should listen for fallacious reasoning used by other group members. Recognizing fallacies and using logical reasoning patterns will keep your group on course and help it reach its goals.

GROUP MEMBERS

Whenever there is a job to get done and several people willing to help, the first thing you probably do is divide up the work. Each person takes on a specific task, and when put together these tasks complete the job. Similarly, when you are involved in a group discussion you will find members assuming different roles. Some people primarily express opinions while others offer facts. One member might try to tie together the many ideas expressed and other members will react to those ideas. Few groups can work efficiently without someone to take notes as people talk. Equally vital to the group's success is the person who keeps the participants' spirits up and stimulates them to accomplish their purpose.

Members' Roles

Group members may assume any of twelve different roles, each of which makes a specific contribution to the functioning of the group. They may fill various roles at different times and in different groups. Study the following list carefully because an understanding of the different ways you can function within a group will help you to make worthwhile contributions and to respect the contributions made by others.

1. The *initiator-contributor* suggests or proposes to the group new ideas or a changed way of regarding the group problem or goal. The novelty proposed may take the form of suggestions of a new group goal or a new definition of the problem. It may take the form of a suggested solution or some way of handling a difficulty that the group has encountered. Or it may take the form of a proposed new procedure for the group, a new way of organizing the group for the task ahead.
2. The *information seeker* asks for clarification of suggestions made in terms of their factual adequacy, for authoritative information, and for facts pertinent to the problem being discussed.
3. The *opinion seeker* asks not primarily for the facts of the case but for a clarification of the values pertinent to what the group is undertaking or of values involved in a suggestion made or in alternative suggestions.
4. The *information giver* offers facts or generalizations which are "authoritative" or relates his own experience pertinently to the group problem.
5. The *opinion giver* states his belief or opinion pertinently to a suggestion made or to alternate suggestions. The emphasis is on his proposal of what should become the group's view of pertinent values, not primarily upon relevant facts or information.
6. The *elaborator* spells out suggestions in terms of examples or developed meanings, offers a rationale for suggestions previously made, and tries to deduce how an idea or suggestion would work out if adopted by the group.
7. The *coordinator* shows or clarifies the relationships among various ideas and suggestions, tries to pull ideas and suggestions together, or tries to coordinate the activities of various members or subgroups.

8. The *orienter* defines the position of the group with respect to its goals by summarizing what has occurred, points to departures from agreed-upon directions or goals, or raises questions about the direction which the group discussion is taking.

9. The *evaluator-critic* subjects the accomplishment of the group to some standard or set of standards of group-functioning in the context of the group task. Thus, he may evaluate or question the "practicality," the "logic," the "facts," or the "procedure" of a suggestion or of some unit of group discussion.

10. The *energizer* prods the group to action or decision, attempts to stimulate or arouse the group to "greater" or "higher quality" activity.

11. The *procedural technician* expedites group movements by doing things for the group—performing routine tasks, e.g., distributing materials, or manipulating objects for the group, e.g., rearranging the seating or running the recording machine, etc.

12. The *recorder* writes down suggestions, makes a record of group decisions, or writes down the product of discussion. The recorder role is the "group memory."[5]

Members' Influence on Group

You have probably noticed that some people in a group tend to make everyone else "feel good" while other people seem to destroy the harmony of the group. During a discussion you may remember identifying with one person in particular who seemed to be the group's ideal. You may also remember times when one person seemed to demoralize the entire group, perhaps by complaining a lot or trying to dominate the discussion.

Participants may influence their group positively or negatively depending on whether they are interested in building the group's morale or fulfilling individual needs. Some of the positive and negative behavior you may observe in group members is listed below. These two lists will help you recognize different types of behavior so you can respond constructively to the various positions group members assume.

Positive Influence

1. The *encourager* praises, agrees with, and accepts the contribution of others. He indicates warmth and solidarity in his attitude toward other group members, offers commendation and praise, and in various ways indicates understanding and acceptance of other points of view, ideas, and suggestions.

2. The *harmonizer* mediates the differences between other members, attempts to reconcile disagreements, relieves tension in conflict situations through jesting or pouring oil in the troubled waters, and the like.

3. The *compromiser* operates from within a conflict in which his idea or position is involved. He may offer compromise by yielding status, admitting his error, disciplining himself to maintain group harmony, or "coming halfway" in moving along with the group.

[5] *Ibid.*, pp. 94–95.

4. The *gate-keeper* and *expediter* attempts to keep communication channels open by encouraging or facilitating the participation of others ("We haven't got the ideas of Mr. X yet") or by proposing regulation of the flow of communication ("Why don't we limit the length of our contributions so that everyone will have a chance to contribute?").

5. The *standard setter* or *ego ideal* expresses standards for the group to attempt to achieve in its functioning or applies standards in evaluating the quality of group processes.

6. The *group observer* and *commentator* keeps records of various aspects of group process and feeds such data with proposed interpretations into the group's evaluation of its own procedures.

7. The *follower* goes along with the movement of the group, more or less passively accepting the ideas of others, serving as an audience in group discussion and decision.

Negative Influence

1. The *aggressor* may work in many ways: deflating the status of others, expressing disapproval of the values, acts, or feelings of others, attacking the group or the problem it is working on, joking aggressively, showing envy toward another's contribution by trying to take credit for it, and so on.

2. The *blocker* tends to be negativistic and stubbornly resistant, disagreeing and opposing without or beyond reason and attempting to maintain or bring back an issue after the group had rejected or by-passed it.

3. The *recognition seeker* works in various ways to call attention to himself, whether through boasting, reporting on personal achievements, acting in unusual ways, struggling to prevent his being placed in an "inferior" position, or similar behavior.

4. The *self-confessor* uses the audience opportunity which the group setting provides to express personal, nongroup oriented "feeling," "insight," or "ideology."

5. The *playboy* makes a display of his lack of involvement in the group's processes. This may take the form of cynicism, nonchalance, horseplay, and other more or less studied forms of "out of field" behavior.

6. The *dominator* tries to assert authority or superiority in manipulating the group or certain members of the group. This domination may take the form of flattery, of asserting a superior status or right to attention, giving directions authoritatively, interrupting the contributions of others, and the like.

7. The *help seeker* attempts to call forth sympathy response from others, whether through expressions of unsurety, personal confusion, or depreciation of himself beyond reason.

8. The *special interest pleader* speaks for the "small businessman," the "grass roots" community, the "housewife," "labor," or other cause, usually cloaking his own biases in the stereotype that best fits his individual need.[6]

GROUP LEADER

Getting a job done may be easier when several people share the work load, but group efforts can also be unproductive and chaotic. You may have worked in groups where tasks overlapped or where no one knew what anyone else was doing. Probably

[6] *Ibid.*, pp. 95–97.

no one took charge of the group. People did their own thing rather than follow any planned direction.

To work effectively, a group must be organized around an efficient leader, who plans the group's activities and keeps members working toward a common goal. The leader is responsible for drawing out opinions from quieter members of the group and for summarizing the main points of the discussion.

Because the leader is such an important member of a group, let's look closely at the leader's role.

First, the leader starts the discussion. We have all sat around in loosely structured groups, chatting casually, until someone said, "All right, let's get started." That person was assuming leadership of the group. To get a group started, the leader should state the problem that members will be discussing and relate the importance of that problem to the group. At this time the leader should also set a time limit for the discussion. Participants will tackle a problem more enthusiastically if they know the group will not drag on indefinitely. When the purpose and conditions of the group have been clearly defined, the leader usually asks the group a question which starts the discussion moving.

During the discussion the leader maintains a positive feeling among members of the group toward both their subject and each other. When conflicts occur, the leader tries to help the group benefit from the opposing viewpoints. The difference of opinion should be kept to the subject and not allowed to reflect on the personalities of the participants.

The leader keeps the discussion organized and summarizes main points periodically. Asking questions, volunteering information, and making sure every member of the group contributes are also the leader's responsibilities.

Finally, the leader concludes the discussion, summarizing the group's progress. The leader should end the discussion on a friendly note and set a time for the next meeting, if one is needed. As the group breaks up, members should feel as though they have accomplished their purpose, and they should look forward to meeting again to continue the discussion.

REACHING A DECISION

The goal of a problem-solving group is to reach a decision. This decision can be made in several ways.

Majority Vote

First, the leader or another group member can call for a vote near the end of the discussion. In this case, whatever the majority decides is accepted by the group. When a definite decision is needed and time is limited, a majority vote is an efficient way of making a decision.

Consensus

Decisions can also be made through consensus, which means that all members agree on one solution, as opposed to a majority vote, where only most of the members must agree. Arriving at a consensus usually requires members to compromise until one solution is acceptable to all. This can be time consuming, especially if members cling to opposing views, but it is usually worth the extra effort, because it may also be more in keeping with the general goals of the group and because members leave the group feeling they have reached a decision acceptable to everyone. Decisions reached by consensus tend to solidify the group and help members work effectively together on other occasions.

One Person's Decision

Decisions may also be made by one person in the group, either the leader or some other respected group member. Usually the group agrees ahead of time that one person will make the final decision. Sometimes, though, when a group is near the end of a discussion and can't reach a consensus or a majority, they may turn the problem over to one person whom they think has special authority or insight concerning the problem.

Any one of these ways of reaching a decision may be used effectively, depending on the situation.

ADVANTAGES AND DISADVANTAGES OF GROUP DISCUSSION

Advantages of Group Discussion

Increasingly, business and industry are turning to discussion groups as a way to solve problems. Evidently, they recognize that groups have some advantages over individuals in the decision-making process.

First, a group can gather more information than an individual can. Several people working together can collect more statistics and present more ideas than one person working alone. A wider range of viewpoints are also considered, because each member shares attitudes and experiences which influence the decision. One person working alone usually bases decisions on a more limited perspective.

Groups also seem to feel a greater commitment to solving a problem. That group spirit or camaraderie helps a group keep at a problem until it is solved. When a few members become discouraged, other people in the group bolster their spirits. On the other hand, one person working alone may become discouraged and abandon the project because no one else is involved. For all these reasons, group discussions are often the preferred means of solving problems.

Disadvantages of Groups

Groups can also hinder the decision-making process. One disadvantage often mentioned about a group is that it takes more time to reach a decision than one person working alone. Time is needed for group members to express their ideas and share information. Especially if a group intends to reach a consensus, time is spent clarifying, explaining ideas, and reassuring and convincing each other. Even the most efficient group gets off the track occasionally. Casual chatter as the discussion gets started, or "conversation on the side" during the discussion, extends the work time. A statement like "That reminds me" or "Just let me say this one thing before we get started" can cost a group half an hour.

Another disadvantage of a group is the chance of conflict. The many viewpoints which can be an asset to decision making can also cause conflict, which can slow down the decision-making process and, in some cases, even cause the group to break up. Participants who understand the potential problems conflict may cause can help their leader recognize potential disagreements and keep them within constructive limits.

A third disadvantage often mentioned about groups is that they tend to make riskier decisions than individuals working alone. The camaraderie that is a positive feature of a group might also contribute to members' willingness to take risks. When they can share the responsibility for the decision with a number of people, they are more likely to agree to solutions that they would not make alone.

An awareness of the advantages and disadvantages of group problem solving will help you use groups to discuss problems effectively. You can use the strengths of a group and work around its weaknesses to reach constructive solutions to everyday problems.

SUMMARY

A discussion group is defined as "two or more people who are interacting with one another in such a manner that each person influences and is influenced by every other person." When a group's goal is to find a solution to a problem, we call it a problem-solving group. Interaction of members is one of the most important differences between a gathering of people and a group discussion. This group interaction can be divided into four stages: (1) orientation, (2) conflict, (3) emergence, and (4) reinforcement.

Organization also contributes to a group's effectiveness. A problem-solving group is often organized on John Dewey's process of reflective thinking, which involves five steps: (1) identify the problem, (2) describe the problem, (3) set up standards by which to evaluate solutions, (4) discuss each solution according to these standards, and (5) decide on one solution. Brainstorming and logical thinking techniques will help you introduce and evaluate important ideas. Although some people may want to be a member of a group so they "don't have to do anything," group members actually have specific responsibilities which must be fulfilled so the group can work effectively. The responsibilities, along with examples of positive and negative behavior are listed in the chapter.

Every group also needs a leader to keep it working toward its goal. A leader introduces the problem, asks questions, contributes ideas, and concludes the discussion. The leader should encourage all members of the group to participate and limit conflict to the topic rather than allowing personalities to interfere with the discussion.

The goal of a problem-solving group is to reach a decision. Decisions can be made by: (1) majority vote, (2) consensus, or (3) individual decision. Usually the group agrees at the start of the discussion on how the decision will be made.

Both advantages and disadvantages can be seen in using group discussion to solve problems. Some of the advantages of discussion groups are: (1) groups can gather more information, (2) they can present more viewpoints, (3) they may feel a greater commitment to finishing the project. On the other hand, some of the disadvantages are: (1) groups are more time-consuming than one person working alone, (2) there is more chance for conflict, and (3) groups tend to make riskier decisions than one person acting alone.

When you understand how group members interact, how a group is organized, and the responsibilities of group members and leaders, you can use group discussions to solve problems on the job and in your personal life.

REVIEW QUESTIONS

1. How is a discussion group different from a gathering of people?
2. How does a discussion group change from the beginning to the end of the discussion? List and explain the four stages of interaction.
3. Discuss how Dewey's theory of reflective thinking relates to problem-solving groups.
4. What is brainstorming? When is it useful in group discussion?
5. As a group member, what are your responsibilities to the group? How can you influence the group positively? How might you influence it negatively?
6. How is a leader's responsibility to a group different than a member's role? How is it the same?
7. What are the advantages and disadvantages of group discussion? If you were a manager with a problem to solve, would you form a group of your employees to help you make the decision or would you make the decision yourself? Give reasons for your answer and discuss them with other members of your class.

ACTIVITIES

1. Contact local businesses or industries related to your major area to find out if they have discussion groups functioning. When you find a discussion group, ask if you can join it once as an observer. Keep a log of the group's interaction and problem-solving organization. Did they follow a logical problem-solving pattern? Did members contribute constructively to the discussion? What positive and negative behavior did you recognize? How was the decision finally made? Use Table 9–1 or one of your own design to help you keep track of the group's discussion.

2. Groups may be formed to identify problems or to solve them. Form a group with four or five other people in your major area. Identify three problems that may occur in your field and choose one as the basis for activity 3, below.
3. Form a group with four or five people in your major area. Discuss the problem you identified in activity number 2. Limit your discussion to 25 minutes and choose one person to lead your group and another member to take notes. Be sure to follow Dewey's pattern of reflective thinking discussed in this chapter. When you have finished, analyze the roles of members and leader using Table 9-2.
4. Form small groups of three or four class members. Identify the problems presented by the scenario at the beginning of this section. Reorganize the scenario following productive discussion practices described in this chapter. Present the improved scenario for your class.

Table 9-1 Group Discussion Log

Discussion topic:
Number of members:
Length of time for discussion:

INTERACTION	PROBLEM-SOLVING ORGANIZATION
Summarize comments made during *orientation*.	What comments are made to help everyone understand the problem?
Record the first statement that started *conflict*.	List the main points discussed.
	What standards are set for evaluation?
What tells you that the group is moving into *emergence?*	What solutions are offered?
What ideas are preferred in *reinforcement?*	What solution is chosen?

	MEMBERS' ROLES	
	Positive Behavior	*Negative Behavior*
Member 1		
Member 2		
Member 3		
Member 4		

Table 9-2 Leadership Role

LEADERSHIP TASK	EVALUATION	
	(Rate effectiveness of the task described in first column)	
How does the leader introduce problem?	Excellent Fair	Very good Poor
Give examples of techniques the leader used to encourage participation.	Excellent Fair	Very good Poor
How does the leader smooth over areas of conflict?	Excellent Fair	Very good Poor
List main points of the leader's summary.	Excellent Fair	Very good Poor

Group Decision

What is the group's decision?
How is it made?

Members' Roles

Use the lists on page 000–000 to help you identify member roles and positive or negative behavior. As you fill in the chart, remember that each group member may play several roles throughout the discussion.

Description of Role	*Evaluation of Behavior (Positive/Negative)*
Member 1	
Member 2	
Member 3	
Member 4	

PART IV   Writing

As a career placement counselor, Maxine receives many requests each day.

"Has the Johnson Company hired a secretary?"

"Are there any openings for accountants?"

"Will you look at my resumé and tell me what you think?"

These are examples of the questions Maxine answers quickly and efficiently either on the phone or in person each day. But whenever Maxine has to write a letter in answer to a request, she has a problem wording her answer. For example, one day she received this request from Mrs. Wolhert, den mother of Boy Scout Troop 4:

Dear Maxine,

Last spring you helped my daughter write a letter of application and get her first job. She found your information very helpful and I appreciate the interest you took in her job search.

My son and his best friend are now thinking about getting their first jobs, and they have been talking about job seeking skills in their Boy Scout Troop. Since they are just entering high school, they are interested in part-time jobs. As a den mother for their troop, I think a letter from you on how to find a job would be very interesting to them. Will you write a few tips on a page or two and send it to us in time for our next club meeting on January 20?

We'll all appreciate any information you can send us.

Sincerely,

Roxanne Wolhert

Roxanne Wolhert

"What can I say about how to get a job in one letter?" Maxine wonders as she reads Mrs. Wolhert's letter a second time. "Well," she thinks, reaching for her pen, "the letter won't write itself. I'd better get started."

Following is the letter Maxine sends to Mrs. Wolhert:

Dear Mrs. Wolhert,

Thank you for asking me to write to your Boy Scout Troop. There are numerous things your scouts should know about getting a job. They should make the best utilization of appropriate dress and language when they participate in an interview situation. To get invited to the interview in the first place, they will need a professionally prepared resume and letter. We can help them prepare their resumes. Classes are also available in resume writing. I'm glad you asked me to send you this information because I remember the first time I went for an interview. What a disaster! I want to encourage you to prepare for job interviews. Employers expect a thoroughly prepared applicant. You should take a class or get some professional counseling before you go into an interview. It is well worth the money it costs. You should never go to an interview without careful planning. No one is ever successful when they talk to an employer before they are adequately prepared.

I hope this will help. Good luck!

Sincerely,

Maxine Klopp

Maxine Klopp

"There, that's done," Maxine says as she signs the letter. "I hope Mrs. Wolhert is satisfied."

DISCUSSION OF SCENARIO

If you were Mrs. Wolhert, would you be satisfied with Maxine's letter? Is it well organized and informative? Does it relate well to her audience?

You probably noticed that Maxine started to write immediately. She did not think about what she should say first or reread what she had written.

Although this incident is fictional, situations like it occur all too often in the work place. In a recent survey by Communispond, Inc., a personal communications firm located in New York, 200 executives were asked to rate their writing skills. Fifty-five percent rated them "poor to fair." Even though they recognized that their writing skills were ineffective, 60 percent of the executives surveyed indicated that they are writing more letters, memos, and reports than they were a year ago. Some of them said they write as many as 40 different items each week. That's eight items every day.[1]

Ineffective writing was also evident in the written communication they received. Fifty-five percent rated that written communication "poor to fair." They said it was wordy

---

[1] "Executives Acknowlege their Lack of Business Writing Skills," *Supervision*, September 9, 1982, p. 9.

and unclear.[2] In another survey, conducted by University of Texas faculty, clarity was again mentioned as a major concern, followed by grammar, mechanics, and usage.[3]

People responding to this survey indicated that ineffective writing causes misunderstanding at work and wastes employees' time. People take longer to read poorly written documents, misunderstand them, and have to rewrite them. Because ineffective writing takes more time, it costs extra money.

HOW WELL DO YOU WRITE?

Does Maxine's situation remind you of a time when your writing could have been more clearly organized? Maybe you could have prevented clients from complaining to your manager if you had answered their first claim letters clearly. You might have saved yourself time in rewriting if you had paid attention to the mechanics of good writing the first time. How would you rate your writing skills?

Take a few minutes now to use your knowledge of writing to evaluate Maxine's letter. Consider the focus of her material, the ideas she presents, and the word choices she makes. Is her letter clear and easy to follow? Does she give helpful information? Are her statements accurate and concise?

Write a brief evaluation of Maxine's letter from Mrs. Wolhert's point of view. Then discuss your ideas with other members of your class.

In this section on writing we will discuss the writing process. After reading this discussion, you should be able to rewrite Maxine's letter effectively.

[2] Ibid.

[3] L. Faigley and T. P. Miller, "What We Learn from Writing on the Job," *College English*, October 1982, p. 561.

10

SENTENCES AND PARAGRAPHS

Writing has laws of perspective, of light and shade, just as painting does, or music.
If you are born knowing them, fine. If not, learn them. . . .

Truman Capote

After studying this chapter you should understand:
1. How to write a sentence using phrases and clauses
2. How to recognize and correct problem sentences
3. How to combine phrases and clauses into various sentence patterns
4. How to punctuate sentences correctly
5. The definition and conventions of a paragraph
6. Three requirements of a paragraph

People who can't write don't last very long around here. We can't afford them. We're a small company compared to our competitors. We work on a close profit margin. If a person writes poorly, then another person of similar technical competence has to be put on the same job, a person who can understand and translate what the first person has written. This means two people are doing the job of one. We don't enjoy that kind of luxury around here.

An executive at a scientific
consulting firm[1]

Many times the only communication we have with an individual is by writing.

A secretary[2]

[1] Lester Faigley and Thomas P. Miller, "What We Learn from Writing on the Job," *College English*, October 1982, p. 565. Reprinted with the permission of the National Council of Teachers of English.
[2] Faigley and Miller, "What We Learn from Writing on the Job," p. 563.

It [bad writing] causes misunderstanding between the taxpayer and this office. This leads many times to unnecessary litigation.

A tax examiner[3]

Statements like these emphasize the importance of writing on the job. One study revealed that workers spend 23.1 percent of their work time writing—the equivalent of more than one workday a week.

Although this study showed that people in the professional and technical occupations write more than people in the trades, most occupations require some writing. One of the most interesting things this study indicated was that the amount of writing you do increases as you move up in a company. One respondent explained it this way:

Many companies, ours included, do not require written reports by their employees who are involved in the actual sales or promotion process. Everything is communicated orally, the purpose being to eliminate the paperwork load, thus allowing more time at the point of contact. The real problem I see is one that develops later in an individual's career, after he has been on the street for several years with no need of written communication. The individual is promoted to a management-level position and charged with the responsibility of written documentation without having recent training or experience in written communication. The ability of the individual to move readily into management is more often than not hampered by that individual's lack of written communication skills than by the understanding of the job itself.[4]

Consequently, if you want to get a job, keep a job, or move ahead in your career, you must know how to write effectively. We have already discussed logical thinking, effective word choice, and correct spelling as aids to written communication. In this chapter we will discuss how to put those elements together into sentences and paragraphs to express thoughts.

SENTENCES

We express thoughts by grouping words into phrases, clauses, and sentences. Sometimes one clause is a sentence by itself, but usually a sentence is formed by joining phrases and clauses together to form one complete thought.

Phrases

A *phrase* is a group of words containing either a noun or a verbal. There are two kinds of phrases: a prepositional phrase and a verbal phrase. A *prepositional phrase* is made up of a preposition (words like to, from, before, of, etc.), a noun that acts as the object of the preposition, and words that modify the noun.

[3] Faigley and Miller, "What We Learn from Writing on the Job," p. 565.
[4] *Ibid.*

A *verbal phrase* consists of a verbal and its modifiers. A *verbal* is a form of a verb that functions as another part of speech. Infinitives, participles, and gerunds are verbals.

To run is the best exercise.

To run is an infinitive (*to* + verb) functioning as a noun.

To run with a friend is the best exercise.

To run with a friend is an infinitive phrase: the verbal plus its modifiers.

Running, Tom twisted his ankle.

Running is a participle (-*ing, -ed,* or -*en* form of the verb) functioning as a modifier. In this sentence *running* tells something about Tom.

Running around the block, Tom twisted his ankle.

Running around the block is a participial phrase (a participle plus its modifiers) telling something about Tom.

Running is my favorite hobby.

Running is a gerund (the -*ing* form of the verb) functioning as a noun. Although participles and gerunds may both be -*ing* forms of the verb, the gerund always functions as a noun, and the participle always functions as a modifier.

Running for my health is my doctor's idea.

Running for my health is a gerund phrase functioning as the subject of the sentence.
    In each example the phrase is a part of a sentence. When the phrase stands alone it does not convey a complete thought.

To run with a friend
Running around the block
Running for my health

In each case we ask the question "What about it?" or "What happened?" A phrase alone does not express a complete thought.

Clauses

    A *clause* is a group of words containing a subject and a verb. There are two kinds of clauses: independent clauses and dependent clauses. An *independent clause* can stand alone to express a complete thought.

Mary cashed her check.

    A *dependent clause* must depend on other parts of a sentence to convey a complete thought.

When Mary cashed her check, the clerk asked to see her ID.

By itself, the second clause, "the clerk asked to see her ID," conveys a complete thought. You know what the clerk did (asked to see Mary's ID) and you know who asked to see the ID (the clerk). "When Mary cashed her check" also contains a subject (*Mary*) and a verb (*cashed*), but it is not a complete thought. We wonder what happened when Mary cashed her check. The rest of the sentence answers that question: "the clerk asked to see her ID."

Independent clauses are actually sentences and will be discussed more thoroughly later in this chapter.

A dependent clause may serve as an adverb or an adjective.

Anne went home early *because she had finished all of her work.*

". . . because she had finished all of her work" is an adverbial clause. It explains why she went home early.

Anne, who had all of her work finished, went home early.

In this example the clause ". . . who had all of her work finished" functions as an adjective. It tells us something about Anne.

You will notice in each of these examples the dependent clause does not express a complete thought.

. . . because she had finished all of her work
. . . who had all of her work done early

They both leave questions in the reader's mind.

Dependent clauses usually begin with an introductory word such as *that, because, who, which, when,* or *since.* Knowing this can help you identify a dependent clause in a sentence.

Sentence Defined

An understanding of clauses and phrases and their uses in a sentence is important if we are to observe another convention of effective written communication: to write in complete sentences. Writers can group their words into three different patterns: sentences, fragments, and run-ons. Of these three, only the sentence is accepted.

A *sentence* expresses one complete thought. It contains a subject and a verb and is usually punctuated at the end by a period.

Bob found the error.

This expresses a complete thought. You know what Bob did. (He found the error).

Bob found the error when he balanced his checkbook.

This is also a complete sentence. "When he balanced his checkbook" simply explains in more detail when Bob found the error.

when he balanced his checkbook

This is not a complete sentence even though it contains a subject (*he*) and a verb (*balanced*). You should recognize it as a dependent clause. We also call it a fragment if it is punctuated as a sentence by mistake.

Sentence Problems

Fragment   A *fragment* is any group of words that is punctuated like a sentence but does not express a complete thought.

Riding down the road
When we went on vacation
Because she passed the entrance exam

These express only a part of (a fragment of) the complete thought. Punctuating them to look like sentences with a capital letter at the beginning and a period at the end does not make them complete thoughts. You will recognize the first as a phrase and the second and third examples as clauses.

Because fragments cause confusion, they should be avoided. Readers wonder, "Who was riding down the road?" and "What happened when you went on vacation?" Complete sentences will answer these questions and prevent confusion for the reader.

Run-on Sentences   You have probably met people who don't know when to stop talking. Writers can have the same problem. They string phrases and clauses together in a continuous flow of written words much as the nonstop talker runs thought after thought together without ever seeming to draw a breath. Numerous complete thoughts that run together without proper punctuation are called a *run-on sentence*.

Ron fed the data into the computer, then he waited until the computer printed out the results so he could take the findings to his supervisor.

In this example there are three complete thoughts:

Ron fed the data into the computer
he waited until the computer printed out the results
he took the findings to his supervisor

punctuated as one sentence.

You can improve the sentence several ways: correct the punctuation in a run-on sentence. First you can separate the complete thoughts with periods.

Ron fed the data into the computer. He waited for the results. He took the findings to his supervisor.

The second way to correct a run-on is to use a conjunction to join two similar complete thoughts.

Ron fed the data into the computer *and* waited for the results. Then he took the results to his supervisor.

The conjunction *and* joins the first two thoughts, making this one sentence with a compound verb; the third thought becomes a sentence of its own. You will notice that the second example is more effective. Although the first example is punctuated correctly, the style is choppy.

Numerous other techniques can be used for improving run-ons. For example, you could make the second sentence into a dependent clause.

Ron fed the data into the computer. *When the computer printed out the results,* Ron took them to his supervisor.

The way you make the correction will depend on the clauses and phrases that are in the run-on. As a guide, remember that your sentence should convey accurate meaning quickly and be interesting to read.

COMBINING PHRASES AND CLAUSES

Many factors make your sentences interesting to read. Word choice and selection of details are two of those factors. Another way to increase the interest of your writing is to vary the types of sentences in each paragraph. Clauses can be combined in different ways to form four types of sentences: simple, compound, complex, and compound-complex.

A *simple sentence* is one independent clause:

TO: Connie
FROM: Jack
SUBJECT: Luncheon Meeting to Discuss Johnson Contract
DATE: December 10, 1985
       S   V
    Mary will meet you for lunch at 1 p.m.

A simple sentence may contain a compound subject:

TO: Connie
FROM: Jack
SUBJECT: Luncheon Meeting to Discuss Johnson Contract
DATE: December 10, 1985
     S   S   V
   Mary and Bob will meet you for lunch at 1 p.m.

or a compound verb:

```
TO:       Connie
FROM:     Jack
SUBJECT:  Luncheon Meeting to Discuss Johnson Contract
DATE:     December 10, 1985
          S    V                      V
          Mary will meet you for lunch and bring the Johnson contract with her.
```

or a compound subject and a compound verb:

```
TO:       Connie
FROM:     Jack
SUBJECT:  Luncheon Meeting to Discuss Johnson Contract
DATE:     December 10, 1985
          S        S    V
          Mary and Bob will meet you for lunch and bring the Johnson contract with them.
```

Even though the sentence mentions two people who did two things it is *one* independent clause; therefore, it is a simple sentence.

A *compound sentence* has *two* independent clauses. Notice there is a subject and a verb on each side of the conjunction.

```
TO:       Connie
FROM:     Jack
SUBJECT:  Luncheon Meeting to Discuss Johnson Contract
DATE:     December 10, 1985
          S    V                           S    V
          Mary will meet you for lunch at 1 p.m., and Bob will call you later this afternoon.
```

A *complex sentence* has one independent clause and at least one dependent clause.

```
TO:       Connie
FROM:     Jack
SUBJECT:  Luncheon Meeting to Discuss Johnson Contract
DATE:     December 10, 1985
                    dependent
          Although Bob wants to talk over the Johnson contract with you,/he can't meet you
          for lunch today.                                    independent
```

A *compound-complex sentence* has at least one dependent clause and two independent clauses.

TO: Connie
FROM: Jack
SUBJECT: Luncheon Meeting to Discuss Johnson Contract
DATE: December 10, 1985

                         dependent   independent
    Although Bob wants to talk over the Johnson Contract, he can't meet you for lunch,
but Mary will meet you at 1 p.m.
                         independent

When you write paragraphs and essays, you should construct sentences from each of these types to avoid monotony in your writing. The following two paragraphs show how a variety of sentence types can make your writing more interesting. The first paragraph is written in simple sentences. The second paragraph says the same thing with a variety of sentence types.

A group of electrical cable fabricators, all of them women, formed a (quality) circle. Their supervisor had an intuitive grasp of the quality circle concept. She soon became an able leader. She controlled the regular meetings firmly. She never dominated them. Participation was strong. The circle quickly produced its first proposal. The proposal was about the problems created by their need to cover some of their cable assemblies with a protective material composed primarily of fiberglass. Whenever they did this, they wore protective clothing and masks. But they still got bits of fiberglass on their hands, arms and faces. Some of it even got into their eyes and down their throats. To protect themselves, they devised a "glove box." It was a sealed plastic box. It had rubber gloves inserted into it. They wanted to isolate the fiberglass. They did not want to bury themselves in protective clothing. They presented their proposal. They discussed it with management. Finally, management agreed to implement it.[5]

A group of electrical cable fabricators, all of them women, formed a circle. Their supervisor had an intuitive grasp of the quality circle concept and soon became an able leader. She controlled the regular meetings firmly, but never dominated them. Participation was strong, and the circle quickly produced its first proposal, which concerned the problems created by their need to cover some of their cable assemblies with a protective material composed primarily of fiberglass. Whenever they did this, they got bits of fiberglass on their hands, arms, and faces—despite protective clothing and masks. Some of it even got into their eyes and down their throats. To protect themselves, they devised a "glove box," a sealed plastic box with rubber gloves inserted into it. They reasoned that the best thing to do was to isolate the fiberglass, rather than bury themselves in more protective clothing. They presented their proposal and, after discussion of the costs, management agreed to implement it.[6]

[5] This paragraph is adapted from *Quality Circles* by Philip C. Thompson, p. 120. © 1962 by Philip C. Thompson. Published by AMACOM, a division of American Management Association, New York. All rights reserved.
[6] Reprinted by permission of the publisher, from *Quality Circles* by Philip C. Thompson, p. 120. © 1982 Philip C. Thompson. Published by AMACOM, a division of American Management Associations, New York. All rights reserved.

PUNCTUATION

As we have seen in the case of run-ons, correct punctuation is important to effective written communication. A comma or period can make the difference between an easily understood statement and one that is misunderstood.

Punctuation marks are like road signs. They give direction and organization to our writing just as road signs help maintain order on our highways. End marks (periods, question marks, and exclamation marks) tell us when an idea has been completed. Commas, colons, and semicolons help us understand the relationships between ideas; they indicate which ideas are most important and help readers follow the writer's reasoning process.

On the next few pages the most frequently used punctuation marks for letter and report writing are reviewed.

End Marks

End marks signal the completion of a thought. The two most common end marks are periods and question marks. A *period* indicates the end of a statement.

Mr. Roberts hired Michael for the manager's job.

A period should be used only to end a complete thought, a statement that contains a subject and a verb and is understandable when read by itself.

Complete   Renee sent out twenty application letters before an employer asked
Sentence: her to come for an interview.
Fragment: Before an employer asked her to come for an interview

A *question mark* should be used to indicate a question, a plea for an answer.

When are you going to finish that report?

Question marks may be used when you expect a direct answer.

Are you going to the show Friday night?

They may also be used when you want to make your reader think about something.

How much control of your life are you willing to give the computer?

Questions like this are called *rhetorical questions.* You use them to make your reader think about the topic. You do not expect an immediate answer.

Exclamation marks are used for commands.

Go!

They are also used to show excitement.

Hey! I got the job!

Exclamation marks give extreme emphasis to statements; therefore, use them sparingly. If they appear too often in your writing they fail to signal the need for special attention because the reader thinks of them as usual rather than special end marks.

Commas

Commas indicate short rests rather than complete stops. They are appropriate signals in many different situations. Because they are used so often, they are also often abused by a writer. Following are some typical instances when commas should be used to give order to writing.

1. Commas are used before a conjunction to separate two independent clauses.

   Their careers are less likely to tempt them into the tunnel vision of material advance they decried in their parents, and many of them have delayed careers and families to develop alternative interests.[7]

2. Commas are used to set off dependent clauses used as adjectives when they add extra information to the sentence.

   You hear about the sumptuous parties the rich old people throw at Palm Springs, where the wealthiest gather to do nothing that could be called purposeful.[8]

The clause adds to our information about Palm Springs but it is not necessary to our identification of Palm Springs.

3. Commas are used to set off introductory phrases and clauses.

   Up to now, the babies of the postwar boom have changed the conventions of every age they have been through.[9]

   When unemployment is chronic, we can no longer rely on the market to do this job fairly.[10]

4. Commas are used to set off a series.

   Schools, colleges, military service, marriage, and jobs are permanently less constricting than they were before the boom babies hit them.[11]

5. Commas are used to set off transitions, words that link ideas in a sentence or paragraph together.

   So many factors go into the equation that there is no reason to assume that fewer adults won't be able to support a growing retired population. This ability depends, among other things, on how many of them work, how much they earn, and how productive they are. On the other side of the equation, we know how many old people

[7]From THE GOOD YEARS by Caroline Bird, copyright © 1983 by Caroline Bird. Reprinted by permission of the publisher, E. P. Dutton, Inc.
[8]*Ibid.*, p. 103.
[9]*Ibid.*, p. 49.
[10]*Ibid.*, p. 45.
[11]*Ibid.*, p. 49.

there are likely to be, but we don't know how long they will live, how many will continue to earn, how many dependents (including former spouses) will have to be cared for, and how their benefits will be adjusted to reflect the changing purchasing power of the dollar.[12]

Semicolons

Semicolons are used to separate two closely related independent clauses.

Correct:

Moralists distinguish between two kinds of love; the first is a deep understanding and concern for the welfare of the beloved; the other, more dubious variety is the psychological state of bewitchment with the idea of a relationship with the beloved.[13]

When to use a semicolon is often confusing. Just remember that a semi-colon can be used only to separate *independent* clauses, and those clauses *must be closely related.*

Incorrect:

It is possible to fall in love when you are older; in the future people will retire later.

Although both these thoughts concern the activities of older people, the types of activities are not closely enough related to be connected by a semicolon. Also, do not use semicolons to separate dependent clauses.

Incorrect:

When moralists talk about love; they distinguish between two kinds or ideas that are dissimilar.

If you keep those two guidelines in mind, you should use semicolons cor-rectly.

Colons

The most common use for a colon is to introduce a list of items from other parts of the sentence.

None of the worriers has any very explicit suggestions for the score or more of active years newly available to most Americans after middle age. Based on the past, these later stages are usually filled with negatives: retirement, disengagement, retrospec-tion. But the postwar babies have improved the options of every age they have

[12]*Ibid.,* p. 38.
[13]*Ibid.,* p. 142.

passed through so far, and there is every reason to believe that their later years will be no exception.[14]

Notice that the material to the left of the colon contains a subject and a verb and is a complete thought. The material to the right of the colon is the list.

A colon can also be used to introduce a series of dependent clauses. Notice these clauses are connected by semicolons.

> In the 1980s we are going through a similar crisis. This time, circumstances are forcing us to doubt a number of basic principles: that economic growth can continue indefinitely; that it solved our most pressing problems in the past; that the market will create enough jobs to go around and allocate income fairly; that we would be better off with less government; that you earn your money by your efforts alone and have a right to spend it any way you please; that your money income is a rough but generally reliable measure of the quality of your life and your value to the community; that the Gross National Product is a measure of the well-being of the nation.[15]

Standard punctuation can make your ideas easier to follow and thus increase the effectiveness of your writing.

CONVENTIONS OF THE STANDARD PARAGRAPH

Students sometimes think English teachers invented paragraphs to make their students miserable. Actually paragraphs were "invented" by printers who began to use indentations as a way of breaking up the printed page and making it easier to read. Eventually certain conventions were applied to paragraphing in the same way that conventions are applied to sentence structure, spelling, and punctuation.

Definition

A *paragraph* is a group of sentences on one specific topic. For example these sentences all discuss the same topic.

Imported mineral water must be taken from unpolluted springs.
It must be sanitary and free of coliform bacteria.
Imported mineral water must be bottled under sanitary conditions.

All three sentences discuss regulations governing imported mineral water. On the other hand, look at this sentence:

Mineral water is my favorite summertime drink.

[14]*Ibid.*, p. 33.
[15]*Ibid.*, p. 35.

It does not say anything about regulations. It is, therefore, off the topic and should not be included with the group of sentences above.

Topic Sentence

The topic of a paragraph is clearly stated in one sentence. This sentence is called the *topic sentence*. The topic sentence points the direction the rest of the sentences will take. For example:

Computers make office work easier.

leads to quite a different discussion than

Computers replace people in the office.

The first of these topic sentences will lead you to a discussion of time-saving features of the computer. The second sentence leads to a discussion of how computers are taking over people's jobs.

Because the topic sentence leads the way, it is usually the first or second sentence in the paragraph.

topic sentence

While soft-drink producers are cheered by the fact that overall annual per capita consumption has grown from 33 gal. in 1975 to 40 gal. today, other trends are giving them pause. *A number of different beverages—notably wine, bottled waters and juices—are being consumed in greater quantities than ever before.* Part of the reason is that as the population matures, health and fitness are its new bywords. Calorie-counting accounts for the surge in diet drinks, which grew at a 10% rate last year, far outpacing the 1.4% rise that sugared products eked out. And the public's perception that caffeine is harmful has given rise to a host of decaffeinated drinks.[16]

Actually, the topic sentence may be placed anywhere in the paragraph. The second most common position for it is as the last sentence in the paragraph.

topic sentence

THC (tetrahydrocannabinol), the most important active ingredient in marijuana, can cross the placental barrier between mother and unformed child. The THC is definitely carried in mother's milk. There is some disputed evidence that marijuana produces a higher rate of miscarriages and stillbirths in monkeys. Because of the risks to the unborn child, evidence of birth defects is difficult to obtain. But fetal tissue is extremely sensitive to foreign chemicals. Experience has shown that many substances which are safe for adults are teratogenic (capable of producing birth defects). *Even NORML agrees that pregnant or nursing women should avoid marijuana.*[17]

[16]"The Top 10 Soft Drink Brands," *Business Week*, May 30, 1983, p. 60.
[17]Richard Vigilante, "Pot Talk—Is Decriminalization Advisable?" © 1983 by National Review, Inc., 150 East 35 Street, New York, NY 10016. Reprinted with permission.

Discussion

The other sentences in the paragraph discuss the topic stated in the topic sentence. The last sentence of a paragraph often restates the topic expressed in the first or second sentence. Note the function of each sentence in the following example:

topic sentence

discussion

During the years since World War II, bird feeding has developed into such a popular hobby that surveys are being conducted to determine how much is being spent annually by bird lovers on food and equipment. A recent study by the United States Forest Service shows that 43 percent of the households in the town of Amherst, Massachusetts, feed birds. Each household spent an average of $8.80 per year on bird food. This means that residents of this town spend at least $20,000 a year on food for birds. In a survey by an independent market research agency, it was found that bird feeding was conducted by 24 percent of the 861,000 households in the city of Boston. The average amount expended per household was approximately the same as for Amherst. The figures showed that residents of Boston spent about $1.7 million per year on bird food. If the Boston figures were projected on a statewide level, the amount spent annually for bird food in Massachusetts would come to about $3.4 million a year.[18]

In summary, a paragraph is a group of sentences all on one topic. The topic is expressed in one sentence called the topic sentence. The other sentences in the paragraph develop the topic with relevant details. Especially in longer paragraphs, the last sentence restates the topic.

THREE REQUIREMENTS OF A PARAGRAPH

A good paragraph meets three requirements: it is unified, it is coherent, and it offers sufficient discussion of the topic.

Unified

In a paragraph that is *unified,* all the sentences are on one topic, each contributing to the discussion of the topic expressed by the topic sentence. As you read the following paragraph, decide whether it is unified. Are all the sentences on the same topic?

Computers make office work easier. The computer will search its files for you. All you have to do is type in the name of the file you need. This saves a lot of time you would otherwise spend searching by hand through extensive storage files. The computer will also answer your question immediately. The computer doesn't say: "Ask me tomorrow," "I'll have to look that up," or "Maybe Kay knows." The computer answers your question from its stored data bank immediately. This prevents frustration among employees. The computer will print out

[18]John V. Dennis, *A Complete Guide to Bird Feeding* (New York: Alfred A. Knopf, Inc., 1981), p. 103.

information for you. Then you don't have to type it or copy it from the file. This is the third way a computer makes office work easier. In fact, the computer has made our office work so much easier that we don't need as many secretaries. Last month two secretaries were laid off from my department. I hope I am not laid off. My fiance and I want to get married next year, and I need this job to save money for the wedding. But computers certainly are convenient. They help us with a lot of office tasks.

As you read this paragraph you probably noticed that several sentences near the end were off the topic stated in the first sentence. Read these sentences again.

In fact, the computer has made our office work so much easier that we don't need as many secretaries. Last month two secretaries were laid off from my department.

They are actually discussing the topic, "Computers replace people in the work place."

The sentences:

I hope I am not laid off. My fiance and I want to get married next year, and I need this job to save money for the wedding.

discussed yet another topic: reasons why the writer needs her job.

As you read the paragraph you saw how easy it was to "slide" from one topic into another. The efficiency of the computer led the writer to a discussion of layoffs caused by the use of computers in her office. This, in turn, led to a statement of her concern for her own job. When writing your paragraphs, continually check the statements you make against the idea you have expressed in the topic sentence. Make sure all the sentences in the paragraph relate to that same idea.

Coherence

The second feature of a good paragraph is *coherence,* which means that all the thoughts stick together. Even though your thoughts are unified (all on the same topic) they do not necessarily stick together. There are several ways to achieve coherence in a paragraph.

One way to achieve coherence is through the use of transitional words or phrases, which act as bridges between thoughts. *For example, on the other hand, however, therefore, as a result,* and *consequently* are examples of transitional phrases. Using these words as bridges between ideas will keep your thoughts flowing smoothly and help your reader to follow along with you. Without such transitions, your reader may have difficulty following your ideas.

Numbering your ideas is another transitional device.

First you cream the sugar and shortening. *Second* you add the vanilla and eggs. *Third* you put in the flour and soda.

Words like *then, next,* and *last* can be substituted for the numbers.

A third way to establish coherence is to repeat key words. For example, in the paragraph on computers, *computer* is a key word and is repeated several times in the paragraph.

The computer will search its files for you. All you have to do is type in the name of the file you need. This saves a lot of time you would otherwise spend searching by hand through extensive storage files. The computer will also answer your question immediately. The computer doesn't say: "Ask me tomorrow," "I'll have to look that up," or "Maybe Kay knows." The computer answers your question from its stored data bank immediately. This prevents frustration among employees. The computer will print out information for you. Then you don't have to type it or copy it from the file. This is the third way a computer makes office work easier. In fact, the computer has made our office work so much easier that we don't need as many secretaries. Last month two secretaries were laid off from my department. I hope I am not laid off. My fiance and I want to get married next year, and I need this job to save money for the wedding. But computers certainly are convenient. They help us with a lot of office tasks.

Pronouns or synonyms can also be used to take the place of key words.

Pronoun used as transition:

The computer makes office work easier. *It* will search its files for you.

Synonyms used as transition:

The computer makes office work easier. *This machine* will search its files for you.

Sufficient Discussion

The third element of an effective paragraph is *sufficient discussion*. One detail is usually not enough to clarify the idea expressed by the topic sentence. For example, the following paragraph is not effective.

Computers make office work easier. They print out information and save the secretary typing time.

The one detail is not enough to prove that "computers make office work easier." Paragraphs are usually developed with a series of details.

Computer graphics have many applications. Managers use computer graphics to condense volumes of data into trend-line charts, graphs and diagrams—often in color. Landscape designers draw simulated cities with buildings, streets and plantings, rotating the simulation on the screen to view all sides and dimensions. Using computer-aided design (CAD), engineers design an auto part, display it on the computer screen, view it from all sides, modify it easily, save it for later reference. The computer can be programmed to calculate all types of stress points and even determine if one part meshes with another. Buildings, shoes, machine tools, airplane parts, bridges, textiles, clothing, needlepoint—all can be designed and modified using the computer. Even artists are using computer graphics in their work.[19]

[19]Elaine F. Uthe, "The Computer in Our Lives," *VocEd*, April 1982, pp. 26–27.

In this example the author shows how managers, landscape designers, engineers, and artists use computers in their work. Many other people may also use computers in their work, but the author could not mention all of them so she has selected representatives from people in business, design, and art. This selection emphasizes the main idea that computers have *many* applications. On the other hand, if the author had shown only how landscape designers use computers, for example, she would not have adequately discussed her main idea.

Sometimes one example may be sufficient if it is discussed in detail.

> If properly placed, city trees can significantly reduce energy consumption. By shielding a house from cold wind, trees may lower heating bills as much as 15 percent; conversely, by shading a house from direct sunlight, they may cut cooling costs 50 percent or more. A prime example is found in Sacramento, California, a city which, next to Paris, France, may be the most heavily forested urban area in the world. The 350-acre park surrounding the state capitol has more than 300 trees made up of some 200 species. Authorities estimate that each park tree annually saves the equivalent of from 7.4 million to 54.8 million BTUs (a measurement of energy consumption) of fossil fuel energy that would otherwise be used for cooling and heating. "On a hot day here in summer, you can count on the capitol grounds being about 10 degrees cooler than nearby neighborhoods," notes Authur May, park grounds supervisor.[20]

In this paragraph the one example is discussed in enough detail to adequately support the main assertion.

Counting words is not the best guide to deciding whether a paragraph is effective. Ask yourself if you have adequately discussed your main ideas. Have you given enough examples so the reader understands the topic thoroughly? Have you mentioned enough facts to prove your main point? If you can answer "yes" to these questions, then your paragraph is probably adequately developed.

When you are familiar with parts of the paragraph—topic sentence, discussion, and restatement of main idea—and understand the elements of an effective paragraph—unity, coherence, and adequate discussion—you are ready to organize this material into a logical pattern.

PARAGRAPH DEVELOPMENT

There are two basic patterns of paragraph development: general to specific, and specific to general.

General-to-specific paragraph development can be compared to deductive reasoning. This type of paragraph begins with a general statement.

The loss of the American chestnut has been called the worst known ecological disaster.

This general statement is clarified through discussion of specific details:

[20]Dennis Hanson, "Never Underestimate the Value of a Tree." Copyright 1983 by the National Wildlife Federation. Reprinted from the June–July issue of National Wildlife Magazine.

It was used for rail fences, log cabins, etc.

It was prized for furniture, interior trim, railroad ties and mine shorings.

The bark provided tannin for leather.

Sweet nuts were food for man, turkeys, and animals.

The finished paragraph reads like this:

> The loss of the American chestnut has been called the worst known ecological disaster. The tall, straight-trunked tree was the predominant species of the vast eastern hardwood forest that awaited the early settlers. It was the tree of most uses, durable for rail fences, log cabins, house and barn timbers and sidings. It was prized for furniture and beautiful interior trim, railroad ties, and mine shorings (for which it was especially valued for its resistance to dampness). The bark provided tannin for curing leather. The sweet nuts were food for man, deer, turkeys, and roaming hogs.[21]

In the second basic pattern of paragraph development, *specific to general,* the topic sentence concludes the paragraph. As with inductive reasoning, the specific example precedes the general statement.

These two basic patterns can be varied to fit the writer's purpose. Following are a few of the more usual variations.

Description

If your purpose is to help your reader visualize a place or repeat a process, you will write a descriptive paragraph. Description can be accomplished in two ways: (1) space order, and (2) time order.

Space Order   Space order is usually used to help the reader visualize a place. When you organize details according to space, you create a three-dimensional image for the reader. For example, if you are describing your work area, you might start at the door and guide the reader around the room from left to right, floor to ceiling, or front to back. Following is an example of a paragraph organized according to space.

Our insurance office is carefully planned to make our clients feel comfortable. As you walk into the office, the first thing you see is the receptionist's desk in front of the door. If you have any questions, she can help you immediately. To the right of her desk is an informal grouping of chairs around a low table. Here you can relax or read a magazine while you wait. Behind the receptionist's desk there are three partitioned offices for our agents. Here you can discuss your concerns about your policy in private. To the left of the receptionist's desk is a computer. This computer is connected to the terminal in our home office, so we can answer your questions quickly while you wait.

You can see how this organization allows the reader to easily visualize the office.

[21]Howard Bloomfield, "Elm Update; Is DED Dead?" *American Forests,* April 1983, p. 22.

Time Order   Time order or *chronological order,* as it is often called, may be used to describe a process or an event. When you organize according to time, you begin with the first activity and relate each step until you reach the end. Occasionally you may start at the end and relate each step backwards to the beginning. The following paragraph illustrates time order.

> I also use a scarecrow when the corn is coming up. Laugh if you want, but my scarecrow, moved to a new position every day or so, does fool pheasants into staying away from newly sprouted seed. And we have lots of pheasants. My scarecrow is partially mobile, but easy to make. First drive a stake firmly into the ground (but not too deep, because you will want to move the scarecrow around). Now imagine a clothes hanger hanging from the top of the stake. But instead of a clothes hanger, substitute a thin board half as long as your out-stretched arms. By means of a piece of heavy string attached to both ends of the board, hang it from the top of the stake. On this crude "clothes hanger," put an old shirt, the board running through from sleeve to sleeve. Then pin an old pair of pants to the bottom of the shirt. Because the whole thing hangs loosely from the string over the top of the stake, the slightest breeze will make the "arms" wave back and forth rather realistically. I pin a shiny piece of aluminum foil on the end of each sleeve and put an old hat on top of the stake. I tie the bottoms of the trouser legs together around the bottom of the stake so they don't flap loose. My Frankenstein monster does not scare crows, but he does scare pheasants.[22]

The key to effective organization according to time is to move forward or backward systematically.

Definition

Paragraphs may also be organized to define a word. Sometimes an unfamiliar term can be defined with a few words or a sentence. Other times the definition is more complex and an entire paragraph is needed. A definition paragraph answers the question "What is it?" The term is usually mentioned in the topic sentence, and the other sentences establish a clear definition for the term. Following is an example of a definition paragraph. Note the term is mentioned in the first sentence.

> Word processing is a term used to refer to the computerized creation of all types of text—letters, books, legal contracts, etc. It allows the writer to type the text completely, then edit it, correct spelling and grammar, and make other changes before printing the text. This eliminates the chore of retyping pages to make corrections. Retyping caused by moving text around is made much easier with word processing since whole sentences, paragraphs, and even pages can be moved from one spot in the document to another with just a few commands to the computer—again before actually printing the text.[23]

[22]Gene Logsdon, *Homesteading: How to Find New Independence on the Land* (Emmaus. Penn.: Rodale Press, Inc., 1973), p. 127. Reprinted by permission of the author, Gene Logsden.
[23]Carole B. Matthews, "Home Computer Programs," *Consumer Research Magazine,* May 1983, p. 21.

On page 000 is another example of a definition paragraph. In the example the topic sentence, which includes the term, is stated at the end.

Comparison and Contrast

Another variation of paragraph development is comparison and contrast. A *comparison* paragraph shows how two things are *similar,* and a *contrast* paragraph shows how two things are *different.* Sometimes these patterns may be combined and you can show both similarities and differences in the same paragraph. Following are examples of comparison and contrast paragraphs.

The first shows how two things can be compared. In this paragraph the author compares the rewards of aging for both men and women. Through the comparison, the author shows differences in society's view of aging for men and women.

> This society offers even fewer rewards for aging to women than it does to men. Being physically attractive counts much more in a woman's life than in a man's, but beauty, identified, as it is for women, with youthfulness, does not stand up well to age. Exceptional mental powers can increase with age, but women are rarely encouraged to develop their minds above dilettante standards. Because the wisdom considered the special province of women is "eternal," an age-old, intuitive knowledge about the emotions to which a repertoire of facts, worldly experience, and the methods of rational analysis have nothing to contribute, living a long time does not promise women an increase in wisdom either. The private skills expected of women are exercised early and, with the exception of a talent for making love, are not the kind that enlarge with experience. "Masculinity" is identified with competence, autonomy, self-control—qualities which the disappearance of youth does not threaten. Competence in most of the activities expected from men, physical sports excepted, increases with age. "Femininity" is identified with incompetence, helplessness, passivity, noncompetitiveness, being nice. Age does not improve these qualities.[24]

The next paragraph illustrates the technique of contrast.

> The big difference between entertainment today and entertainment in the future will be our participation. Today we sit back and watch other people act out stories on a screen. In the future we will take part in the story. Today, we listen to records. In the future we will be a member of the orchestra. We will write novels as we read them and travel to distant countries just by walking across the street. Our entertainment will be as varied as our imagination wants it to be.[25]

The last paragraph shows how comparison and contrast can be combined. In this paragraph the author discusses similarities and differences alternately.

---

[24]Susan Sontag, "The Double Standard of Aging," *Saturday Review* September 23, 1975. Copyright © 1975 by *Saturday Review.* All rights reserved. Reprinted by permission of *Saturday Review,* New York, N.Y.

[25]Kathleen S. Abrams and Lawrence F. Abrams, *100 Years from Now* (New York: Julian Messner, 1983) p. 78.

So many of the activities of the computer resemble human cognitive processes that the comparison between man and machine has never been more apt. Never mind that the brain's architecture is different from that of the computer; never mind that wetware (brain cells) is not the hardware. Both mind and machine accept information, manipulate symbols, store items in memory and retrieve them again. Whether machines do these things like people do is less significant than that they do them at all. "Obviously, people don't think the same way as machines," said Papert during a symposium on the impact of the computer. "People are biological. When we ask if a machine thinks, we are asking whether we would like to extend the notion of thinking to include what machines might do. That is the only meaningful sense of the question: Do machines think? When Newton said the sun exerts a force on the Earth, he introduced a new technical concept of force. Artificial intelligence, in a similar way, is introducing a new technical concept of thinking.[26]

Cause–Effect

Cause–effect paragraphs show how certain factors (causes) bring about a result (effect). This development is similar to cause–effect reasoning discussed in Chapter 3. For example, you might wonder why your last school dance was poorly attended. Then you consider:

When it was held:	the night before final exams started
Where it was held:	off campus
The music played:	fox trots and waltzes

As a result you understand why the dance was poorly attended.

Following is an example of a cause–effect paragraph.

Growth in the employment of computer and peripheral equipment operators will result from the increased amount of computer hardware, such as terminals, in use. Computer operator employment will rise from 393,000 in 1978 to 850,000 in 1990. The growing number of computers will also stimulate the demand for computer service technicians. In addition, as more and more small systems are installed, the amount of time technicians spend traveling between clients will increase, further intensifying demand for these workers. The employment of computer service technicians is therefore expected to show the largest percentage of increase of all the computer occupations, growing from 63,000 in 1978 to 160,000 in 1990—a 154 percent rise.[27]

Combining Patterns of Development

Two or more patterns of organization are often combined in one paragraph. The following paragraph illustrates the technique of combining two patterns of development.

[26] © Patrick Huyghe, "Of Two Minds," *Psychology Today*, December, 1983, p. 28. Reprinted by permission of the author, Patrick Hughes.

[27] "Jobs for Two Million Workers," *VocEd*, April 1982, p. 31.

Once, after presenting the quality circle concept to a group of forklift drivers, I turned the meeting over to them for discussion on whether they wanted to form a circle. One side quickly decided in favor. The other side, the minority, argued that this kind of work was management's job, not theirs. They saw quality circles as just another management "scam." Yes, they knew ways to improve their job, but why should they? The argument continued, and it seemed that they would never reach a decision. Finally, an older man, who had been listening patiently, commented that he had worked for many companies in which he was prohibited from speaking his mind and voicing his ideas about how to do the work. "Here is a chance to have a say, and I'm going to take it." All of them eventually joined the circle.[28]

What patterns of development can you identify in this paragraph?

Argumentative Paragraphs

As we have seen, paragraphs serve many purposes. They may define a term or describe a process or an event. They may add to our understanding through comparison and contrast or they may explain an occurrence by relating the causes. Any of these types of paragraphs may also be organized to prove a point. Such paragraphs are called *argumentative paragraphs*. An agrumentative paragraph differs from other paragraphs in that its topic sentence states an opinion. The rest of the sentences in the paragraph support or refute that opinion.

Following is an example of an argumentative paragraph developed by reasons. Notice that an opinion is stated in the first sentence and then the rest of the sentences give reasons why that opinion is not correct.

It's possible that some people buy bottled water because they believe it's therapeutic. However, an article in *Consumer Reports* in September 1980 reported the burgeoning sales of bottled water (Perrier, for instance, zoomed from 3 million bottles in 1976 to 200 million bottles in 1979) were due to two reasons: dissatisfaction with the taste of tap water and worries about chemical contamination of municipal water supplies. The article said: "After trichloroethylene, an industrial solvent, was found in the wells near Los Angeles, southern California bulkwater companies reported new customers at a rate up to five times the usual." Another reason for the popularity of bottled water may be that drinking water—particularly mineral water with a twist of lime—is "in" and is advertised as more healthful than drinking alcohol or sweetened drinks.[29]

Order of Importance

At the beginning of this section on paragraph development we mentioned two basic patterns: general to specific, and specific to general. A third kind of pattern, one that is especially effective for argumentative paragraphs, is *order of impor-*

---

[28]Thompson, *Quality Circles*, p. 13.
[29]Carol L. Ballentine and Michael L. Herndon, "The Water that Goes into Bottles," *FDA Consumer*, May 1983, p. 7.

tance. Order-of-importance organization, as the name implies, is a method of organizing details according to their importance.

Whenever you consider the reasons for doing something, certain of those reasons stand out as more important to you than others. For example, if you were defining a regular exercise program, your reasons for exercising regularly might be:

> Weight control
> Health maintenance
> Muscle tone
> "In" thing to do

If you were organizing those details by order of importance, you would decide which reason was most important to you, decide which was least important, and rank the other details in order between the least and most important.

Usually when you organize a paragraph by order of importance, you start with the least important detail and progress to the most important. The rationale for this is that readers will best remember the last statement you make; therefore, you want to leave them with your most convincing support foremost in their minds. Nevertheless, the key to the effective use of this type of organization is to consider your readers. Will your readers be hostile to your opinion? If so, perhaps it would be best for you to secure their attention with your most powerful defense first.

The ranking of your details may also be influenced by who your audience is. For example, if your paragraph on exercise is intended for a weight watchers newsletter, you will probably emphasize regular exercise as a means of weight control. If you are writing for a medical magazine, on the other hand, you will probably emphasize the health benefits of regular exercise.

The following paragraph shows how details can be organized by order of importance.

Establishing quality circles in our factories may be an important way to increase productivity. These discussion groups give workers and management a chance to resolve minor problems before they become major grievances. This is one reason why quality circles can help increase productivity. People tend to work harder when conditions are pleasant. These discussion groups are also important to worker morale. When workers know that management is listening to them, they have a more positive attitude toward their jobs. But quality circles are most important to the work place because they allow employees a chance to have some input into decisions made about working conditions and production. When workers can express ideas and have those ideas seriously considered by management, they feel involved in the company. Then when the company is successful, the worker feels successful also. Providing this discussion time, therefore, can help establish a "partnership" between workers and management. For all these reasons quality circles can help increase productivity.

SUMMARY

Effective writing is important to career success. Studies show that workers spend almost one-fourth of their time on the job writing. In writing we use sentences and paragraphs to express our ideas.

A sentence is a group of words that includes a subject and a verb and that expresses a complete thought. When a group of words is punctuated as a sentence but does not express a complete thought, it is called a sentence fragment. A fragment may be either a phrase (a group of words with *either* a subject or a verbal) or a dependent clause (a group of words that contain both a subject and a verb but depends on another part of a sentence to make the thought complete).

Many thoughts punctuated as one sentence are called a run-on sentence. The main thoughts in a run-on sentence should be separated with proper punctuation to make the writing clear.

Using a variety of sentence types will make your writing more interesting. There are four sentence types: simple, compound, complex, and compound-complex. A simple sentence has one independent clause. A compound has more than one independent clause joined by a conjunction. A complex sentence has one independent and at least one dependent clause, and a compound-complex combines at least one dependent clause with two independent clauses.

Correct punctuation directs the reader from idea to idea much as road signs direct the traveler from place to place. Review the uses for punctuation marks discussed in detail in this chapter.

A group of sentences all on the same topic is called a paragraph. A good paragraph is unified, coherent, and adequately developed. All paragraphs have two parts: a sentence that states the topic, and sentences that discuss the topic, and most paragraphs also have concluding sentences that restate the main idea.

The topic sentence states the main idea of the paragraph. Because it leads the discussion, the topic sentence is often the first sentence in the paragraph, but it may occur anywhere in the paragraph. The second most usual place is the last sentence.

The sentences that discuss the paragraph are usually organized in one of two ways: General to specific, or specific to general. Order of importance is a third kind of organization pattern. These patterns of development can be varied to fit the writer's purpose. Some of the variations are comparison, contrast, and cause–effect. Use one of these patterns or combine them to accomplish your purpose for writing. This was shown specifically in the chapter with the discussion of argumentative paragraphs.

REVIEW QUESTIONS

1. From your reading of this chapter, how would you rank the importance of writing ability to success on the job? Support your answer with details from this chapter.
2. When is a clause also a sentence fragment? Give an example.
3. What is a run-on sentence? Give an example. What is the best way to correct a run-on sentence? Correct the example you listed in the first part of this question.
4. Explain why standard punctuation is an important factor in writing effectively.
5. What is a paragraph?
6. How is a topic sentence different from the other sentences in a paragraph?
7. What patterns are used to organize paragraphs? Briefly describe each pattern.

ACTIVITIES

1. Decide which of these word groups are sentences, which are fragments, and which are run-on. Underline the subject of each sentence once and the verb twice. Make the fragments into complete sentences and correct the run-on sentences with proper punctuation.
   a. When I went swimming.
   b. My first day on the job was a disaster I overcharged a customer and broke a teapot then I quit before I was fired.
   c. Threatened by his forceful manner.
   d. At work.
   e. The lifeguard taught the children to swim.
   f. Depending on John for a ride.
   g. Jack slept peacefully.
   h. In the bottom of the boat.
   i. Hopefully, when I graduate from college I'll get a good job so I can afford my own apartment and have some money to spend on travel.
   j. Such as: sorting, typing, and filing.
   k. Audrey's first day on the job.
   l. I'm eating.
   m. After skiing all weekend, Mary and Bob drove nonstop two hundred miles because they wanted to be to work on time Monday morning.
   n. Both of us enjoyed the show.
   o. We went to San Francisco first, then we drove up the coast to Oregon.
   p. Go!
   q. Preoccupied by thoughts of a promotion.
   r. Because unemployment is high, workers must be skilled at finding jobs they have to sell themselves or they are lost in the crowd.
   s. After Mary signed the contract.
   t. Jogging for her health.
2. Using the sentence models on pages 000–000, write two sentences in each pattern: simple, compound, complex, and compound-complex. At least one sentence in each pattern should relate to your major area of study.
3. Select a term related to your major area and write a paragraph defining that term. The word may be a tool or machine such as *ohmeter* or *off-set press.* It may also be a term used to describe a process, such as *silk-screening* or *threading a pipe.*
4. Imagine that you are leaving instructions for a new employee. Write a process paragraph describing a technique or activity related to your major area.
5. Write a comparison or contrast paragraph or a combination of the two for one of the following pairs:
   a. Mopeds and bicycles
   b. Computers and typewriters
   c. Hospitals and hospices
   d. Speeding and jaywalking
   e. Craft boutiques and large department stores
   f. Electric typewriters and electronic typewriters
   g. Calculators and slide rules
6. Select an article from a national news magazine such as *Time, Newsweek,* or *U.S. News and World Report* that discusses an incident using cause–effect development. Write a summary of the way the magazine writer develops the cause–effect relationship.

11

THE WRITING PROCESS

Most people won't realize that writing is a craft. You have to take your apprenticeship in it like anything else.

Katherine Anne Porter

After studying this chapter you should understand:

1. Your responsibility as a writer
2. How written expression develops through three stages:
   Initial planning
   Writing
   Rewriting
3. The content of a written message:
   Introduction
   Discussion
   Conclusion
4. How the three stages of the writing process interact

PETE: Say, Skip, don't forget to pick up a copy of that report on the new shipping and receiving procedures.

SKIP: Where can I find one?

PETE: On Mike's desk in Shipping and Receiving.

SKIP: Thanks for reminding me. I'll go down right now and get one.

PETE: Hey! Wait a minute! I didn't mean you should go down right now. The copies won't be ready until four this afternoon. I just wanted to remind you now because I probably won't see you again today.

What if Pete and Skip had not met in the hall and Pete had sent Skip a written message instead:

```
To:        Skip
From:      Pete
Subject:   Shipping and Receiving Procedures
Date:      1/10/85
Skip, don't forget to pick up your copy of the new Shipping and Receiving Procedures.
```

This is the same message Pete initially sent Skip when they met in the hall. As in the initial spoken message, two important items of information are missing from the written message: where Skip can find a copy of the new procedures, and the fact that the copies will not be ready until 4:00 o'clock in the afternoon. Unlike the spoken message, however, the written message leaves no chance to clarify this vagueness. Skip cannot say, as he does when he and Pete meet in the hall: "Where are the copies?" Also Pete cannot correct Skip's assumption that the copies are ready now by saying:

Hey! Wait a minute! I didn't mean you should go right now. The copies won't be ready until four this afternoon.

YOUR RESPONSIBILITY AS A WRITER

Express Ideas Exactly

When you send a written message, you must be sure it expresses your ideas exactly. Unlike a spoken message, a written message cannot be modified in response to the receiver's body language nor can it be clarified to increase the receiver's understanding. Because a written message "speaks" for you when you are not present, you must use organization and word choice to present your message effectively. You have only one chance to impress your readers. If you frustrate them with poor organization or confuse them with vagueness, they may ignore your message entirely.

Discuss Ideas Thoroughly

You also have a responsibility to discuss thoroughly the message you set out to send. If you are giving directions, discuss each step in detail; if you are persuading your reader to adopt your opinion, present your reasons clearly and support them logically; if you are describing a place or a procedure, present enough details so your readers can picture what you are describing.

Establish Credibility

Your third responsibility as a writer is to establish credibility. You can help your readers gain confidence in you by paying attention to three things as you write.

First, know who your audience is and use language they will understand. If you are writing to a general audience, choose everyday wording and adopt a conversational tone. If you are writing to a professional group about a topic in their field, use the technical wording they understand. Chapter 4 presents a thorough discussion of word choice.

The second way to establish credibility is to support the assertions you make. Research your topic carefully and present details, numbers, and other information to back up your main ideas. If you are describing a process, know the process thoroughly before you begin to write a description; if your purpose is to persuade your readers, use supportive material logically to convince them.

The third way to establish credibility is to make sure you can accomplish your stated purpose. Don't try to prove that *all* joggers *are healthier* when your supportive evidence indicates that jogging *helps many* people *feel better*.

Remember that a written message is permanent. It remains available for people to read and reread without the benefit of your interpretation. You cannot say, "That's not what I mean" or "Let me start over," as you would if you were talking to someone. You cannot shout: "Hey, wait a minute! Listen to me!" as the reader tosses your letter in the wastebasket.

As a writer, you do have one important advantage over the speaker: you can plan, write, and change your message many times before you send it. Unlike a speaker, you have the time to think through your ideas carefully and be sure you express them properly to someone else.

Thus you have both a special responsibility and a unique opportunity to present your written messages effectively. An understanding of the writing process will help you take advantage of these opportunities and fulfill these responsibilities. In this chapter we will discuss the three stages of the writing process and show how they interact to produce an effective message.

PLANNING YOUR WRITTEN MESSAGE

Have you ever thought, "If only I had planned this better, I could have. . . ." You may have been thinking about a side trip you could have taken on your vacation, a class you could have added to your schedule, or a wait at the airport you could have avoided. Planning is an important part of our daily lives. It helps us use our time efficiently and achieve the most we can with the time we have.

Just as planning is important to a happy, productive lifestyle, it is also important to effective writing. Careful planning will save you time during the actual writing process and help you state your message clearly.

As in other situations, planning your writing requires discipline. The planning stage of anything takes time and gives back very little concrete material. It is difficult to point to the result of an hour's thinking and say, "Here's what I have accomplished." For that reason we often find planning difficult. We sort through the many thoughts running through our minds, discarding some and expanding on others. We use our imagination to explore some of the ideas. We decide what's workable and what isn't. We question our beliefs. Then, eventually, after what seems a very long time, we are ready to write. If we have planned carefully, the writing goes surprisingly well. If we haven't planned carefully, the writing process breaks down and adds to our frustration.

You will find many of the ideas in this section regarding planning are also presented in the section on oral communication and in the report writing chapter. Planning is an integral part of many of the things we do.

Consider Your Purpose

The first step in the planning stage of writing is to decide on your purpose. Do you intend to convince your audience to adopt your viewpoint on an issue? Do you want to persuade them to do something? Is your purpose to entertain, describe a process, or give information about an event? State your purpose clearly and keep it in mind while you plan, write, and rewrite your message.

For example, if Maxine, the writer in the scenario beginning this section had clearly understood her purpose before she began writing (Mrs. Wolhert asked her to send information but Maxine also attempts to persuade and entertain), she would have saved herself time during the writing process.

Know Your Audience

Next you should have an idea of who your audience will be. Are you writing this message for your boss? Your co-worker? Your best friend? What does your audience know about your subject? What do you want them to know? Your audience's background and interests will affect your word choice and the details you present. Since Maxine was writing to a youth group, she should choose a conversational tone and everyday language. Her inappropriate word choice hinders communication. For a more thorough discussion of audience and how it affects word choice see Chapter 4. Audience analysis as it applies to the speaking situation is discussed in Chapter 8.

Brainstorm

When you know your purpose and who your audience will be, you should write down all the ideas that come to your mind about your topic. This is called *brainstorming* and it helps you organize the jumble of thoughts presenting themselves. When you brainstorm, you record every idea that comes to you. Don't worry if some of the ideas sound silly or don't seem to fit. Your purpose here is just to record everything so you don't forget anything that might be helpful later. Later you will discard many of the ideas as you focus on one central thought for discussion.

Mrs. Wolhert asked Maxine to write a letter to the youth group on the broad topic, "How to get a job." Maxine is understandably a little overwhelmed by that request. She would have made her job easier if she had brainstormed her topic before she began writing. Her list might look something like this:

How to Get a Job
Interview
Dress right
Learn something about company
Apply
Know how to greet the interviewer
Prepare a resumé
Write an effective letter
Think up questions you would like answered in the interview
Prepare for the interview

Before Maxine can begin writing, she should organize this random listing of topics. The list she will use to write her letter might look like this:

How to Get a Job
Prepare
Dress right
Learn something about company
Write an effective letter
Prepare a resumé
Think up questions you would like answered in the interview
Apply
Know how to greet the interviewer
Take the interview

Brainstorming is applicable to many situations and can be used either in individual writing situations or in group writing or discussions. Its application to oral communication is discussed in Chapter 9.

Focus Your Discussion

The fourth step in planning your written message is to focus your discussion on one central idea.

Because an effective written message discusses the topic thoroughly, you must limit the topic before you start writing. If you choose "Job-seeking skills" as the topic for a two-page letter, you will give your readers only a superficial idea about the subject. They will not be receiving specific information, and you will be frustrated because you have "so much to include in such a short paper."

In order to focus on one central idea, first look at your list and try grouping the topics under general headings. Which groupings interest you most? What topics would interest your audience most?

When you have focused on one area, decide how long your message will be; then limit your topic to fit that length.

For example, you could write hundreds of pages on job-seeking skills. If your intent is to write a book, "Job-seeking skills" would be an appropriate topic. If, on the other hand, your intent is to write a five-page report, you need to limit the larger topic to something like "Writing a resume" or "Dressing for an interview." If you want to write a two-page letter as Maxine did, you would settle on even a more limited topic such as "What to include under personal data," or "How I dressed for my first interview."

A general topic may be limited in a variety of ways. Maxine, for example, may have limited her broad topic of "Tips on job-seeking skills" to "Five things junior high school students should know when they look for part-time work."

Beginning writers tend to cover too much material in one message. Although it may be difficult to do at first, try applying this guide, continuing to narrow the focus of your subject until you think you will not have enough material to write the number of pages you intend. When you reach that point, you have usually limited your topic successfully and can begin writing. You will probably be surprised to find that you have more than enough to say on the subject.

Research

Keeping the limited topic clearly in mind, you should research the area thoroughly before beginning to write. Research skills and techniques are thoroughly discussed in Chapter 2. Your personal experiences can be used to supplement material you find in the library and gather from talking to experts. Researching is one of the most time-consuming parts of the writing process, so plan to spend adequate time on it. Without details, examples, and other information, your writing will be superficial and you will lose credibility as a writer.

Develop a Purpose Statement

When you have limited the focus of your message, state your reason for writing the message clearly in one sentence. This sentence is the most important sentence in your message because it establishes the boundaries for your discussion and tells the reader what direction your writing will take. Like the topic sentence in a paragraph, the purpose statement in an essay controls the organization of the material, and for that reason it is often called the *controlling idea.* You may have also heard the purpose statement referred to as the *thesis statement.* The variety of names given to this one sentence indicates its importance to the success of the written message.

The purpose statement is one of the first sentences you will write. Place it where you will see it as you write and refer to it as you start each new paragraph. Use it as a guide to keep your essay on the path you have established for it.

Let's say you limited the general topic "Job-seeking skills" to "Writing a resumé." A purpose statement for this topic might be "You should write a resumé that highlights your special skills." The message would discuss techniques such as arrangement of data, selection of references, and information included, which show your skills as a worker to best advantage.

With the purpose statement clearly in front of you, you are ready to begin writing your message.

WRITING THE MESSAGE

If you have planned carefully before you sit down to write, you may expect the words to come to mind as quickly as you can move your pen across the paper. Sometimes that will happen, but just as often you will find that your thoughts come reluctantly.

Even professional writers find putting thoughts on paper difficult; therefore, we can all expect to experience some difficulty during our writing. But understanding how people actually write can help make your experience writing easier.

Many of us think writing is like jogging: the faster you write the better; the steadier your pace, the more efficient you are. Actually writing is more like wine tasting. When tasting wine, you drink from the glass, evaluate the taste, and either take another drink or set the glass down, depending upon your evaluation. Writing, too, is a process of stops and starts. You express an idea, reread what you have written, and either expand on it or reject it and start over.

A study of the way college students write revealed that those who were usually successful as writers followed a pattern of writing: pausing, rereading, pausing once more, and then starting to write again. The study showed that their success as writers depended upon how well they used their pauses. Those who paused to reread what they had just written as a way of helping them plan what to say next had more writing success than those who did not reread their writing.[1]

If you expect writing to be a series of stops and starts rather than one continuous flow, you will be more relaxed and content to spend the time you need to write effectively. During this writing stage your main concern is putting your thoughts on paper. Although you should attempt to follow the patterns of sentence and paragraph development and organize your thoughts, you need not attempt to polish your style during this time. If you wait until you have the "perfect" wording in mind, you may block the flow of your thoughts and make writing unnecessarily difficult.

THE CONTENT OF A WRITTEN MESSAGE

Most written messages whether they are letters, reports, or essays, have a beginning, a middle, and an ending. As you plan your message, you should keep these divisions in mind. How will you start your message? What will your discussion include? How

[1] Sharon Planko, "Reflection: A Critical Component of the Composing Process," *College Composition and Communication*, October 1979, p. 276.

will you end your paper? Following are some thoughts on organizing the content of your written message.

Introduction

Your written message should start with an introductory statement for the purpose of catching the reader's attention and indicating the purpose of the message. This introduction may be one or two sentences, in the case of letters or other short messages, or a couple of paragraphs or even several pages in longer reports or essays. Whatever its length, certain conventions hold true for the introduction. Use startling statistics, quote an authority, or tell a brief, exciting story to capture the reader's attention. Then lead into the discussion by stating your purpose clearly. Usually you should not reveal your topic immediately with a statement such as, "Today I'm going to tell you how to write a resumé." Instead begin with an attention getter:

Last week 4,000 people applied for 200 jobs at a Milwaukee company.

Then discuss the significance of this statement to your topic:

This is only one of the many incidents indicating that the competition for jobs is keen throughout the country.

Next lead into your purpose statement:

In order to get a job today, you have to be as skilled in seeking the job as you are in doing the job itself. The right kind of resumé can give you an edge over your competition.

Now you can present your purpose statement:

You should learn to write a resumé that highlights your special skills.

When you combine these sentences, you have the following introductory paragraph.

Last week 4,000 people applied for 200 jobs at a Milwaukee company. This is only one of many incidents indicating that competition for jobs today is keen throughout the country. In order to get a job today, you have to be as skilled in seeking the job as you are in doing the job itself. The right kind of resumé can give you an edge over your competition. You should learn to write a resumé that highlights your special skills.

Discussion

The discussion paragraphs satisfy the curiosity you have aroused in the first paragraph. They accomplish the purpose you established with your purpose statement. Discussion paragraphs may use any of the means of development mentioned in Chapter 10. You may use as many discussion paragraphs as you need to cover the topic and organize them in whatever way seems most effective to you, but make sure all the paragraphs relate specifically to the purpose statement. As you write each topic sentence, check it against the purpose statement. Does the topic sentence discuss an aspect of the topic stated in the purpose statement? If it does not, eliminate that paragraph from your discussion.

As an example, let's look at the following topic sentences.

Purpose statement:

You should learn to write a resumé that highlights your special skills.

Discussion Paragraph 1:

Learn to arrange the information so your best features stand out.

Discussion Paragraph 2:

In personal data include information that shows special aptitudes for the job you are seeking.

Discussion Paragraph 3:

Select references that can vouch for your reliability.

Each of these topic sentences tells a way you can use a resumé to highlight special skills; therefore, you will expect each paragraph to contribute important information to the discussion.

On the other hand, a topic sentence like, "It's doubtful that employers even look at resumés" will not add to the discussion. Although it is on the general topic of resumés, it certainly will not lead to a discusion on how resumés can highlight special skills.

Concluding Paragraph

Last, sum up the discussion paragraphs by restating the main points. Avoid using the same wording in both the discussion paragraphs and the concluding statement. Instead, paraphrase your main ideas. Your conclusion will lose impact if it is simply a repetition of the discussion. Remember, the conclusion is your last chance to convince your readers. Make it count.

REWRITING

In the rewriting stage of the writing process you will make the revisions that polish your writing style. Notice we have used the word *revision* because rewriting is more than correcting spelling and punctuation. It is actually changing what you have just written to improve the effectiveness of your communication.

Following are some student descriptions of the revision process:

Scratch out and do over again: "I say scratch out and do over, and that means what it says—scratching out and cutting out. I read what I have written and I cross out a word and put another word in—a more decent word or a better word. Then if there is somewhere to use a sentence that I have crossed out, I will put it there."[2]

Reviewing: "I just review every word and make sure that everything is worded right. I see if I am rambling; I see if I can put a better word in or leave one out. Usually when I read what I have written, I say to myself, 'That word is so bland or so trite,' and then I go and get my thesaurus."[3]

Redoing: "Redoing means cleaning up the paper and crossing out. It is looking at something and saying, 'No, that has to go,' or 'No, that is not right.' "[4]

Several important ideas about the revision process are brought out in these statements.

First, revision is rearranging: ". . . if there is somewhere to use a sentence that I have crossed out, I will put it there." During the revision you will polish the organization of your paper, rearranging sentences and paragraphs so your thoughts are expressed logically.

Second, revision is rewording: "Usually when I read what I have written, I say to myself, 'That word is so bland or so trite,' and then I go and get my thesaurus," and "I read what I have written and I cross out a word and put another word in—a more decent word or a better word." During the revision process you will polish your word choice, crossing out and substituting words until your thoughts are expressed clearly and concisely. Use a dictionary and thesaurus to help you vary your wording and choose the most effective language for your purpose.

Third, revision is cutting: "Redoing means cleaning up the paper and crossing out. It is looking at something and saying, 'No, that has to go.' " Cutting is probably the most difficult of all steps in the revision process. We tend to think everything we write is special. However, we usually write more than is needed: we might say the same thing twice in slightly different words; we might use words or phrases with tiresome repetition throughout the paper. Reread your entire paper with an awareness of these repetitions and wording constructions. Cross them out and polish your sentence structure until your message is concisely written.

Proofing

When you have made the necessary changes and your paper is in final form, you should proof it. Proofing is the correction of mechanical errors such as spelling, punctuation, and paragraph development. Use a dictionary to help with spelling and a usage handbook for information on punctuation and grammatical structure. When you are certain your paper is mechanically correct, you are ready to write or type it in final form so your audience can read it.

---

[2]Nancy Sommer, "Revision Strategies of Student Writers and Experienced Adult Writers," *College Composition and Communication,* December 1980, p. 381. Reprinted with the permission of the National Council of Teachers of English.
[3]*Ibid.*
[4]*Ibid.*

INTERACTION OF THE THREE STAGES
OF THE WRITING PROCESS

For instruction purposes, we have discussed each step of the writing process separately, but when you actually write a message you will find that these three stages interact. You will revise during the writing stage and write during the planning stage. You may stop in the midst of writing and go back to planning. Especially, you will find revising merges into all areas. You will revise both your plan and your writing. You may even revise as you proof.

One of the keys to effective writing is to feel comfortable with this ongoing process of stops and starts. Don't try to confine your writing to a rigid structure; do plan carefully before you begin writing; then write, pause, reread, and write again confident that you can express a message effectively through writing.

SUMMARY

When you write, you should express ideas exactly and discuss them thoroughly. You should also establish credibility by writing to a specific audience and supporting and qualifying assertions.

The writing process includes three areas: planning, writing, and rewriting. In the planning stage you should consider your audience and purpose for writing, then brainstorm ideas, focus on a topic that can be covered adequately in the number of pages you anticipate, and research that topic thoroughly. When you rewrite your paper, you should change wording and organization to improve the communication, then proofread what you have written for mechanical errors. While you are writing and proofing, observe the aspects of good sentence and paragraph structure discussed in Chapter 10.

A written message, like other forms of communication, has a beginning, a middle, and an ending. Use an attention getter to introduce your topic, discuss it thoroughly in the body of your paper, and sum up your main points as you conclude the message.

REVIEW QUESTIONS

1. What are the three steps in the writing process? Briefly describe what the writer does in each step. Show how these three stages interact.
2. What is the difference between revising and proofreading? How are they both necessary to the rewriting step of the writing process?
3. What are the three parts of the content of a written message? What is the purpose of each part?

ACTIVITIES

1. Write two purpose statements for each of the following topics. Be prepared to describe the direction your essay would take for each of these purpose statements.
   a. Automation in the work place
   b. Foreign competition in the auto industry
   c. Walking as exercise
   d. Tax breaks for private schools
   e. Studying at a two-year school
2. Select an essay from a current magazine. (Editorials in news magazines and speeches in *Vital Speeches of the Day* are good sources for short essays.) Identify the parts of the essay: introduction, discussion, conclusion. Find the controlling idea. List the topic sentences.
3. Now that you understand the writing process, refer to your evaluation of Maxine's letters to the Boy Scouts. What additional comments can you add to your evaluation? When you have thoroughly evaluated the problems with Maxine's letter, rewrite the letter using the purpose statement: "You should learn to write a resumé that highlights your special skills." You may have to do some research. Include an introductory paragraph, at least three discussion paragraphs, and a concluding paragraph. Observe all the aspects of word choice we discussed in Chapter 4.

12

WRITING REPORTS

The secret of all good writing is sound judgment.
                                        Horace

After studying this chapter you should understand:
1. The definition of a report
2. The importance of audience analysis
3. The development of a purpose statement
4. How to organize and develop an outline
5. Writing the report from an outline
6. How to document sources

Can you imagine yourself writing as many as 40 letters, memos, and reports each week? A business writing survey by Communispond, Inc., of New York showed this to be true for some executives. Sixty percent of the executives surveyed said they are writing more letters, memos, and reports today than they wrote a year ago. Some of them said they write as many as 40 items each week.[1]

The opportunity for writing probably increases as you move ahead in your career, but almost all employees are required to write at some time in their jobs. Filling out work orders, writing a memo to request a vacation day, and documenting an incident with a letter are all examples of on-the-job writing. Report writing techniques can also be applied to a variety of technical material such as product manuals and regulation handbooks.

[1] "Executives Acknowledge Their Lack of Business Writing Skills," *Supervision*, September 1982, p. 9.

In this chapter we will discuss the basics of report writing. To illustrate this type of writing, we will use the 1982 annual report from Sentry Insurance. Items are quoted from the report throughout the discussion. Then the entire report is printed at the end of the chapter so you can see how the process can be used to complete an actual report.

REPORTS DEFINED

Reports can be informational or persuasive, long or short, formal or informal. In some ways you might think of a report as a long essay, because many of the techniques of sentence structure and paragraphing used in other written messages are also necessary for report writing. However, a report is usually more structured than an essay. It usually includes documentation of the facts used and a list of sources. Formal reports also include a variety of explanatory material such as a letter of transmittal, an abstract, and a synopsis.

Persuasive Reports

When changes are considered in your company or when problems arise, one way of coping is to prepare a report. The report discusses the situation clearly and helps the people involved make a logical decision. Reports can describe a situation, explain the reasons for a condition, or suggest ways of dealing with a problem. In the scenario that introduced the first section, Preparing, Theresa attempted to prepare a persuasive report.

Informational Reports

Informational reports attempt to update the readers with details and descriptions. The purpose of this type of report is to add to the reader's knowledge. Companies' annual reports are an example of informational reports.

AUDIENCE ANALYSIS

"Who will read this report?" is the first question you should ask yourself as you begin to prepare your report. Your message must be clear to your audience; therefore, you must use words and writing style they can understand. We explain things differently to children than we do to adults. We choose different words to communicate to lay people with a limited knowledge of our subject than we do when dealing with technicians who are familiar with all the aspects of our topic. You are probably aware that you talk differently to your supervisor than you do to your co-workers. In the same way, you will use a more formal tone when you are writing a report for your supervisor than when you are writing a memo to a co-worker.

Consider the following ways to define "oscilloscope."

A scope is a little box. It has a screen on it. The screen looks like a TV. The scope tells us how much electrical power there is in a machine. The scope is hooked up to a machine. Then it turns the electricity from the machine into lines. These lines make patterns on the scope's screen. You can tell how much power the machine has by looking at the pattern on the screen.

An oscilloscope is an electronic device used to measure changes in electric current. These changes are shown on a screen similar to our TV screens. The scope records the electric current in the form of a thin line. The patterns of these lines shown on the TV screen indicate the variation in electrical charge.

An oscilloscope is an electronic device depicting periodic changes in electronic quantity. These oscillations are changed into electrical voltage which can be shown on the screen of a cathode ray tube.

The first is an explanation a child can understand. Notice the brief sentences and the short, familiar words. The second is geared toward an adult lay person. You will notice that the sentences are longer and some of the thoughts have been combined, but the terminology remains familiar. The third definition is written for technicians. Here no attempt has been made to define technical terms or simplify the concepts. The writer expects the technician to understand the terminology used.

What if a technician wrote a definition like the first one and sent it to an electronics engineer? The recipient would probably be insulted. He might also decide that the technician didn't know anything about an oscilloscope. He might even label the person simpleminded and tell his superior he does not want him transferred to his department.

The problem here is not that the technician is simpleminded or even uninformed about the workings of an oscilloscope. The problem is that the person did not keep the audience in mind while writing the definition. If the technician had remembered to write for someone knowledgeable about electricity, the style and tone of the writing would have suited the reader better.

Before you begin writing your report, learn all you can about your audience. This effort may require some research, but it will be worthwhile. Ask the person who assigned the report the question, "Who will read this material?" Learn whether your report is destined for:

1. A general audience
2. The board of directors
3. Technicians who confront the problem daily
4. Your supervisor, who wants to know more about the situation

When you know the knowledge level of your audience, you will know:

1. How many terms you will need to define in the text
2. How detailed your explanations should be
3. What terminology to use
4. The style and tone you should use in your writing

When preparing an annual report, for example, you should keep in mind that it will be read by stockholders and other lay people who are especially interested in the company. It will also probably be used as source of public information and given to people who tour the company or who request information about the company but who are not directly involved in the workings of the business.

DEFINING THE PURPOSE

The second question you should ask yourself is, "Why am I writing this report?" Your immediate response may be, "My supervisor told me to" or "We write an annual report each year," but these are only superficial replies. Your real reason for asking this question is to determine the focus of the report.

Set a Goal

The purpose statement of a report is a sentence or brief paragraph stating the direction your report will follow. You must decide specifically what you want the report to accomplish. In other words, you must set a goal or purpose for the report. Then, no matter how many other topics come up as you are writing, you can keep your goal firmly in mind and remain true to the purpose you have set for your report.

Determine the Purpose

To determine the purpose of the report, first make sure that you understand the assignment. Ask the person making the assignment exactly what the report should accomplish, and write down what you are told. This information will help you later when you write the purpose statement.

Often determining the purpose is one of the easiest parts of writing the report because the person who assigns the report will state the purpose clearly. For example, your supervisor may send you the following memo:

```
To:       Ron Smyth

From:     Mrs. Alice Raymond

Subject:  Annual Report

Date:     October 20, 1982


    We should begin preparing our annual report for 1982.  This year I
think we should emphasize the way Sentry has diversified to stay
competitive in the next decade.  Let's give an overview of Sentry
```

enterprises. Contact the chairman for his introductory comments. The
accounting department should be able to supply all the financial figures
you will need. I will look forward to discussing your first draft with
you by November 20, 1982.

In this case you know exactly what you should accomplish when writing the
report.

At other times, however, you might be given an assignment like this:

Ron, it's time we started thinking about that annual report. Can you look into it and get me
something in writing before the next board meeting?

In this case you will have to determine your own the purpose of the
report. How many different directions can you imagine this report taking? After you
have thought of a few goals for your report, look at the list below for some other
ideas of purpose statements.

The purpose of this report is to describe the most recent legal decisions affecting the
insurance business.

The purpose of this report is to discuss the way Sentry Insurance has adapted to a tight
economy.

The purpose of this report is to relate ways the computer is used at Sentry.

The purpose of this report is to compare Sentry's financial picture this year with last year's
financial status.

The purpose of this report is to describe the four locations of Sentry headquarters.

The purpose of this report is to sum up Sentry's philosophy of selling insurance.

You can see that your job is more complicated with the second example. If
you have an assignment like this, you should question your supervisor about the ex-
pectations for the report. You will talk to other people who are involved in the decision. You will also want to do some reading on the topic. This is an excellent opportunity to use the prereading, skipping, and skimming skills we discuss in Chapter 15.
Until you know the exact direction your report will take, you will not want to spend
a lot of time doing in-depth reading, but you will want to do some general reading on
the topic to help you determine your purpose.

Write a Purpose Statement

As you read and think about your report, you will determine a goal for the
report, but this goal may be difficult to express in something as structured as a purpose statement. It may help to begin your purpose statement with the words: "The
purpose of this report is to," but ending that sentence can still be troublesome. Be
sure to limit your purpose to a goal you can accomplish in the number of pages and
amount of time available for your project. Also be sure to use concise wording when
stating your purpose. Remember, statements including words like *all* or *never* are
very difficult to support, so qualify your purpose and be sure it is a goal you can adequately support.

Let's go back to the memo on pages 214–215. You will notice the focus of the report was clearly defined:

This year I think we should emphasize the way Sentry has diversified to stay competitive in the next decade. Let's give an overview of Sentry Enterprises.

From that direction and after some initial research on the subject you could develop the following purpose statement:

To better understand Sentry's commitment to diversification, let's take a closer look at some of Sentry's major enterprises.

When you are sure of the direction you want your report to take and you have written it clearly in a sentence or two, copy that purpose statement in bold letters on a note card and keep it in front of you as you research and write the report. Look at it often. It will help you stay on one specific topic.

RESEARCH

The research techniques that are discussed in Chapter 2 should be used here in the planning stage of your report.

ORGANIZING THE REPORT

When your research is completed, your next step is organizing the report. As you researched, you formed many ideas about the topic. Now these ideas must be organized into a logical pattern so your reader can follow your thoughts easily.

Brainstorm

The first thing you will do is write down all the ideas that come to mind on your topic. Write them down as fast as you think of them. Don't worry about putting them in any special order at this time. From Chapter 11 you will recognize this activity as brainstorming. It gives you a chance to clear your mind of all ideas you have been forming while you researched. It also helps if you remember all the important ideas about your subject.

After brainstorming on the topic of diversification, your list may look like this:

Diversification
Recreation
Sentry World Golf Course
Consulting
Communications
Crestline

Wood products
SENCO
Reed Industries
Vitter
Transportation
Midstate
Centerpoint
Sentry Broadcasting
George Segal movies
Sports Center
Landscaped grounds
Financial services
Foreign markets
Work—management systems
Home security
Manufacturing
Produce series, movies, and specials

Outline

When you have a list of ideas, you will group them into main headings, subtopics, and details and will organize these into an outline. An outline is the pattern of the report. As you write, you will follow your outline as a contractor follows a blueprint. For that reason it is important that the outline be carefully developed.

The main ideas are developed by the subpoints, and the subpoints are supported by the details. In an outline the main ideas are designated by Roman numerals, the subpoints by capital letters, and the details by Arabic numerals. An outline might look like this:

I. Main idea
  A. Subpoint
  B. Subpoint
    1. Detail
    2. Detail
II. Main idea
  A. Subpoint
    1. Detail
    2. Detail
    3. Detail
  B. Subpoint

One of the conventions of an outline is that the same structure must be used throughout. That is, if you start writing in sentences, you must state all the ideas in complete sentences. If you write the main heads in phrases, you can also list the subpoints and details in phrases or single words.

Another convention of an outline concerns the number of items listed. You must have at least two main headings and at least two subpoints under each main heading. You must be able to support each subpoint with at least two details. This convention ensures that you have adequate development for each idea. If you have only one detail, it would have to be powerful, indeed, to support a subpoint all by itself. If you have only one subpoint under a main heading, your development is most certainly weak; and, of course, you could not write an entire paper from one main heading.

Keeping your purpose in mind:

To better understand Sentry's commitment to diversification, let's take a closer look at some of Sentry's major enterprises.

You select the major enterprises from the list on pages 216–217. These are your main topics (the Roman numerals in your outline). You may organize them like this:

   I. Transportation
  II. Communications
 III. Recreation
 IV. Financial Services
  V. Wood Products
 VI. Manufacturing
VII. Consulting

When you have your main topics selected and organized, you should arrange the supportive details under each topic. Using the list you made during brainstorming and adding to it as you work, you will eventually develop an outline that looks something like this.

  I. Transportation
    A. Midstate increases passengers
       1. Increase 66%
       2. Increase miles 81%
       3. Double revenue
    B. Midstate located at Central Wisconsin Airport
       1. 22,000-square-foot hangar
       2. 8 airplanes
 II. Communications
    A. Sentry Broadcasting
       1. WYBR-FM (Sentry's 11th radio station)
       2. 9.9% sales increase last year
    B. Centerpoint
       1. Opened offices in New York, Los Angeles
       2. Goals to produce series, movies, and specials
       3. First production—George Segal movie,
          special for dub and series pilot for pay cable
III. Recreation
    A. Sentry World sports complex
       1. 65,000-square-foot center
       2. Total sports facility
    B. Sentry World Golf Course

1. 18 championship holes
2. Designed by Robert Trent Jones II
C. Landscape grounds—5 acres
IV. Financial Services
    A. Sentry Financial Services
        1. 13.4% gain
        2. Provide money to borrowers planning a major purchase
    B. Sentry Leasing Company
        1. 18.4% gain
        2. Lease automobiles, office equipment, farm machinery, and medical tech
V. Wood Products
    A. Includes Vitter and Crestline
    B. Consolidated their operations
VI. Manufacturing
    A. Reed Industries
        1. Beverage equipment
        2. Security Systems
    B. Will be introducing new products and developing foreign markets
VII. Consulting
    A. Creative Management Alternative—management system to improve white-collar performance
    B. CMA promoting new business

WRITING THE REPORT

Finally, you are ready to write the report. You will want to refer to Chapter 10 on sentence structure and paragraphing and Chapter 11 on essay writing. Remember that just as a paragraph is a collection of sentences on one topic, a report is a collection of paragraphs on one topic. The same guidelines that apply to paragraphing, such as complete thoughts, linking statements, and development of ideas, also apply to report writing. If you follow your outline and approach report writing one paragraph at a time, you will find your report is soon written. You will also want to remember that the first written copy is a rough draft. Don't be too concerned with style here. Get your ideas down in an organized manner. Write quickly. You can polish your sentences, paragraphs, and even organization during the rewriting.

Introductory Paragraph

The first paragraph or paragraphs in your report are introductory paragraphs. Here you will use one of the attention getters we discussed in Chapter 8 to capture your reader's interest. In this section you will also introduce the topic of your report and lead up to the specific purpose. The purpose statement should be placed at the end of your introduction; it signals the beginning of the discussion. Remember to make a smooth transition from the introduction to the purpose statement.

Developmental Paragraphs

Next come the developmental paragraphs, in which you will discuss the topic and accomplish the purpose of your report. These paragraphs are developed by detail, statistics, and illustrations, all of which you will find in your research notes. If you have done your job as a researcher well, you will have an excellent selection of details. Choose only those quotes, statistics, and illustrations that you think will best support your purpose. Be selective; you do not want to burden your readers with more material than they can absorb. At the same time, be sure that each paragraph is thoroughly developed with ample detail. Back up each assertion with facts and reasoning. Quotes from recognized authorities in your field will lend credibility to your assertions. To refresh your memory on developing paragraphs with details and logic see pages 192–195.

Crediting Sources: Footnotes

Remember to give credit to your sources for any quotes, controversial or unique ideas, and statistics that are not common knowledge. Your readers will want to be able to check on your source and verify the credibility of your information. Formal reports use footnotes and bibliographical references to credit sources. In reports written for a general audience, the source is often credited in the report itself. Sentry's annual report gives reference to sources in the text. Look carefully at the example to see how this can be done effectively.

If you want to footnote your sources, the examples below illustrate how to make formal footnote reference.

The first time you refer to a source, identify it completely.

Book

[1] David Lewis, How to Be a Gifted Parent (New York: Berkley Books, 1979), p. 21.

The footnote includes:

1. Author's full name, first name first
2. Title of the book underlined
3. Place of publication, publisher, and date of publication in parentheses
4. Page reference

Note that a comma separates the author's name from the title of the book and the publication information from the page reference. A period marks the end of the reference.

Magazine or Newspaper Article

[2] Peter O. Whitmer, "Ken Kesey's Search for the American Frontier," Saturday Review, May–June 1983, p. 23.

The footnote includes:

1. Author's full name, first name first
2. Title of the article in quotation marks
3. Title of the magazine underlined
4. Date of the magazine
5. Page number for the reference

Note that commas are used to separate the parts of the reference. A period marks the end of the reference.

Newspaper

[10]"Popular Ice Cream Is Still a Royal Treat," The Daily Herald, 22 June 1983, Sec. 2, p. 29, Col. 5.

Note the use of commas to separate items. Also, many newspaper articles do not give credit to the author. In these cases begin with the title of the article. If an author's name is mentioned, begin with the name as in a magazine article reference. Notice that the section and column number of the article are also mentioned.

Concluding Paragraphs

When you have discussed your topic thoroughly, you should end the report with one or more concluding paragraphs. Depending on your purpose, these paragraphs may be recommendations for action, solutions to a problem, or merely summary paragraphs. Whatever method you use to end your report, be sure to give your readers a sense of conclusion. The material on concluding paragraphs in Chapter 11 will be helpful to you as you conclude your report.

Bibliography

Included as the last page of your report will be a bibliography, a list of the sources you used in writing the report.

A bibliographical reference for a book differs from a footnote in three ways:

1. The author's last name goes first.
2. No page number is given because you are not making one specific reference.
3. Periods separate the main parts of the reference.

Lewis, David. *How to Be a Gifted Parent.* New York: Berkley Books, 1979.

A bibliographical reference for a magazine or newspaper is similar to that for a book except the complete number of pages included in the article is also mentioned.

Whitmer, Peter O. "Ken Kesey's Search for the American Frontier," *Saturday Review,* May–June 1983, pp. 23–31.

REWRITING THE REPORT

As you write the last sentence of your report, you probably draw a breath of relief and say, "I'm finally finished." But remember you have just finished the rough draft. Now you must polish your sentence structure and paragraph organization. You must make sure all your ideas are clearly stated and developed.

Although the topics and purposes differ, good reports have some elements in common. As you are rereading your report, check for the following things:

1. Have you used adequate detail (facts, quotes, examples, and illustrations) to develop each idea?
2. Are your ideas unified within the paragraph and from paragraph to paragraph?
3. Have you cited all the sources necessary and included a list of the sources you used as the final page of your report?
4. Is your paper readable? Have you written in a clear, concise style and a tone appropriate to your audience?
5. Is your paper mechanically correct?
6. Does your discussion satisfy the goal you set for yourself with the purpose statement?

When you are sure that your report meets these requirements, you are ready to type the paper and submit it to your supervisor.

EXAMPLE OF A REPORT

On the following pages you can read part of an annual report published by Sentry Insurance. Comments are included to help you relate the report to the information you have just studied.

Attention getter

A Closer Look At Diversification
Sentry Builds For The 21st Century[2]

"By year 2000, Sentry Enterprises will generate one-third of all Sentry revenues."

Notice the quote used as attention getter

That promise from Tom Jirous, *Sentry Executive Vice President and head of Sentry Enterprises,* clearly indicates Sentry's commitment to diversification. With over 15 separate, fully-owned "noninsurance" holdings, 1982 marked a year of continued growth and development. New additions to the Enterprise family ranged from a recreational golf/tennis complex, to a new radio station, to a white-collar consulting firm. In short, diversification continued to highlight Sentry's revenue plans for the future.

Identify the person quoted

Interesting details

Diversification, however, is hardly a new word to Sentry. Since 1967, Sentry has been carefully building an attractive portfolio of enterprises. With the insurance industry periodically encountering

Background information

[2] *Sentry Annual Report* 1982, pp. 9–13. Sentry Insurance, Stevens Point, Wisc.

down cycles, diversification into other markets establishes revenue not totally reliant on insurance. Thus, by "spreading our risk," Sentry can better strengthen itself for the challenges of the next century.

Purpose statement
To better understand Sentry's commitment to diversification, let's take a closer look at some of Sentry's major enterprises.

Transportation

Sentry's regional airline, Midstate, enjoyed a healthy year in 1982. Its growth—in the face of the troubled airline industry—has been encouraging. *Since June 1980, when Sentry added Midstate to its enterprise fold, the company has taken off.*

Main assertion

Supporting details
For example, Midstate carried over 200,000 passengers in 1982—an *increase of 66%.* Air service stretched out to Kansas City, Duluth, Waterloo and Cedar Rapids. Green Bay and Madison have been recently added. With seven midwestern states serviced, Midstate's *passenger miles increased 81%.* Revenues nearly doubled. The once tiny commuter is quickly becoming regionally known. Careful planning and controlled expansion have been keys to Midstate's success.

Supporting detail

Quote
"When you consider how unstable the airline industry has been the past few years, Midstate's growth is really impressive," *says Midstate President Bryce Appleton.* "We fully believe we can attain our goal as a top carrier in the upper midwest."

Credit reference

Supporting detail
Another 1982 highlight for Midstate was the opening and dedication of the maintenance and operations center at Central Wisconsin Airport. *The 22,000*-square foot hangar/office structure can house up to eight Fairchild Metroliners and a large inventory of parts.

A close relationship with Sentry continues to be an important factor in Midstate's success. The parent company not only represents financial strength and commitment to the airline, but shares many of its goods and services. Human resources, training, and processing equipment have greatly aided Midstate, whose employee count has reached 240.

Entering its 20th year of service, the future looks very bright at Midstate Airlines. The industry may be turbulent at present, but Midstate is quickly establishing its reputation as a strong and dependable airline.

Communications

Communications continued to be an important Sentry enterprise. *Sentry Broadcasting added a new radio station, and Centerpoint, Sentry's new television production company, made impressive strides.*

Main assertion

WYBR-FM in Rockford, Illinois, became Sentry's eleventh radio station. The new station joins AM-FM operations in Stevens Point, Eau Claire, Racine, Springfield (IL) and Sioux City (IA), with new acquisitions being eyed. Sentry Broadcasting showed *a 9.9%* sales increase last year.

Supporting detail

Centerpoint's entry into the world of television programming was one of Sentry Enterprises' more exciting stories. Opening offices in New York and Los Angeles, Centerpoint has assembled a staff of successful television executives. In addition, joint ventures to develop programming have been formed with such noted motion picture and television producers as Blake Edwards, Guber/Peters, Foreman/Jones and Grasso/Jacobson.

Centerpoint's goals are to produce series, movies and specials for the networks, cable/pay television, and video cassettes and disks.

Supporting details

Centerpoint's first productions are now completed. A two-hour made-for-TV movie starring George Segal will air on CBS in fall, 1983. A special for disk is finished, and so is a series pilot for pay cable. In addition, miniseries are being readied for NBC and CBS, and a broadway play is scheduled for the Canadian and U.S. cable markets.

Quote

"We have over 80 creative projects in the developmental stage," says *William Ellis, CEO of Centerpoint.* "The deals we've signed and the people we've hired are quickly establishing us as an important programming source in the entertainment business."

Reference

Recreation

Major topic

The SentryWorld sports complex in Stevens Point *opened to the public in 1982.* With a 65,000 square foot sports center featuring six indoor (and six outdoor) tennis courts, five racquetball courts, a restaurant and lounge, pro shop, and complete locker facilities, SentryWorld's reputation as a total sports facility spread quickly— and that's *before* the golf course opened.

Descriptive details

The SentryWorld Golf Course—18 championship holes designed by noted architect, Robert Trent Jones II—was immensely popular with the golf-playing public. From its opening in July until the winds of October ended the season, reservations were quickly filled.

Nothing characterizes SentryWorld like its floral motif. Five acres of flowers color the course and grounds, and glacial boulders border the four lakes. Magnificent sand traps and undulating greens dot the landscape. Four tees per hole let the golfer select the degree of difficulty.

For 1983, SentryWorld has a variety of golf, tennis, and racquetball tournaments planned. For sport or for spectating, the public is welcome at SentryWorld.

Financial Services

Sentry Financial Services and Sentry Leasing Company (SENCO) *recorded strong performances in 1982.* Sentry Financial Services showed a 13.4% gain (well ahead of GNP totals), and SENCO increased 18.4%. To further strengthen each company, their merger was announced January 1, 1983. This allows both distribution forces to sell each other's products to their customers.

Main assertion

Supporting details

Sentry Financial Services provides money to borrowers planning a major purchase. For example, SFS loans money for cars, campers, mobile homes, boats, and other recreational vehicles. SENCO leases a wide variety of equipment including automobiles, office equipment, farm machinery, and medical technology to a wide range of businesses.

Wood Products

Year-end looked encouraging and inventories are being stocked up in expectation of an improving market. Although U.S. housing starts

Main assertion

were down, Crestline and Vetter streamlined their operations *to better prepare for new jobs in 1983.*

      To strengthen the wood products division, Vetter and Crestline consolidated many of their operations including DP, personnel, engineering, office management, and accounting systems. Production methods have also merged to avoid unnecessary duplication. However, each brand will continue to be marketed separately.

Supporting details

Manufacturing

Reed Industries, Sentry's beverage equipment and security systems enterprise, underwent an investment year in 1982 in anticipation of big sales. This meant retooling and expansion, especially at Reed's headquarters in Stone Mountain, Georgia.

      New products will be introduced this year including home security systems, electronic controls on vending equipment, and the replacement of metal parts and products with equally durable plastics. Although based in the U.S., Reed will be actively developing foreign markets in 1983.

Descriptive details

Consulting

A new diversification project led to formation of *Creative Management Alternatives,* productivity consultants to business and industry. CMA operates under a nontraditional premise: it believes American workers aren't the reason for slumping productivity. Management is. So they've designed work management systems to improve white-collar performance. Currently, CMA is promoting its new business to potential clients.

Main topic

      Sentry is clearly much more than an insurance company. And while we haven't forgotten what made us successful, we look to a carefully planned diversification program to make us an even stronger organization in the next century.

Concluding paragraph

SUMMARY

A report is a highly structured essay including documentation of the facts used and a list of sources. A successful report is a multistep process.

      Before you begin writing the report, decide who will read it. Then choose your words and writing style to fit your audience.

      Next determine your purpose. Ask yourself, "Why am I writing this report?" State your purpose clearly in one or two sentences and keep that statement in front of you as you research and write the report.

      When you know your purpose, begin to research the report. When your research is completed, you should organize your material into a pattern that your essay will follow. This organizational pattern, called an outline, includes main ideas, supporting points, and details. Write your paper following the outline you have prepared. A report follows a typical essay plan. Introduce your paper with a paragraph or two in the beginning, state your purpose and discuss it using good paragraph form, and end your report with a summary paragraph.

When the first draft is written, rewrite for clarity and accuracy. Be sure to give credit to sources of specific information either in the text itself or with footnotes throughout the paper. List your sources at the end.

REVIEW QUESTIONS

1. Explain how the way you write your report is influenced by your knowledge of your audience.
2. How is brainstorming used to organize a report?
3. What are the methods of documenting sources? How does the type of report you are writing influence the method of documentation you use?

ACTIVITIES

1. Prepare either a persuasive or an informational report. Consider yourself part of a business or industry, either a company you have worked for or one you would like to work for. Then choose one of the following projects and prepare a five- to ten-page report including parenthetical references and bibliography.
   a. Choose a problem concerning employees or management at the company. Describe that problem. Offer two or three solutions to the problem and evaluate those solutions. Choose one solution over the others and recommend it to your readers.
   b. Choose a machine, tool, or process that your company is thinking of implementing. Prepare a report evaluating that item. Describe the item in detail and discuss its advantages and disadvantages. Be sure to give enough information about the item so your supervisor can form an opinion.
   c. Select a management concept that your company has implemented to increase productivity. This may be something like quality circles or just-in-time assembly-line arrangement. Write a report explaining the concept so a lay audience can understand it.
      When writing your report, remember to follow the steps discussed in this chapter:
      (1) Analyze your audience
      (2) State your purpose clearly
      (3) Organize carefully
      (4) Document your sources
      (5) Rewrite to polish your organization and sources

13

WRITING BUSINESS LETTERS

In good writing words become one with things.

Emerson

After reading this chapter you should understand:
1. The standard form for business letters
2. How and when to use the direct approach
3. How and when to use the indirect approach

For many people writing letters is a difficult task. We save writing our business letters until late in our workday and put off indefinitely writing letters to our friends. If you approach this chapter reluctantly you are certainly not alone. When asked how they felt about business writing, 71 percent of 200 executives surveyed by Communispond, Inc., a New York communications firm, said they hated or just tolerated writing business correspondence themselves, and 81 percent said the business communication they received was poor to fair.[1] These findings seem to indicate a connection between the executives' reluctance to write and their ability to produce effective letters. Since we usually enjoy the tasks we can do easily and efficiently, it is reasonable to assume that understanding the basics of business letter writing will increase your enjoyment of the task. If you are still reluctant to approach this chapter, remember some findings quoted elsewhere in this section: executives have to write as many as 40 items each week, and that number is on the in-

[1] "Executives Acknowledge Their Lack of Business Writing Skills," *Supervision,* September 1982, p. 9.

crease. You will not be able to avoid writing on the job. Knowing the basics will help you approach your writing tasks more confidently.

BUSINESS LETTER FORM

We often form impressions of people on the basis of how they look. We label well-dressed people as successful or intelligent and poorly dressed people as "down-and-out" or uninformed. Although these labels are often incorrect, we use them all too often to evaluate people. The same is true of business letters. If your letter "looks like" a business letter, it is more likely to get a careful reading. The first step in writing an effective business letter, therefore, is to make it look like a business letter.

There are various patterns to business letters, but each one should include the following:

> Letterhead or return address
> Inside address
> Greeting
> Content
> Closing
> Signature and typed name

Many letters also include the typist's initials, an enclosure notation, and an indication of anyone else who may be receiving copies.

Letters may be physically set up in one of three basic patterns. Figure 13–1 is an example of a *modified-blocked* pattern. Notice that the return address and the signature are on the right hand side of the page and the paragraphs are indented.

This is the most common pattern for business letters. The paragraphs are indented just as the paragraphs of a newspaper or magazine are; therefore, they appear familiar to readers and help them feel more comfortable as they read.

Figure 13–2 illustrates the *blocked* pattern. In this letter the return address and the signature are brought to the left margin, but the paragraphs are indented as they were in the modified-block pattern.

A third pattern, the *full block*, is similar to the block pattern, but everything, including the opening line of each paragraph, is brought to the left margin. It is shown in Figure 13–3. This is a more formal pattern. Because the paragraphs are not indented, we tend to look twice. The pattern seems unusual to us. Consequently, this form is often used for important messages intended for careful reading. Because the typist sets only one margin, the letter can be typed faster and there is less chance for error; therefore, this form is also usually more economical than forms that require indentation.

Whatever form you use, the spacing is the same. Business letters are single spaced with double spacing between paragraphs. Complete standards for spacing are shown in Figure 13–1.

1410 Second Ave.
Milwaukee, WI 53215
February 13, 1984

Ronda Atkins, Superviser
Communications Department
Milwaukee Area Technical College
Milwaukee, WI 53215

Dear Ms. Atkins:

Your correspondence course "Writing Effective Business Letters" sounds interesting, but I would like to know more about course content, tuition, and credits. Your answers to the following questions would help me make a decision about the course.

1. Will the course cover currently preferred letter forms? I have been away from the business world for ten years and I want to be brought up to date on current practices.

2. Will the course discuss ways to write specific letters? In the job I am considering I would have to answer numerous claim letters. I hope to find a course that discusses this subject specifically.

3. Will the course discuss acceptable usages and effective wording of letters? I need a refresher course in those areas.

4. How many credits are offered for the course and can those credits be transferred to an associate degree program at your day school? I am thinking about returning to school in a year or two and I would like to apply credits I earn now on a part-time basis to a full-time program.

5. How much does the course cost? Are books included in the tuition? If not, what are the extra costs for books and materials?

I am very interested in updating my skills and returning to work in the business community. I appreciate whatever information you can give me and look forward to your reply.

Sincerely,

Mary Cotter

Mary Cotter

Figure 13-1 Direct Approach

1410 Second Ave.
Milwaukee, WI 53215
February 13, 1984

Ronda Atkins, Supervisor
Communications Department
Milwaukee Area Technical College
Milwaukee, WI 53215

Dear Ms. Atkins:

    I would like to take your correspondence course in business letter writing. I have been home with my children but they are growing up now--the youngest went to first grade this fall--and I am thinking about going back to work. A refresher course would probably be a good idea for me.

    I am also thinking about returning to school in the Secretarial Science Program but I can't afford it right now so I want to take something that will apply to the program when I can afford to go back to school full-time.

    I'll appreciate any information you can send me about the course. Also, how much does it cost?

    Thanks a lot for your help.

Sincerely,

Mary Cotter

Mary Cotter

Figure 13-2   Indirect Approach

WORDING

Proper form is important to the success of your business letters, but you must also pay close attention to wording. Remember that you will not be sitting next to your readers when they receive your letters. You must choose your words carefully so there is no doubt about your meaning.

All the factors of wording we have discussed elsewhere in this section can be applied to letter writing. Use familiar language and accurate wording.

You must also word your letters so they hold your reader's attention. The best way to make your reader "listen" to you is to word your sentences with the

1410 Second Ave.
Milwaukee, WI 53215
February 13, 1984

Karen Thompson, Personnel Director
Advanced Communications, Inc.
1520 Park St.
Milwaukee, WI 53215

Dear Ms. Thompson:

The position you have offered me as assistant to your media supervisor
sounds like interesting, challenging work. I know I would enjoy working
for a young, forward looking company like yours.

As you know, I have been away from the business world for ten years.
Although the refresher course I took in business letter writing was
helpful, I feel the need to acquire more work-related skills before
accepting a job.

For that reason, I have decided to return to school. I have enrolled in
the Secretarial Science Program at Milwaukee Area Technical College and
will be looking for work again in about two years when I finish the
program.

I appreciate the confidence you have shown in me by offering me this job.
I hope we can discuss job opportunities with your company again when I
have earned an associate degree.

Sincerely,

Mary Cotter

Mary Cotter

Figure 13-3   Three-step Indirect Approach

reader in mind. We call this the *you-focus*. Present your ideas from the reader's viewpoint rather than your own. For example, rather than writing:

It's easier for us to balance our books if you pay cash.

write:

You will receive a 10 percent discount when you save us time by paying in cash.

The wording of the second sentence makes paying in cash desirable for the reader.

In an application letter show the employer how your skills will benefit the company. Rather than writing:

I have managed three different restaurants.

write:

My experience in managing three different restaurants will help me maintain effective organization in your food chain.

Word your letter so the reader is included in your ideas.

ORGANIZATIONAL PATTERNS

Direct Approach

With the direct approach, as the name implies, you come directly to the point. This approach is used in writing most letters of request. It is also used for response letters when you can do what the person making the request wants you to do.

When you are making a request, you should keep the readers' time in mind. Mention your request immediately and tell your readers exactly what you want. Don't expect them to second-guess you. Stay on the topic of the request. Include only ideas and information that pertain directly to the request. Illustrated are two examples of request letters. One is written directly (Figure 13–1), the other is not (Figure 13–2). You can see how much easier the direct letter is to read. You probably find yourself more willing to respond to it also. Because the other letter rambles from idea to idea, it is frustrating and easy to ignore.

When you are responding to a request, you should also keep your reader's time firmly in mind. Answer your reader's questions immediately. Give only the information that has been requested, and make that information easy to find.

Indirect Approach

Although most people usually appreciate a quick and honest answer to their questions, there are times when responding in an indirect manner is more effective.

When you must refuse a request, for example, your refusal will often be accepted better if you use the indirect approach. Direct refusals can cause misunderstandings and hurt feelings. The indirect approach attempts to "soften the blow."

The organizational pattern consists of three steps.

1. Begin with a neutral opening.
2. Give reasons for your refusal.
3. Clearly state your refusal.

Figure 13–3 illustrates this three-step process. The neutral opening eases the readers into the letter. They cannot be sure from reading this paragraph whether you will accept or refuse the request.

Next, give reasons for your refusal before you actually refuse. Most of us dislike being told "no." It is a negative word that tends to prevent further communication. We often are too angry or disappointed to let the person explain the refusal. If your readers can read the reasons before they are actually turned down, and thus have a chance to understand your reasoning, they will accept your refusal more easily.

Another tactic that makes a refusal easier to accept is positive wording of the refusal. You might wonder how you can use positive language to say no; it is really quite easy. Tell people what they *can* do instead of what they *can't do*. For example, you can say:

Positive: Use the sidewalks please.

rather than:

Negative: Keep off the grass.

or:

Positive: Please smoke in the student lounge only.

rather than:

Negative: No smoking is allowed in the library.

Although you will use positive language, make sure your refusal is clear. Sometimes people confuse positive wording with ambiguity. A positively worded refusal should leave no doubt on the reader's mind.

Clear refusal: Until you pay off your current loan of $750.00, we can serve you on a cash-and-carry basis only.
Ambiguous refusal: Currently, we are offering loans to our preferred customers. We may be able to include you in this list sometime.

In the second example your readers are not sure what they should do to become preferred customers or when they will be given a loan. Ambiguous answers will confuse your reader. Confusion leads to frustration and frustration to anger. Since you want to avoid anger when you refuse someone, you will also want to avoid noncommittal statements.

The indirect approach may also be used in sales letters where your purpose is to sell your reader a product or a service. In a sales letter you start out describing the benefits of the product or service, and you tell your readers what you want them to do at the end of the letter. You *convince* them to do something before you *tell* them to do it.

SUMMARY

Writing business letters is easier if you understand a few mechanical and organizational techniques of letter writing. First, be sure you follow an acceptable pattern for business letters. Second, choose either the direct or indirect approach to organization. The direct approach allows you to come immediately to the point. It saves you and the reader time and is an efficient organization for most request and response letters.

The indirect approach is appropriate for sales letters and for letters where you must refuse a request. It allows you to give reasons for the refusal first. This usually makes the refusal easier to accept.

DISCUSSION QUESTIONS

1. Which of the two letter patterns presented in this chapter do you prefer? Explain your answer.
2. How is the direct approach different from the indirect approach?
3. Can you think of a time when you received an indirect answer and you would have appreciated a direct answer? What are some of the problems that may be encountered with the indirect approach? How can these be overcome?

ACTIVITIES

1. Rewrite the following statements so they are focused on the reader.
   a. We are offering you $200 off on a microwave oven when you buy a dishwasher from us.
   b. Our beautiful city has everything a tourist could want.
   c. I have five years' experience as a computer programmer.
   d. We can offer you a wholesale price of $10 per jacket. They sell retail for $20 each.
   e. We will deliver your chair on Thursday.
   f. We ask you to walk slowly near the pool.
   g. Our records show that you are behind with your January payment.
   h. Our company policy allows men or women to take a leave of absence for child care.
2. Change the following statements from negative to positive wording.
   a. I'm sorry, but I cannot keep our appointment today.
   b. Because you misunderstood my directions, you took the wrong turn.
   c. I regret our delay in sending you the merchandise.
   d. You cannot tour our factory except during the regularly scheduled tours on Tuesday and Thursday.
   e. You arrived late for our appointment. That's why I was not in my office.
   f. Don't go near the restricted area.
   g. You won't gain weight eating our sugarless candy.
   h. Please be patient with the inconvenience our remodeling causes.

3. Write a letter requesting information about a product or service. Use the direct approach and follow all the techniques of writing a letter of request discussed in this chapter.
4. Write a letter refusing a request. Use the indirect approach and follow all the techniques of writing a letter of refusal discussed in this chapter. Use one of the following ideas or choose a topic of your own.
   Refuse a request to:
   a. Speak at a convention related to your major area.
   b. Donate money to a charity of your choice
   c. Buy a set of encyclopedias
   d. Enroll your child in a special school
   e. Join the YMCA
   f. Serve on the Board of Education at your church or synagogue
   g. Take a job in another city

PART V   Reading

Carol is a buyer for Teddies & Trains, a chain of boutiques specializing in unique children's toys. She is responsible for the Great Lakes division, five stores located in Michigan and Wisconsin.

July is an especially busy time for Carol. During that month she orders toys for the holiday season, when Teddies & Trains does 50 percent of its business. Carol's boss has told her, "If we don't have merchandise that sells well during November and December, we won't make it through the next summer." Every July Carol studies the toy catalogs, trying to decide what children will want from Santa next Christmas.

In July, though, Carol also likes to work on her tan, so one especially hot afternoon, when the airconditioner seems to have given up keeping her office cool, Carol takes her duffel bag from the closet, stuffs some toy catalogs in with her swimsuit and beach towel, and heads for the ocean.

Soon Carol is comfortably settled in the soft sand. As the sun warms her back, she reluctantly pulls the toy catalogs from her bag.

Just as she opens the first catalog, Jack shouts, "Hey, Carol! How about a game of volleyball?"

"No, thanks," Carol answers, "I have to read these catalogs."

"Too bad," Jack says, "we're going to win this one. Just watch!"

Keeping one eye on the game, Carol leafs idly through the pamphlets and brochures she has brought from the office. Briefly she looks at a brochure describing a new game called Castles and Ghosts. A salesman from Games Gallery had dropped it on her desk a few days ago.

"A great game," he had said. But when she tried to ask him more about it, he had answered, "I'm in a hurry. Just read the brochure. Everything's written up in there."

"Look at this! Look at this!" a shrill voice calls, and Carol's attention snaps back to the beach. A little boy is proudly showing a sand castle to his mother.

Then she hears Jack's excited voice. "Carol, we won," he yells. "Losers are treating us to a pizza in town. Want to come along?"

"As soon as I finish my reading," Carol answers.

As the volleyball team noisily leaves for its pizza and the little boy and his mother head home for a nap, Carol settles down to finish her reading. But the warm sun makes her drowsy.

"Castles and Ghosts," she murmurs dreamily. "Sounds like a good game." Then she writes her secretary a note: "Order 20 of these games!"

Two weeks later Carol is in one of the stores when Castles and Ghosts arrives. Twenty castles, each four feet high, fill the storeroom and clutter the hall.

"What is this?" Carol asks as the delivery man unloads the last castle.

"It's the game you ordered," Dan, the delivery man, tells her.

"A game," Carol says, surprised. "I wouldn't have ordered a game with a four-foot castle. No mother has room for a game like that in her house."

Dan shrugs. "Your name is on the order," he says. Then he adds, "It's sent to you C.O.D., so I'll just wait for the cash."

"C.O.D.!" Carol exclaims. "Our policy is to pay 60 days after we receive the merchandise."

"Not from this company," Dan explains. Out of his pocket he pulls a crumbled brochure just like the one Carol had taken to the beach. "See, it says right here: 'Terms— Cash on delivery.' "

"I suppose it also says the castles are four feet high," Carol says, ruefully.

"Sure does," Dan says. He points to the caption under one of the pictures.

"I guess I didn't read the brochure very carefully," Carol says as she goes to the office to write Dan a check.

DISCUSSION OF SCENARIO

When Dan leaves, Carol thinks about the situation.

Her inefficient reading has caused many problems:

First, she has ordered a game that she knows will be very difficult to sell.

Second, she has twenty—not just one or two—of these games on her hands.

Third, she has been required to pay cash for the games several months before she can actually begin to sell them.

"How could I have made such a costly mistake?" Carol asks herself. "I read the brochure."

But did Carol read the brochure? Let's go back to that day at the beach.

The first mistake Carol makes is trying to read the brochure at the beach. She is immediately distracted from her reading, first by Jack and the volleyball game and then by the little boy building sand castles. Everyone except Carol is playing. As a result, she has a difficult time concentrating on her work.

Even when most of the people leave and the beach is quieter, Carol has difficulty concentrating. The sun lulls her toward sleep. Although her eyes see the words, her drowsy brain does not register what she is reading.

Carol's mistake is not entirely her fault, though. The salesman who left her the brochure must assume some of the responsibility. Because he was in a hurry, he did not take time to introduce the reading material to her. If he had said, "We've made some changes in our payment policy" or "This game is a little different from the games we've sold in the past," Carol would have been alerted to reading specifically for that information.

HOW WELL DO YOU READ?

Although fictional, Carol's problem may have reminded you of a time when you could have read more efficiently. Maybe you would have made better connections if you had read a bus schedule more carefully. You might have gotten a job or won a sweepstakes contest if you had read the directions on the form thoroughly.

How would you rate your reading skills? The following test will help you evaluate your reading efficiency. First, read the selection through as quickly as you can. Be sure to check the time immediately before you start reading and as soon as you stop. When you finish reading, write down the number of seconds it took you to read the passage. Divide 41,700 (695 words x 60) by the number of seconds you needed to read the passage. This will give you the number of words you read per minute in this instance. Your score on this passage is an indication of how many words per minute you usually read.

You Can Beat That Beat Feeling

All too often doctors hear complaints like this: "I feel so tired, I just can't get going. . . . Even after a night's sleep, I can barely drag myself out of bed. . . . During the day, I often nod off when I should be working."

Whether you call it fatigue or exhaustion, that tired feeling ranks near the top of a list of reasons Americans say they seek medical help. Concern over fatigue each year sends more than eight million people to the doctor seeking relief.

If you feel bushed after mowing the lawn, painting the living room or jogging a couple of miles around the neighborhood, you know the reason for your weariness and you forget it. With rest and a night's sleep, your body overcomes the draining biochemical changes that muscular exertion produces and you are primed for the beginning of a new day.

But chronic fatigue leaves its victims with a washed-out feeling that won't go away. "It seems that such fatigue overtaxes the body somewhat the way the heart can be overtaxed in physical disease," says Dr. John L. Bulette, an authority on fatigue and chairman of the Department of Psychiatry at the Allentown Hospital in Pennsylvania.

Debilitating tiredness can also be a warning signal of a plethora of conditions listed in the medical textbooks. At the University of Colorado's Department of Family Medicine, medical reasons accounted for just over half of the 176 cases of fatigue diagnosed in a year-long study, which found the condition predominantly among patients age 15 to 34. Although more than half of those were blamed on prolonged recuperation from viruses, doctors also picked up cases of more serious underlying diseases.

The longer fatigue lasts, the greater chance that the cause is psychological, not medical. Telling the two apart is not always easy. But Dr. Frederick Lewis, a Denver psychiatrist, starts with two questions. "I ask whether fatigue gets worse when you do something physical. If it does, the cause is probably something physical. Or I ask whether tiredness gets better if you exert yourself. If it does, then the cause is probably psychological". . . .

Many Faces of Fatigue

Because fatigue occurs in so many guises and can be linked to nearly every medical condition imaginable, diagnosis must boil down to a process of elimination. For the sake of simplicity, doctors separate fatigue into several main categories, though the symptoms may overlap.

Psychological fatigue. Overextenders often manage to work themselves into a state of physical exhaustion without ever being aware of the reason. They burn the candle at both ends, stinting on sleep, perhaps while holding a job and going to school part-time. Other gluttons are zealous exercisers, who have to hear from a doctor that they're taking their bodies beyond reasonable limits in trying to achieve fitness.

Mental fatigue. "Contrary to psychological fatigue, mental fatigue responds best to action," writes Dr. Marion Graham in *Inner Energy: How to Overcome Fatigue* (Sterling Publishing Co.). Mental exhaustion frequently shows up as a result of concentrating intensely while doing a boring and repetitious task. Typing or standing for hours on an assembly line, for example, is likely to bring it on—and with it headaches and eyestrain. The longer the repetition, the greater the fatigue.

Emotional fatigue. A more ominous kind of exhaustion is commonly associated with inner stress. Unrelenting anxiety saps the body's energy. Emotional fatigue often shows up in people who are irritable and restless and who concentrate, sleep and eat poorly. Of such anxiety-ridden patients, Graham writes: "Careful questioning of a completely honest person commonly reveals a deep-seated job dislike or disinterest, either as a result of a square-peg-in-a-round-hole syndrome or of repeated frustrations or hostilities in connection with the job."

But it's not always so simple. Emotional fatigue sometimes stems from depression—a deeper mental disturbance. One common type, endogenous depression, arises from within and can't be pinned on environmental stresses. Insomnia is one telltale symptom of depression and by itself may account for otherwise unexplained fatigue. Hearing the doctor suggest that fatigue might be depression in disguise comes as a complete surprise to some patients.[1]

· · ·

How did you do? You may be surprised to learn that the average reading speed for a high school graduate is 250–300 words per minute. Do you read faster or slower than average?

Reading speed, of course, is not the only indicator of your reading efficiency. Comprehension, or how well you understand the material, is another factor in rating how skillfully you read. The average comprehension rate for a high school graduate is 75 percent.

To test your comprehension, answer the following questions about the selection you have just read.

Test

1. How many people see doctors each year because of fatigue? (5 points)
2. What is chronic fatigue? (10 points)
3. According to a study done at the University of Colorado, what age group is most subject to fatigue? (10 points)
4. If tiredness gets better when you exert yourself, the cause of your fatigue is probably _____. (10 points)
5. What are the three main categories into which doctors separate fatigue?
   _____ (5 points)
   _____ (5 points)
   _____ (5 points)
6. When you overexert yourself, you can suffer from _____ fatigue. (10 points)
7. What fatigue is cured quickest by getting some exercise or doing other activities? (10 points)
8. Standing for hours on an assembly line can result in _____ fatigue. (10 points)
9. Inner stress results in _____ fatigue. (10 points)

[1]Reprinted with permission from *Changing Times* Magazine, © 1983 Kiplinger Washington Editors, Inc., Apr., 1983. This reprint is not to be altered in any way, except with permission from *Changing Times.*

10. _____ is a symptom of depression that may also cause fatigue. (10 points)

Total points: _____

Now compare your answers with the answers given at the bottom of the page. Total the points of your correct answers to find out your percentage of comprehension. Then compare your reading speed with your reading comprehension. Did you fall within the average range of 250–300 w.p.m. and 75–80% comprehension? If both your reading rate and your reading comprehension were lower than average, you should begin now to improve your reading skills.

Comparing your speed and comprehension may indicate other problems. It may show that you are reading rapidly but not understanding what you read (high reading rate, low comprehension score), or it might indicate just the opposite, that even though you are comprehending what you read, your slow reading rate shows inefficient reading practice. Even if your scores fall within the average range, you can increase your reading rate and sharpen your comprehension skills by understanding some of the techniques of efficient reading. You may want to set a goal for yourself of increasing your reading rate by 50 or 100 words per minute while you maintain 75–80% comprehension. The material discussed in the next two chapters will help you reach your personal reading goal.

Answers to quiz for "You Can Beat That Beat Feeling"

1. 8 million
2. Tiredness that won't go away; seems to affect the body in a way similar to heart disease
3. 15–34 years of age
4. Mental fatigue
5. Mental, Emotional, Physiological
6. Physiological
7. Mental
8. Mental
9. Emotional
10. Insomnia

14

THE READING PROCESS

"What is reading but silent conversation?"

Walter Savage Landar

After studying this chapter you should understand:
1. Reasons for learning to read efficiently
2. The physical process of reading
3. Efficient reading habits including eye fixations, phrase reading, and pacing
4. How unproductive reading habits hinder efficient reading

Most of us learned to read so long ago that we have forgotten that reading is a learned skill. Reading seems as natural to us as breathing. But reading is not a natural bodily function like breathing; it is a technique we learn and refine with practice.

REASONS FOR LEARNING TO READ EFFICIENTLY

There are many reasons why we should practice reading. The ability to do a job more efficiently is probably the reason foremost in your mind. Workers must read memos, reports, service manuals, and catalogs daily in order to complete their work assignments. A department chief at Western Electric estimates that his managers spend one-third to one-half of their working day reading. Another study of 100 workers from a variety of occupations reveals that they spend an average of 113 minutes (nearly 2 hours) per day reading.[1] The more skillfully you can do your work-related reading, the easier your job will be.

There are also other reasons for refining your reading skills. To keep our country running smoothly, we must stay informed about national and international issues. Every day we are confronted with numerous newspapers and magazines, each filled with the events of the day and opinions about them. Often we are asked to make decisions that affect the direction the country will take on major issues. We must read efficiently to keep up with the current news so we can make informed decisions.

A third reason to read efficiently is to increase enjoyment of our leisure time. The latest books are often a topic of social conversation. Efficient readers will have time and energy after they have finished their work-related reading to read for enjoyment. When you read efficiently, you do not have to be left out of a conversation about a good book because you have not had time to read it. Refining your reading skills will add to your efficiency at work and your enjoyment of leisure time.

THE READING PROCESS

There are three stages in the process of developing and refining reading techniques.

Motor Stage

Most of us began reading by saying each word to ourselves. This is the motor stage of reading development. Motor readers say aloud, whisper, or just form each word with their mouths. They can read only as fast as they can say each word. You may remember your first-grade teacher telling you to keep your lips together during silent reading time. She may have told you that you bother your neighbor when you whisper. Actually, your teacher was probably more concerned with your reading development than with your classmate's concentration. She knew if she could encourage you to stop saying each word as you read it, you would improve your reading technique.

Auditory Stage

When you learned to read "instantly," you probably moved into the second stage of reading development, the auditory stage. Auditory readers do not whisper the words they read, but they still hear the words. Auditory readers must think each word as they read it. They actually "hear" the word echoed in their minds.

You can probably think of times when you have been an auditory reader. Maybe you were reading a difficult chapter in a textbook, or you may have been try-

---

[1] Larry Mikulecky, "Job Literacy: The Relationship Between School Preparation and Workplace Actuality," Reading Research Quarterly, 1982, 17, No. 3, p. 402.

ing to repair your car following the directions in a do-it-yourself manual. You read slowly, letting each word sink in. Auditory readers read faster than motor readers, but because they must "hear" each word in their thoughts, they do not read as efficiently as they could.

Sight Stage

The most efficient reader is the sight reader. Sight reading is the third stage of reading development. These readers use their eyes like cameras: The eye records the image and the reader understands the thought instantly—just like taking a picture with a camera. Click and the image is recorded. Since sight readers do not have to say or think each word, they can read quickly and effortlessly.

Our goal in reading efficiently is to become sight readers. To reach this goal, we must practice the skills of efficient reading.

EFFICIENT READING SKILLS

Increasing Eye Span

One reading skill is the ability to read quickly. In order to increase your reading speed, you should understand the physical process of reading. Let's say that the illustration below indicates possible eye movements along a line of type. The first example shows the eye moving smoothly in a straight line across the page. The second example shows the eye moving in jerks, stopping on one spot, then "leaping" to another spot on the page. In the third example the eye also moves in jerks, but the stops are farther apart, so the leaps are longer.

~~This example shows how the eye moves smoothly.~~

This example shows how the eye moves in short jerks.

This example shows how the eye can move in longer movements.

Which process do you think is the most efficient? Many people would choose the first illustration. We tend to think anything that moves smoothly is efficient. But that is not the way our eyes read.

When we read, our eyes stop at certain places along the line. These stops are called *fixations*. You can't feel your own eyes stopping, then leaping to another place on the page, but you can watch someone else's eyes reading this way. Sit across from someone and watch the person read. You will find that the reader's eyes move across the page in jerks rather than in a smooth line. You may want to watch and compare several readers. You will probably find that some read with fewer fixations than others. The fewer fixations we make, the faster we can read; therefore, the third example shows the most efficient way of reading.

You might compare reading with running errands. The more stops you have to make during the day, the more time it takes you to complete your errands. If you can do everything with two or three stops, you are finished more quickly. You are probably less tired, too, because continually stopping your car and running into a store can be exhausting.

The same is true of reading. The fewer times you have to fixate on a line while you are reading it, the more quickly you will finish the line and the less tired you will be when you have finished reading.

Practice will help you decrease the number of fixations you make. Look at the example below. Each dot represents a fixation. The space between the lines represents the reader's eye span. Now look directly at the first dot. Can you see all the letters between the two lines? If you can, you probably have an eye span equal to that of other college students.

> *The Wired Sky*
>
> Communications companies are
>
> now in the process of replacing the
>
> copper wires in the ground that
>
> carry information by means of elec-
>
> trical impulses with strands of glass
>
> that carry information through
>
> pulses of light. These optical fibers
>
> offer such vastly improved signal-
>
> carrying capacity that a single fiber
>
> one-fifth the thickness of a human
>
> hair can do the work of 10,000 ordi-
>
> nary telephone wires.[2]

Now read the entire passage, fixating your eye on the dots only. Did you understand what you read? If you had difficulty seeing all the letters between the lines, you may want to practice increasing your eye span.

Take a newspaper and draw two evenly spaced lines down one of the col-

---

[2] Charles L. Gould and C. R. Gerber, "Skynet 2000," *The Futurist,* February 1983, p. 5.

umns. Practice fixating your eye on the line until you can take in all the letters on either side of each line. A newspaper works especially well for this because the column width is typically narrow, but any printed page will do, as long as you draw the lines approximately as the example above shows, placing the line about ten or eleven letters apart.

As you develop the ability to read examples like the one above comfortably, increase the number of letters between dots and practice increasing your eye span accordingly.

You will notice that the dots are placed above the line of type rather than on the line. There are two reasons for this. First, it is easier to start slightly above the line of print and allow your eyes to glide down the page naturally. Second, the tops of the letters in our alphabet give a better clue to the entire letter than the bottom of the letters. This is shown in the following example.

Therefore, when you are reading, if you look slightly

Therefore, when you are reading, if you look slightly

Therefore, when you are reading, if you look slightly above, you will see the words more clearly. The more clearly you can see the words, the less effort you need to exert when you read. As a result, you will have more energy to put into thinking about what you read.

Phrase Reading

Closely related to the concept of increasing your eye span is the technique of phrase reading, that is, grouping words together in meaningful phrases. For example, rather than reading each word in the following selection individually and putting the ideas together at the end, you group the words into meaningful phrases as you read. The second illustration shows how you can group these words into phrases.

"Vision is a learned skill. It is not something that is predestined," explains Dr. Stephen Miller, director of the primary care division of the American Optometric Association. "A lot of things that affect our vision are environmental—caused by the way we use our eyes and by the kinds of lives we live." To specialists in a field called behavioral optometry, seeing is not simply a mechanical process but an integrated feedback system between eyes, emotions, and intellect.[3]

"Vision . . learned skill, . . not . . . predestined," explains Dr. Stephen Miller, director . . primary care division . . American Optometric Association. "A lot . things . affect . vision . environmental—caused   by . way . use . eyes . . . kinds . lives . live." . specialists . . . . behavioral optometry, seeing . not . . mechanical process but . integrated feedback system between eyes, emotions, . intellect.[4]

[3] Leonore Levy, "Teach Yourself to See Better," *Science Digest*, August 1982, p. 34.
[4] *Ibid.*

One study of 1,700 college students showed that the average eye span among these college readers was 11.1 words. Another study indicates that we can see about four letters to the left of a fixation and six letters to the right. That's a total of about ten letters per fixation.[5]

You can see that you grasp the meaning of the passage more quickly when you read by phrases. To phrase read effectively, you should overcome the notion that a good reader reads every word. Actually you can skip many words in a paragraph and still grasp the paragraph's meaning.

You will accept the concept of phrase reading more easily when you understand that our language has two kinds of words: key words and function words. *Key words* are words that give meaning to the sentence. They are usually nouns, verbs, and modifying words. They may also be words that signal a comparison or a contrast between ideas such as *however, also,* and *but. Function words,* on the other hand, do not convey meaning. They simply make sentences read smoothly. These words may be prepositions or auxiliary words in verb phrases such as "*in* our house" (*in* is a preposition) or "*has been* walking," (*has been* are auxiliary words in the verb phrase *has been walking*).

Although function words tend to be short, word length should not be your main reason for skipping or including words as you phrase read. For example, *not* is a short word, but in the sentence:

To specialists in a field called behavioral optometry, seeing is *not* simply a mechanical process but an integrated feedback system between eyes, emotions, and intellect.

not and *but* are basic to the meaning of the sentence. If you skip over them, you change the entire meaning of the sentence. Then your thought is:

seeing *is* simply a mechanical process

In that same sentence *an* and *a* are function words. They help the idea flow smoothly but they do not represent the idea themselves. You can leave them out without altering the meaning of the sentences.

Now let's look at the example we used at the beginning of this section. You will remember that we read it in meaningful phrases this way.

"Vision . . learned skill. . . not . . . predestined," explains Dr. Stephen Miller, director . . primary care division . . American Optometric Association. "A lot . things . affect . vision . environmental—caused   by . way . use . eyes . . . kinds . lives . live." . specialists . . . . behavioral optometry, seeing . not . . mechanical process by . integrated feedback system between eyes, emotions, . intellect.[6]

While reading, we kept in mind the difference between key words and function words. As a result, we were able to skip over many words and still retain the meaning.

[5] Walter Pauk, "Reading in Meaningful Phrases," *Reading World,* May 1981, p. 286.
[6] Levy, "Teach Yourself to See Better."

Now let's disregard word meaning and make our selection on word length.

"Vision . . learned skill . . . . something . . predestined," explains . Stephen Miller, director . . primary care division . . American Optometric Association. " . . . things . affect . vision . environmental—caused . . . ." . specialists . . field called behavioral optometry, seeing . . . . mechanical process . . integrated feedback system between eyes, emotions, and intellect.[7]

In this example several important ideas are lost. The grouping of the first two sentences sounds like vision is predestined to be a learned skill. The author's actual meaning is just the opposite. By skipping over the little signal word *not*, we miss the contrast between the two sentences. The same thing happens when we skip *not* in the last sentence. Seeing becomes a mechanical process.

When you phrase read, remember to read key words and signal words. Only function words, those words that do not convey meaning, can be successfully skipped.

Pacing

Thus far we have talked about increasing reading efficiency by understanding the physical process of reading. We discussed how the eye sees things and how it moves across a line of type. Then we applied this process to the concept of phrase reading. Efficient readers make use of these concepts to increase their reading speed.

But speed alone does not make a reader efficient. Efficient readers also understand and remember what they read. They think beyond the process of reading to consider the material they are reading. They know that the type of material will determine how fast they can successfully read. Some material can be grasped more quickly than others. For example, we can understand most ideas in a newspaper more quickly than we can understand the definition of an electrical charge as explained in an electronics test.

Therefore, efficient readers vary the speed at which they read, depending on the type of material they are reading. This technique is called *pacing*. To pace yourself successfully, you need to know the purpose for which you are reading. Are you reading for enjoyment or information? Are you concerned about facts or ideas? Do you intend to evaluate what you read? These are some of the questions you should ask yourself before you begin reading.

If you are reading a novel or magazine article for enjoyment, you can read quickly through the material, savoring the story. A few days later you may not remember details about the selection, but you will remember the story generally and will know whether or not you enjoyed the selection. If, however, you read a training manual in the same casual way, you would probably find that when you finished the reading, you still did not know how to do the task. In this case you

[7] *Ibid.*

needed to read slowly for detail, thinking carefully about the directions and picturing the procedure in your mind as you read. Knowing your purpose for reading the material will help you pace yourself as you read.

Let's think back to the story of Carol at the beginning of the section. If Carol had understood the concept of pacing, she could have avoided the costly mistake she made. Because Carol attempted to read business material at the beach, where she was continually distracted, she gained only a superficial impression of the game she was reading about. She read the advertising report as she would have read a leisure magazine. Her mind was on fun instead of business. If she had understood that efficient readers read different things in different ways, she would have chosen to read her catalogs in her office, where her thoughts were on business. She would have brought a favorite magazine to the beach.

The following example will help you understand how knowing your purpose will help you read efficiently. Here are two similar passages. Read the first one without any advanced preparation. When you have finished, answer the question following the passage and check your answer against answer A on the last page of this chapter.

GI Robots

The speed, precision, and cost-effectiveness that make robots attractive to private manufacturing are also making them attractive to the military.

Robots enhanced with sensors and with artificial intelligence—computer programming that enables them to "think"—would be able to take over many routine or dangerous jobs of soldiers, or even to do things soldiers cannot do, says a report by Dennis V. Crumley of the Futures/Long Range Planning Group of the U.S. Army War College's Strategic Studies Institute. Some tasks that smart robots may be able to perform on the twenty-first century battlefield are:

Identify aircraft, control air traffic, and transmit deceptive noises to confuse the enemy.

Identify and track targets and select the highest-priority target from among several on the battlefield.

Handle materials that have been contaminated during nuclear, chemical, or biological warfare.

Load weapons, set fuses, and transfer rounds of ammunition from storage areas to guns.

Collect, correlate, and transmit information about the enemy to command posts.

Detect enemy minefields and implant "smart" mines capable of recognizing enemy movements.

Dig ditches, make craters, or build obstacles based on the robot's programmed knowledge of the enemy, reducing the need for soldiers to perform these routine tasks.

· · ·

The report emphasizes that research and development of robotic technology have not yet been aggressively pursued in the United States, and, for the Army to take full advantage of robot potential, "an effort on the scale of the Manhattan Project would likely be required." Since such an effort is unrealistic at present, Crumley concludes that to make best use of robots, the Army should establish priorities; the most important potential applications should then be pursued with further research and development.[8]

Now answer this question: Name four of the seven areas in which the military could use robots in the future. Answer A is on the last page of this chapter.

Now read the second selection. Your purpose in reading is to find out what the military may use robots for in the future. When you have finished, answer the question following the passage. Answer B is on the last page of this chapter.

GI Robots

The speed, precision, and cost-effectiveness that make robots attractive to private manufacturing are also making them attractive to the military.

. . .

The greatest near- to mid-term potential applications for robots in the military, however, will probably be off the battlefield, the report notes. For example, physical examinations could be automated—an expansion on the coin-operated blood-pressure machines found in shopping centers today. Robots with artificial intelligence could conduct aptitude tests, process payrolls, issue uniforms or equipment, and perform other administrative chores. Another application could be computer-assisted training in weaponry, with robot targets, automatic scoring, and voice-supported critiques of trainees' performances.

Other military uses of robots could include space exploration, underwater search for enemy mines and submarines, and situation assessment during or after a nuclear strike when people may be under too much stress to make rational judgments.

The report emphasizes that research and development of robotic technology have not yet been aggressively pursued in the United States, and, for the Army to take full advantage of robot potential, "an effort on the scale of the Manhattan Project would likely be required." Since such an effort is unrealistic at present, Crumley concludes that to make best use of robots, the Army should establish priorities; the most important potential applications should then be pursued with further research and development.[9]

Now answer this question:

Name four things the military may use robots for in the future.

Did the first question surprise you? Did you find answering the second question easier? You probably found that knowing your purpose helped you get more from the reading.

UNPRODUCTIVE READING HABITS

Regression

As you read the second passage above, you may have found yourself rereading parts of the selection until you were sure you understood the writer's meaning. Rereading for understanding is a necessary part of efficient reading.

[8] "GI Robots," *The Futurist*, February 1983, p. 29.
[9] *Ibid.*

However, rereading may also be an unproductive reading habit. Sometimes people reread because they have not been paying close attention to the words in the first place. Other times people reread just as a habit rather than for a useful purpose. This unnecessary rereading is called *regression*.

Regression is the tendency to check up on yourself, to do something again just to make sure it was done right the first time. For example, if you start to leave the house, then turn back to make sure you have turned out the lights or locked the door, you are repeating something you have already done. You know the door is locked or the lights turned off, but you feel better after you have checked one more time.

Some people do the same thing when they read. Every few sentences they stop and reread what they have just read. Although they understood the selection the first time, they feel more confident if they reread it. This regression slows down reading speed and makes the reading process inefficient.

Regression should not be confused with rereading for meaning. Rereading a difficult passage to gain understanding is a technique of efficient reading. Rereading passages you can easily understand the first time is an unproductive reading habit.

If you habitually reread, you should begin to break yourself of the habit. When you start reading, tell yourself that you will not reread any part of the selection. Then, regardless of how strong the urge is to reread, do not allow yourself the "luxury" of regressing. Make yourself continue reading ahead. When you have finished the selection, think about what you have read. Recall as many details as you can. Then look over the selection again to see how accurately you grasped the material the first time. You will probably be surprised to discover that you took in most of the material with the first reading. When you feel confident of your ability to grasp meaning with the first reading, you will be encouraged to break the regression habit.

Lack of Concentration

Another unproductive reading habit is lack of concentration. When you allow yourself to daydream while you read, you can't remember what you have read. This habit in turn may lead to regression because you must reread the selection for meaning.

Lack of concentration was one of the problems shown by the scenario at the beginning of this section. Carol couldn't keep her mind on the material she was reading. First the volleyball game, then the little boy shouting to his mother, and finally the invitation to join the team for a pizza distracted her. She lost interest in the brochure and probably told herself she had read it when in reality she had merely turned the pages.

Efficient readers make sure they are ready to concentrate before they begin reading. First they find a place where they can concentrate. A quiet setting, adequately lighted, is necessary for complete concentration. Although you should be comfortable, you may find that sinking into the softest chair in the room hinders rather than helps your concentration. Reading in bed or in an overstuffed lounge chair may put you to sleep.

Know your purpose for reading and choose your setting accordingly. If you are reading for information or ideas, you will probably read most efficiently in a businesslike setting. Choose a desk or table where you can take notes as you read. If you are reading for enjoyment, that lounge chair may be just the thing you need to help you relax and get involved in a good story.

Another important factor in concentration is your state of mind. Are you ready to begin reading? Before you start to read a selection, make sure you are willing to concentrate on your reading. We can all remember times when we have daydreamed through an entire chapter and then had no idea what we had read. If you feel like jogging or making a phone call, perhaps you had better do that before you start reading. Then your mind will be willing to concentrate when you do start to read.

Think of reading as a commitment you have to do a job. Eliminate as many distractions as possible, and then discipline yourself to concentrate on the material you are reading.

Insufficient Vocabulary

A third unproductive reading habit is skimming over words you don't know or phrases you don't understand. Words are the tools a reader uses to put meanings together. Just as a plumber cannot fix a clogged drain without the proper tools, so a reader cannot understand a selection without sufficient vocabulary.

Acquiring vocabulary is an ongoing process; you should continue to add words to your working vocabulary throughout your life. In fact, you must keep adding words to your vocabulary, because many of the words you use today were not used a decade ago. *Petropolitics, careerism* and *stagflation* are examples of words that have been coined recently to meet our need to communicate as the world changes.

You can increase your vocabulary while you read. When you come to an unfamiliar word, ask yourself if you can recognize any part of the word. For example, you can separate *petropolitics* into *petro* and *politics*. You know what *politics* mean. If you also know that *petro* means oil, you can define *petropolitics* as "politics influenced by or concerning oil." In the same way, since you know what *career* means, you can define careerism as "the practice of advancing your career." If looking at the word does not give you enough clue to its meaning, noticing how it is used in the context may help you define it. For example, you might read:

Stagflation is undermining our confidence.

In this case *stagflation* could be many things. It could be violence in the streets, unemployment, or a prophecy about the end of the world. But when we read the next sentence:

This combination of rising unemployment and spiralling inflation makes investors uncertain about the future of the economy.

we know that *stagflation* is an economic condition combining high unemployment with high inflation. Stagflation has been defined in the context of the writing.

If the context does not offer you enough of a clue to the word's meaning, look the word up in the dictionary. A dictionary should be close at hand for words you can't figure out by one of the other techniques. Even when you think you can define a word by looking at its parts or seeing how it is used in context, you should use a dictionary to double check your understanding.

When you learn the meaning of an unfamiliar word, add the word to your working vocabulary. Use the word in your own writing or in your conversation until it comes naturally to you. The more extensive your vocabulary is, the easier it will be for you to read efficiently.

SUMMARY

Since studies show that workers spend between one-quarter and one-half of their workday reading, it is important for us to refine our reading skills.

As readers we move through three stages of development: motor, auditory, and sight. A sight reader is the most efficient reader. Our goal as readers is to learn to read by sight.

Understanding the physical process of reading is an important factor in increasing reading efficiency. Our eyes read by fixating periodically along a line of type. Increasing your eye span and learning to read in phrases will help you read faster. Avoiding unnecessary regression and increasing your vocabulary will help you understand quickly what you are reading.

Control of the reading situation is the key to efficient reading. Choose a place where you can concentrate on the material you are reading. You should know your purpose for reading and should control your reading speed and your reading environment accordingly. For example, read a textbook or work assignment more slowly and with more concentration than a mystery novel you have picked up for fun. The technique of judging how intently you need to read a selection is called *pacing*.

REVIEW QUESTIONS

1. How are the three stages of reading development different? At which stage do you think you read? At what stage should the most efficient reader read?
2. In order to read faster, we can increase our eye span and learn to read in meaningful phrases. How do these two techniques work together to increase our reading efficiency?
3. What is pacing and how is it important to efficient reading?
4. After thinking about what you have just read, what would you say will help us most to achieve reading efficiency?
5. How can the place where you read help or hinder the reading process?

ACTIVITIES

1. Practice increasing your eye span. Fixate your eyes on the dot above each line. Move your eyes steadily down the page. Can you see each entire line with just one fixation?

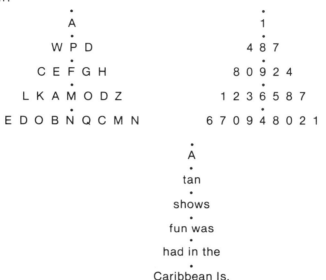

2. Underline the key words in the following paragraph. Then phrase-read using your underlining as a guide. When you have finished, write a brief summary of the paragraph. Then read the paragraph through word for word.

> Tension headaches (or stress headaches) are probably the most common kind. When you get tense, your neck and head muscles tighten and their blood vessels constrict. Then they expand—and you feel a dull, throbbing ache, either in your temples or the back of your head. The obvious way to get rid of a tension headache is to get rid of the tension—by meditating, walking, rubbing your cramped neck muscles, or sitting down with your eyes closed in a dark, quiet room.[10]

Did you miss any key ideas when you phrase-read the material? If you did, reevaluate your phrase-reading technique.

3. Now that you have practiced the individual parts of rapid reading, put the skills you have acquired to use. See how rapidly you can read the following selection. Then take the quiz following it. Remember that you want to increase your reading speed while you maintain at least 75–80 percent comprehension.

    Your purpose in reading is to learn about the different kinds of headaches and their probable causes. When you have finished reading, record your time in seconds here _____. Then divide that number into 19,680 (328 words x 60). That will give you your score in words per minute.

[10]Gabe Mirkin, "Headaches," *Health*, January 1982, p. 48. Copyright 1982 Family Media, Inc. All rights reserved.

What Is a Headache?

It's the commonest ailment in the country, affecting 90 percent of all Americans. Throbbing and pounding, it generates billions of dollars each year for aspirin manufacturers. Yet despite its universality, the simple pain in the head is not completely understood.

"It's only in the past decade that we've begun to understand the pain mechanisms, and there's still a lot to be learned," says Seymour Solomon, director of the headache unit at Montefiore Medical Center, in New York City.

But where does the pain come from in the first place?

Researchers know that people get headaches for all sorts of reasons—anything from muscular tension to brain tumors. For example, tension headache usually results from psychological stress. This in turn may cause scalp muscles to contract too hard or too long. Nerve endings in the scalp, stimulated by the tightened muscles, relay electrochemical impulse to the brain, which interprets the signal as pain.

The notorious and dreaded migraine, which afflicts 25 million Americans, generates pain in a somewhat different way. Blood vessels in the scalp alternately shrink and swell and, while swollen, allow certain biochemicals to seep through the vessel walls to the surrounding tissue. There the chemicals initiate an inflammatory reaction, which stimulates nerve endings to send a signal to the brain.

About 10 percent of all headaches are caused by disease. Tumors can stretch and irritate the covering of the brain. And fever resulting from inflammations, such as those of the eyes, ears, nose, or neck, can swell blood vessels in the head.

In chronic headaches, psychological factors are thought to loom large, aggravating, perpetuating—and at times even initiating—head pain.

But what about the 10 percent of the population that does not get headaches? Says Solomon, "We do not understand why the brain sometimes registers pain and at other times does not. What we can say is that there is a complex interaction between a patient's psychology and the mechanisms of pain."[11]

QUIZ

a. What percentage of Americans are bothered by headaches?	(5 points)
b. How does the tension headache cause pain?	(10 points)
c. How is the migraine different from the tension headache?	(10 points)
d. What percent of headaches are caused by disease?	(10 points)
e. Name one disease that causes headaches.	(5 points)
f. What factor is thought to contribute the most to tension headaches?	(5 points)
g. Why are there some people who never get headaches?	(10 points)

44 pts.—80%

Now compare your reading rate and comprehension with your scores on the pretest at the beginning of this section.

ANSWERS TO GI ROBOTS

Answer A

Identify aircraft, control air traffic, and transmit deceptive noises to confuse the enemy.

[11] Alan Breznick, "What is a Headache?" *Science Digest,* March 1983, p. 96.

Identify and track targets and select the highest-priority target from among several on the battlefield.

Handle materials that have been contaminated during nuclear, chemical, or biological warfare.

Load weapons, set fuses, and transfer rounds of ammunition from storage areas to guns.

Collect, correlate, and transmit information about the enemy to command posts.

Detect enemy minefields and implant "smart" mines capable of recognizing enemy movements.

Dig ditches, make craters, or build obstacles based on the robot's programmed knowledge of the enemy, reducing the need for soldiers to perform these routine tasks.

Answer B

Physical examinations

Aptitude tests

Process payrolls

Issue uniforms or equipment

Weaponry training (robot targets, automatic scoring and critiques)

Space exploration

Underwater search for enemy mines

Situation assessment

15

EFFECTIVE READING TECHNIQUES

"When we read too fast or too slowly, we understand nothing."

Pascal

After reading this chapter you should understand:
1. How to preread
2. How to skip read
3. How to skim
4. How to read critically
5. How to combine these techniques for efficient reading

"Don really makes me mad," Mary complained to her friend Anne. "He spent only two hours researching for this report and I spent two full days." She waved her report in Anne's face. "I got only a C on my report," she continued, "but guess what Don got—an A. Why should he get the A when I spent so much longer researching for mine?"

"I know what you mean," Anne said sympathetically. "I have the same problem. At work Theresa is always finished with her paper work before I am. I don't know how she does it. The worst part is she just got another promotion. That's her second promotion in a year. I've been with the company two years and I'm still waiting for my first promotion."

"Some people are just born under lucky stars, I guess," Mary sighed as she and Anne watched Don walk toward the library.

All of us have probably wondered from time to time why some people seem to get good grades and big promotions so easily. Are they successful because they lead charmed lives? Perhaps, instead, they have developed some special skills that contribute to efficient work habits.

Many things contribute to a person's success in school and on the job. Time management and communication skills are two areas that contribute to success. Another thing that helps us move ahead is skillful reading. Skillful readers can do a more thorough job faster than readers with underdeveloped reading skills. They appear to do their work easily, and, truthfully, they do spend less time and expend less effort accomplishing tasks than unskilled readers do. But that does not mean they are lucky. It means that they have acquired skillful reading techniques.

We can compare reading with playing a sport like racquetball. Learning the basics is fairly simple. We can sign up for a court at the gym and hit a ball against the wall for an hour, then tell everyone we have been playing racquetball. However, developing the footwork and eye–hand coordination that makes you a skilled racquetball player takes study and practice.

The same is true of reading. Although we quickly learn the basics of reading, we must study and practice specific techniques in order to become skilled readers. In this chapter we will show how people use reading in their work. We will also discuss four specific reading techniques that will help you develop your reading skills: prereading, skimming, scanning, and critical reading.

READING ON THE JOB

On-the-job mistakes in reading have cost U.S. business and industry millions of dollars. In fact, one company, JLG Industries, reports spending $1 million correcting literacy mistakes made by their workers. William Baines, vice-president of finance for JLG Industries, says that "poorly educated workers are our number one problem, the main factor slowing our growth."[1] Workers' inability to read the warnings at dangerous job sites or read directions related to job procedures is a problem for employers. So are accidents and reduced production due to inefficient reading.

On the job you will read for two main reasons: to learn something and to do something. When you read to *learn*, your purpose is to acquire information, which you must then remember until you need to use it. Let's say that you are the chief engineer at a sewage treatment plant. Part of your job is to give tours to elementary school children during which you explain the primary, secondary, and tertiary method of sewage treatment. Before you can explain these concepts to the children, you must read articles about the treatment of waste and thoroughly understand the three methods. Your purpose in reading is to learn information you will use when you talk to the children.

When you read to *do*, on the other hand, you put what you are reading to use immediately. Your purpose is to get the information you need to accomplish a

[1]Larry McKulecky, Job Literacy: The Relationship Between School Preparation and Workplace Actuality," *Reading Research Quarterly*, 1982, 17, No. 3, p. 402.

specific task. You read as you do. According to a study done by T. G. Stricht on military occupations, 60 percent of job-related reading is reading to do. Let's say, for example, that you are an electronics technician servicing many different kinds of copy machines each week. You can't possibly remember everything about each machine, so you have a service manual for each copier. When a machine breaks down, you read the service manual to learn how to repair the machine. As you read, you follow the directions given to repair the machine.

Although reading to learn and reading to do require similar skills, these skills vary with the situation. For example, both situations require a good grasp of the vocabulary used in the reading. An extensive vocabulary to draw on plus the ability to figure out the meanings of an unfamiliar word by the way it is used in a sentence are important tools for both types of reading.

You may need a good foundation in a technical vocabulary when you are reading to learn, but you will probably depend on a technical vocabulary more often when you are reading to do.

Since this usually is on-the-job reading, you will need to know those terms related specifically to your field. If you are in electronics, for example, you should understand words like *megawatt* and *transformer,* whereas if you are an insurance agent you would use words like *underwriter* and *policyholder.* Although *risk* has the same general meaning for both occupations, the specific use of *risk* in electronics differs from the use of the word in insurance. For example, in electronics you might say, "Standing in a puddle of water while you wire that circuit is taking a risk," while an insurance agent would say, "Here is a list of the risks covered by this policy."

Both types of reading may require you to read critically. As you read to do, you should ask yourself if the directions sound sensible to you. Consider them in light of the situation and your background material. Similarly, when you read to learn, you should constantly evaluate the author's assertions, seeing how they relate to your own experiences.

Reading to learn usually requires reading longer selections at one time than reading to do. When you read to do, you probably read a short segment, apply what you have just read, then read another short segment, proceeding in this way until you have finished the reading selection and accomplished the task. On the other hand, when you read to learn, you usually read the entire selection at once. Then you think about what you have read and make sure you can remember the material so you can use it later.

You may also find that you are able to read through material faster when you are reading-to-do than when you are reading to learn. The way reading-to-do material is organized usually helps you read it faster. Directions may be written in phrases rather than sentences. Key words may be underlined or capitalized. Summaries may occur periodically throughout the text. These organizational techniques help you skim the material quickly. You should find it easy to spot key words and read just the information that relates to your task.

Reading-to-learn material, on the other hand, is usually organized in traditional paragraphs. Although you can use skipping and skimming techniques, the organization often does not encourage you to do so. The structure of the sentences is important for relaying the author's mood as well as presenting ideas. You will want to read the selection slowly.

Now that you understand some of the differences between reading to do and reading to learn, let's discuss the reading techniques which will help you read more efficiently.

PREREADING

If you have ever browsed through a magazine, you have done some prereading. Many people preread from time to time, but because they have not learned this technique as a specific reading skill, they tend to do it without direction and, therefore, inefficiently. In fact, if you asked these readers what they were doing, they would probably tell you that they were "just browsing" or "just wasting a little time."

Far from being a time waster, prereading, when done correctly, is a time-saver. Its purpose is to give you an idea of the contents of a selection before you spend a lot of time reading it. A general idea of the contents is helpful in two ways. First, you can tell quickly if the material is something you should read carefully. Can you use the information for a report you are writing? Will it help you do your job better? Is it something you are interested in reading for fun? If you think the material will be useful or if it especially interests you, you can read the selection carefully. If you decide the material is unimportant, you have not spent much time on it.

The second way prereading is helpful is as a means of preparing you for a careful reading later. In Chapter 14 you learned that knowing your purpose will help you read more efficiently. Prereading helps you clarify your purpose for reading. You can get an idea about the content of the selection and may also learn something about the author and his or her background. You may understand the article better because you have some idea of the author's purpose in writing it.

Exactly what is prereading? It simply means glancing through the text. First you read the title of the article, report, chapter, or book, and also note the author's name. If there is a sentence or short paragraph under the title which describes the content, read that next. Then turn the pages, reading subheads or any other material that is in bold type. Doing this will give you an idea of the topics covered and the depth in which the author discusses the main idea.

While you are browsing through the selection in this way, be sure to look at all the pictures, charts, graphs, and other illustrations. Read each caption until you are sure you understand what idea or factor it is illustrating. You have probably heard the saying, "A picture is worth a thousand words." In your prereading you may find this to be true. We can learn a lot from studying a photograph or chart. If the selection has numerous illustrations, you may find that you have absorbed most of the major ideas expressed in the selection just from studying the illustrations.

While you are prereading in this manner, keep looking for information about the author. In magazine articles, there may be a brief biographical sketch at the end of the article. In books also a short biography of the author usually appears on the back cover. In reports look for the author's title page. A job description, reason for doing the report, or background the author brings to the subject will probably appear in the pages before the actual report.

Skillful prereading can save you a lot of time. When you are writing a report, for example, you should gather all the information available on the subject. Then, through skillful prereading, you can eliminate material that does not pertain to your subject as well as material that seems superficial or outdated. Preread first to determine what will be appropriate for your report, and save your time for a careful reading of pertinent material only.

Preread the advertisement in Figure 15–1 on pages 262–263. Read the statements in large type and study the illustration. On the basis of your prereading, would you consider Northeastern Indiana as a location for your business?

SKIPPING

Skipping is another reading technique that helps you read more efficiently. To use skipping successfully, you must discard the notion that good readers read every word, because skipping, as its name implies, means that you do not read many words in the selection. This technique, however, is not a haphazard skimming over of words you don't know or ideas that don't interest you. Skipping is a highly developed, efficient reading skill.

Skipping simply means reading for main ideas or for one particular concept and skipping everything else.

Skipping gives you a more thorough understanding of the material than does prereading. You learn the author's main assertions, information that can be especially helpful when you are just beginning to research a subject and are still determining the main focus of your report and forming opinions about your topic. Quickly gaining ideas from a variety of sources will help you decide which ideas you want to pursue more thoroughly.

Skipping is also helpful at a later stage in your research, when you know what you need to supplement the material you already have. You can skip through a selection until you find the ideas that will add information to your project.

Skipping may also be useful in your leisure reading. You can use the technique to gain a general knowledge of current events or to finish a best-selling novel quickly. Let's say you decide to skip-read the current best seller. You want to learn what happens in the story. You don't care how the characters think or feel; you care only about what they do. With that in mind, you skip all the paragraphs that describe feelings or thoughts; you read only those paragraphs that show the action of the story.

To use skipping successfully for the reading you will do on the job you must understand the structure of most nonfiction writing. From your study of writing

Figure 15–1   Source: Authored by Timothy S. Borne, Asher Agency, Inc.

Is there any other prepared to give

The community development leaders of Northeastern Indiana are making an all-out effort to attract your business to our part of America.

To do it, we're finding as many ways as we can to help you relocate, expand and succeed here. You see, it's all part of an unprecedented program we've developed to show corporate America just how much our region has to offer.

A loan package that can pay 100% of your financing costs.

In 1979, our State Legislature passed important new acts which paved the way for loan arrangements to business which are so generous, companies relocating or expanding in our locale can be eligible to receive the full one hundred percent of their fixed asset financing costs.

Up to ten million dollars in loan money is currently available for your business to tap into with money raised through Industrial Revenue Bonds.

This money is for the express use of companies expanding here, building new factories or warehouses, renovating older premises, building offices, developing industrial sites, even for the cost of new machinery and equipment.

A 100% effort to reduce your corporate taxes.

Few states in America, if any, can match the far-reaching program of tax relief, tax credits, and tax abatements which were given the green light by our state government in 1981.

We're allowing your company, for example, to deduct one hundred percent of its costs for property improvements during its first year here, with a "sliding scale" of deductions which continue for the following nine years.

Likewise, a company purchasing new manufacturing equipment is eligible for the same deductions over a five-year period.

We're giving tax breaks of up to twenty-five percent to businesses involved in joint industry-university research and development programs.

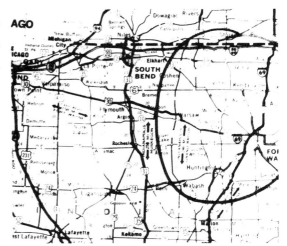

Through our On-the-Job Training Programs we're allowing companies a reimbursement of employee wages up to 50%, and those same companies may also be eligible for state and federal tax credits.

We're also offering unheard of tax credits for companies involved in alternative energy, resource recovery, pollution control, solar power, recycling programs and hydro-electric systems.

Your company will save thousands of dollars every year from these tax breaks alone.

Our workers will give you 100%.

The workers in this part of the country are known for their strong backs and their steady application to the job at hand.

According to a recent report by the Fantus Company, unscheduled absenteeism among our workers was shown to be at a very low four percent overall, and turnover from job to job was among the lowest of all the large industrial states.

Not surprisingly, companies like General Electric, Magnavox, Bowmar, ITT, Phelps Dodge,

region in America your business 100%?

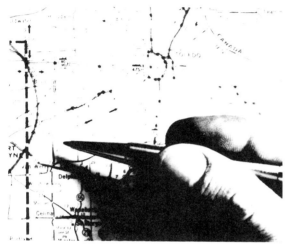

and Tokheim Corporation are some of the prestigious national corporations currently capitalizing on this valuable dependability.

100% accessibility to America's richest markets.

Northeastern Indiana is at the heart of a region of mid-America which is known as "The Golden Zone." A glimpse at the size and wealth of the markets within and surrounding our region explains why this name is so appropriate.

Over eighty-two million people live within a radius of five hundred miles of our area. That's approximately one-third of the entire U.S. population. *One-third.*

Imagine the sheer dollar potential of a market this size for your company's goods and services.

In fact, your company will virtually be on top of every major city in the midwest, with overnight access to the enormous market centers of Chicago, Detroit, Indianapolis, Cincinnati, Cleveland, St. Louis, Pittsburgh, and Milwaukee.

We're cutting red tape by 100%.

In Northeastern Indiana, we're determined to save you the one other business commodity that's as valuable as money. Time.

That's why we've introduced new measures to have all permits to do business here processed and approved within just two and one half working days flat.

Our "One-Stop Shopping" program is also designed to act as your one source of information on any single thing you need to know about this dynamic and still untapped region of America.

Use it to your company's advantage, and clip the coupon now. Or call Mr. Lincoln Schrock, Director, Indiana Northeast Development, direct at **(219) 426-7649.**

It'll be our pleasure to prove to you that here in Northeastern Indiana we really are prepared to give your business everything we've got.

Northeastern Indiana. We're giving your business 100%.

you should remember that nonfiction usually has three parts: an introduction, a body, and a conclusion. Typically, the main idea or thesis of the essay is stated at the end of the introduction. The body of the essay is made up of paragraphs that develop the main idea. Each paragraph consists of a topic sentence and supporting details. The topic sentence is usually the first sentence of the paragraph. The other sentences in the paragraph discuss the topic sentence. Finally, the concluding paragraph sums up main points of the essay.

Magazine articles, reports, textbooks, and other nonfiction reference books are usually written in a structure similar to this; therefore, you can use the following pattern to successfully skip-read most nonfiction writing.

First, read the last sentence of each of the first few paragraphs. If the essay, article, or chapter is short, the thesis statement should come at the end of the first paragraph. In longer selections, the introduction might be several paragraphs long with the main idea for the essay coming at the end. A quick glance through the first few paragraphs should tell you where to find the main idea.

Second, read the first sentence of every paragraph in the body. These should give you an understanding of the ideas the author uses to support the main idea of the essay. If you think that the first sentence of a paragraph does not point directly to the main idea, read the second sentence or the last sentence, since these are alternate placements for the topic sentence.

Finally, read the last paragraph or two, where the main points of the essay are summed up.

In Figure 15–2 you will see the technique of skipping illustrated. The sentences underlined are those you would read if you were skipping the article. When you put these sentences together you have a good understanding of the main ideas. You know that scientists are developing ways to artificially produce gems, and some businessmen are using these gems for jewelry.

Although you can usually skip-read an article successfully this way, you should adapt your skipping techniques to the material you are reading and to your goals for reading the selection. For example, if your goal is to read a best-selling novel for the plot, you should skip over entire paragraphs or pages until you come to a section relating something the characters did. If your goal is to learn how to invest in gold by reading a report that discusses investment strategies, you would turn the pages until you came to the section on gold.

However, you must be careful about using the information you gain from skipping. Remember, skipping does not give you an in-depth understanding of the subject. Even the most skillful skipping gives you only a general idea of the main topics discussed. When you skip-read, you learn the author's main assertion but you do not understand the proof the author uses to support those assertions. You do not pick up any facts the author may use to qualify or clarify the assertions made.

Look at the article on man-made gems again. What information can you add to your general understanding of man-made gems by reading the article word-for-word?

Figure 15-2   World Trends and Forecasts. Source: "Grown Gems: Jewelry of the Future?" *The Futurist,* October 1982, p. 61.

Resources

Grown Gems: Jewelry of the Future?

Gemstones, like many of the earth's natural resources, are becoming scarcer and more expensive. Today, most people cannot afford to buy natural gems, let alone wear them outside a bank vault for fear of robbery. Since people will probably always want something beautiful and affordable to wear, jewelry makers are looking into the possibility of growing gems in laboratories.

Main idea

Supporting idea

Science has known for years how to "grow" minerals in the laboratory. The process, which involves adding common chemicals, heat, and pressure to a "seed" chip of a mined stone, is similar to the methods grade-school "chemists" use to turn sugar into rock candy. Millions of carats of industrial rough diamonds, valued for their hardness, are manufactured each year. Synthetic rubies, made in France as early as the mid-1800s, are used in the jeweled movements of watches. But these stones are not "gem quality," though they are useful in industry.

Supporting idea

Some entrepreneurs have produced laboratory gems that are good enough to wear. Rather than concentrating on the hardness of the stone or on other features that make it useful to industry, the new gem-growers are concentrating on matching the beauty and color of gems found in nature.

In a world that regards anything "man-made" as "fake," however, public acceptance of laboratory-grown gems may be slow in coming. Since the man-made gems sell for only one-tenth the price a natural stone could bring, established jewelers are reluctant to deal with the "fakes."

Supporting idea

One of the new gem-growers, disappointed by this public resistance, hired his own team of gem cutters and jewelry designers and opened his own retail showrooms. Kazuo Inamori, president of Kyoto Ceramics, has carved out a successful market with three showrooms in Japan. The Japanese are attracted to Inamori's created gems because of the perfection and low price of the stones.

Supporting idea

Inamori has recently opened a showroom in Beverly Hills, California, hoping that his laboratory gems will become as well accepted in America as they have been in Japan, just as cultured pearls have become commonplace.

As natural gems become more scarce, Inamori hopes that his man-made gems, designed into unique, "trend setting" jewelry, will become the fashion of the future, an alternative to the plastic and "styrofoam squiggles" to which he believes we could be destined a hundred years from now.

Conclusion

SKIMMING

A third reading technique is skimming. Like slipping, it provides a way for you to acquire information quickly without reading the entire selection.

Skimming differs from skipping in two important ways: (1) when you skim, you glance down the entire page rather than skip entire paragraphs, and (2) you read for details rather than main ideas.

The purpose of skimming is to find specific information quickly. In order to skim successfully, you must know what kind of information you are looking for.

Let's say you want to know if installing a machine in your bank to handle deposits and withdrawals automatically will be cost effective. The only material available on cost effectiveness is included in a much longer report on all aspects of the automatic process. You don't care where the machine will be located, who will install it, or even what the customer reaction has been to the use of similar machines in other banks. You want to know only how much it will cost and how much it will save your bank. As a result, you skim the report, keeping in mind that you are looking for figures. When you see a number, you stop and read that paragraph carefully. In that way, you read only the material dealing with expenses. Later you can compare the cost of the machine with the savings to your bank and determine the cost effectiveness of this device.

You can skim material for dates, names, or other specific details. Skimming can be an especially useful technique when you are studying for an objective test that you know will deal mainly with facts. It is also a useful technique when you need very specific information for a report or discussion.

You might use skimming as a rereading technique too. Perhaps you have read an article carefully; then, let's say a week later, you need a specific date or figure from that article. Rather than reading the entire article again, you skim it until you find the information you need.

To skim successfully, you allow your eyes to move down the page in a rhythmical motion. You are seeing the words but you are not actually reading them. Your mind is concentrating on specific kinds of information. When you see that information, you stop and read it carefully.

The following example illustrates the technique of skimming. Your purpose in reading the article is to compare Japanese IQ scores with American IQ scores. That means you will be reading for numbers. You allow your eyes to skim through the article while your brain is alerted to concentrate on numbers. The first number you see is 11. You stop and read the material before and after 11 carefully. When you understand that material, you continue to skim the article until you come to the next number, 102–105. Then you stop skimming and read the material before and after that number carefully. When you have finished skimming, you should have all the statistics used to compare U.S. and Japanese IQs, but you have actually read less than one-third of the article.

Japanese IQs Rising Fast

IQs in Japan are rising fast, with (the younger generation now scoring <u>11 points</u> above the mean score for similar groups in the United States), according to <u>an article</u> in the British scientific journal *Nature*. The mean Japanese IQ has jumped seven points in recent decades, giving the younger generation the highest IQ recorded for a national population anywhere in the world.

The growing IQ gap is noted by Richard Lynn, a psychologist with the New University of Ulster. Lynn finds a growing disparity between the Japanese and Western populations, with the greatest difference occurring among the samples born most recently. For example, (those Japanese born between 1910 and 1945 have a mean IQ <u>of 102–105</u>, while those born between 1946 and 1969 have a mean IQ of <u>108–115</u>) (The U.S. and European mean is 100.)

The major IQ tests are updated periodically to keep pace with societal changes. Test items for both Japanese and Western cultures have been increasing in difficulty as improvements in such areas as education and nutrition have raised the general intelligence levels. But relatively speaking, the Japanese have forged ahead.

The increasing difference, says Lynn, means that (Japan will have a far higher proportion of people with IQ levels <u>above 130</u>—) the level common among such professionals as research scientists and engineers. He points out that currently only (<u>2%</u> of the American and European populations) fall in this group while the (Japanese have <u>10%</u> in the superior category.) This disparity could have important implications for those societies competing with the Japanese in the area of technological innovation.[2]

CRITICAL READING

The three techniques discussed thus far—prereading, skipping, and skimming—are ways of reading material quickly. The basis for each technique is reading selectively, that is, only specific words or sentences. People who finish reports quickly or clear their desks of paperwork in record time probably use one or more of these techniques. Mary, whom we read about at the beginning of this chapter, would probably get her work done faster and more successfully if she learned how to preread, skip, and skim her reading material.

There are times, however, when you need to read a selection word for word and think carefully about what you have read. We call this *critical reading*.

The purpose of critical reading is to understand thoroughly the author's purpose in writing the material and to evaluate the ideas and opinions the author expresses. When you read critically, you make a judgment about what you have read. The words *critical* and *judgment* may make you think of negative criticism, but you can make a positive judgment also.

Critical reading is helpful when you need to make a decision on a controver-

---

[2] "Japanese IQs Rising Fast," *The Futurist*, February 1983, p. 14.

sial or multisided issue. You will study the facts and evaluate the opinions on all sides of the issue before making a decision.

When you read critically, you pay close attention to details and how those details relate to the author's assertions. That is the difference between critical reading and the other reading techniques discussed in this chapter. In prereading and skipping, for example, you tend to glance over the details. You know what the author's main points are, but you do not understand the reasons for these ideas. In skimming you read the details but you do not try to see them in relation to the author's main ideas. In critical reading, however, you read the details carefully. You learn the reasoning behind the author's main assertions and discover how the author supports the ideas expressed.

Constant questioning is the key to successful critical reading. As you read, ask yourself:

> What is the author's purpose?
> How does the author support this purpose?
> Does the author use facts or opinions as proof?
> Are the author's assertions documented?
> Do I know where the author's material comes from?
> Does the author select the material used as proof fairly or is the material biased?

When you finish reading, recall the conclusions the author presents. Keeping your own experiences and background in mind, do you agree with the author? Compare the author's opinions with your own. What can you learn from the reading? What ideas could you add to the author's material?

Try to recall the main assertions and supporting details. Reread the material to be sure you have it clearly in mind. Then share what you have read with someone else.

By doing these things, you add the material you have just read to your storehouse of knowledge. You can draw on the author's ideas to support decisions you make. The material you have read becomes part of the background information you will use in the future.

Now read the essay in Fig. 15-3 critically. As you read, ask yourself these questions:

> What is the author's main point?
> How does he support his assertions?
> Does he give references for the statistics he uses?
> Does the author use enough statistics to prove his assertions?
> Do I agree or disagree with his conclusion?

When you have finished reading, try to sum up the author's main points and supporting details. Then discuss his opinions with someone else.

When you have done all these things, you have completed the critical

Figure 15-3   Source: Marvin Stone, "Civics Gap: Alarming Challenge,"
U.S. News and World Report, April 25, 1983, p. 80.

One fourth of this nation's 17-year-olds think it is against the law to start a new political party in the United States.

Nearly half of them cannot name their congressman or U.S. senators, and 30 percent of them don't know the name of their governor.

One 17-year-old in 6 thinks Congress can establish a national church. One in 10 says the President has a right to do anything he wants affecting the country, and 4 in 10 think the President can declare an act of Congress unconstitutional. One in 5 does not know that U.S. senators are elected.

Our education editor, Lucia Solorzano, who called these facts to our attention, makes the point that such widespread ignorance among America's high-school students is alarming. It not only raises grave concerns about the quality of the education in civics that the public schools provide; it also can have serious, long-range consequences for a nation whose system of self-government depends so heavily on an informed citizenry.

From Ernest L. Boyer, president of the Carnegie Foundation for the Advancement of Teaching and a former U.S. Commissioner of Education, comes this warning: "Unless we find better ways to educate ourselves as citizens, we run the risk of drifting unwittingly into a new kind of Dark Age."

Nearly all states require some instruction in government for high-school graduation. How, then, is it possible for so many students to know so little and hold such wrong ideas?

Much of the blame is placed by experts on dull teaching methods and on teachers' excessive reliance on textbooks that fail to relate theory to the actual workings of government. Some charge that civics education has given way in recent years to shallow courses in such things as "life adjustment."

Fortunately, some educators are starting to react to the problem. A number of experiments are being tried to make the study of civics more relevant and more interesting to teenagers.

In Oakland, Calif., students got firsthand experience in the workings of the State Legislature by lobbying for a bill to make the birthday of Martin Luther King, Jr., a school holiday.

Waukesha, Wis., school officials found that students thought of government as something existing only in far-off Washington, D.C. So they began teaching how government affects students' own cities and schools. In one exercise, ninth-grade students were asked to act as school-board members wrestling with a 30 percent cut in the school athletics budget. Says social-studies director Phillip Ferguson: "Students . . . are coming out with a stronger attitude about participating in the political process."

In Alexandria, Va., eighth-grade students were assigned to write speeches and issue papers for actual candidates. Reports student Todd Swartz: "Now we know how to tell who the best candidates are."

Despite such local efforts, the nationwide trend remains discouraging. Student knowledge about our government declined in the 1970s, according to periodic tests by the National Assessment of Educational Progress. That decline, the testers say, "should be the cause for a hard reassessment of the social-studies curriculum" in America's public schools.

We heartily agree. Obviously, more and better teaching is required. Yet we find instead that budget reductions have forced cutbacks instead of additions in many schools. Enrollment in civics courses has gone down.

One cost of youthful ignorance about government is reflected in election returns. Fewer than half of the 12.3 million Americans age 18 to 20 are registered to vote, and only 4.4 million of them actually voted in the last presidential election.

We think it's time for Americans to heed the warning of educator Boyer: "This upsurge of apathy and decline in public understanding cannot go unchallenged. In a world where human survival is at stake, ignorance is not an acceptable alternative."

reading process. You understand the author's point of view, you know whether or not you agree with that viewpoint, and you have shared the author's opinion and your response with someone else.

COMBINING TECHNIQUES

You can use any one of the four reading techniques we have discussed in this chapter separately to accomplish a reading goal, but the most successful readers often use these techniques in combination.

For example, you may preread a selection before you read it critically. Prereading prepares you for a thorough reading of the material. It gives you an idea of how long it will take you to read the selection thoroughly and helps you form an opinion about how difficult the concepts will be to understand. Because prereading gives you a general understanding of the material, it helps you to concentrate on specific details when you read through the material completely.

There are times when you might even use all four reading techniques on one selection. For example, you might preread the material to get a general idea of the length and content of the article. Then you might skip through the article to learn the author's main ideas. If you find these ideas interesting or if they add valuable information to the topic you are researching, you will need to read the article thoroughly to understand the author's reasoning. Finally, hours or days later, you might need to skim the article to refresh your memory about certain details.

Just as important as knowing *how* to use these techniques is learning *when* to use them. Prereading, for example, may give you enough knowledge to be able to follow a conversation or discussion on the topic, but it will not give you enough information so you can do well on a test. With skip-reading you will discover the author's main idea, but you will not learn the reasons behind these ideas; you will not learn enough to defend the author's main assertions. If you are using the author's views to help yourself make a decision, you will want to read the material critically; only critical reading gives you enough information to make a judgment about what you have read.

Knowing when to use each technique and combining them when you need to is necessary for efficient reading.

SUMMARY

On the job you will read for two main reasons: to learn something and to do something. Although reading to learn and reading to do require similar skills, these skills vary with the situation. Vocabulary, organization, and length are all ways in which the two types of reading material vary.

There are four reading techniques that help us read more effectively:

prereading, skipping, skimming, and critical reading. The first three techniques help us acquire pertinent information quickly, and critical reading helps us form opinions about what we have read. Prereading and skipping give us a general understanding of the material. Through skimming we can pick out specific facts from a selection, but we do not see how those facts relate to the author's main ideas. When we read critically, we read for details and their relation to the author's main ideas. This is one of the most important differences between critical reading and the other three techniques.

Knowing when to use these techniques is as important as knowing how to use them. You should choose the technique that will help you get the information you need most efficiently. You can use one technique alone or several techniques together. Skillful use of prereading, skipping, skimming, and critical reading should make you a more efficient student and worker as well as a more effective reader.

REVIEW QUESTIONS

1. Define reading to learn and reading to do.
2. What are the differences between reading to do and reading to learn? What are the similarities?
3. You must attend a committee meeting where they will discuss the pros and cons of computerizing your method of billing customers. You have a 30-page report on your desk describing a study done last year on the subject. You have ten minutes before the meeting. What reading techniques would you use? Why?
4. First you skip through an article. Then you read it critically. What additional information do you learn from the critical reading?
5. You have three chapters to read in your insurance textbook. You know you will be tested on these chapters. What combination of reading techniques would you use for the test?
6. What background information do you need to skim successfully?
7. What is the one thing you must do constantly as you read critically?

ACTIVITIES

1. Let's say you were asked to talk to a group of potential investors about the financial stability of the company whose Financial Review follows. You are looking for information. In class with your instructor and other class members, discuss the way you would approach the material in Figure 15-1A. Then, following that approach, take notes on the material. From your notes write two to three paragraphs that you might use in describing the financial state of this company.
2. Imagine you received the memo in Figure 15-2A. How is it organized to make skimming it for information easy?
3. Figure 15-3A shows the directions you have for installing a tilt control knob for venetian blinds. How is it organized to make your job easier?
4. Now select an article from a trade journal in your field of study. Preread, skip, and

skim the article. The chart in Figure 15–4A will help you compare the information you added from each reading. Finally, read the article critically. Then prepare a summary and outline of your reactions. Share what you have learned and your reactions to it with another person in your field.

FINANCIAL REVIEW:

RECORD RESULTS IN LONG-TERM PERSPECTIVE

By every statistical measure of performance, your company's results in 1982 continued the record of consistent improvement since our public offering in June 1971. Our record in recent years has significantly enhanced our very important long-term performance. This has been accomplished despite being measured on a larger base each year.

Compound Growth Rates

	3-year	5-year	10-year
Net sales	21.9%	28.4%	29.4%
Operating income	30.6%	35.7%	26.6%
Earnings pretax	37.7%	40.1%	27.4%
Net earnings	37.2%	38.0%	27.4%
EPS—primary	32.0%	34.0%	24.6%

The Ten Year Review on pages 18 and 19 gives additional statistics with which to evaluate our performance. (The eleventh year is included as a base for computing ten-year compound growth rates.)

Sales

Our sales rose 26.6% to a record $134.5 million for 1982 compared with a 26.9% rise in 1981. The largest gains were achieved in the fabrication of monumental windows and the contract installation of window systems. Significant increases also were achieved in tempered architectural glass. These markets have demanded increasingly sophisticated products and erection and glazing techniques. This adds value and thus sales dollars to our core activities. Our response to these market demands has been the largest contributor to our five- and ten-year growth rates. These growth rates are obviously well ahead of the general level of inflation. However, since many of our products and services are of a custom nature, it is not practical to break down year-to-year sales dollar increases among factors such as inflation, unit growth and product and service sophistication.

Even though some of our other markets have been soft, especially auto glass replacement, our marketing force has a "can-do" attitude. They have sought out new markets, developed new products and devised new selling techniques. The result is consistent sales volumes from these soft markets and, in several areas, small increases.

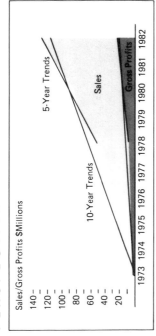

Sales/Gross Profits $Millions

Earnings

In fiscal 1982, our net earnings rose 42.3% to a record $6.4 million. On a per share basis, primary earnings increased 30.1% to $1.08. Net earnings have increased in each of the last ten years, with the exception of 1975, the year most inventories were converted to LIFO accounting. Our net earnings in each of the last four years have grown by over 30%, well ahead of our long-term goal for annual profit growth.

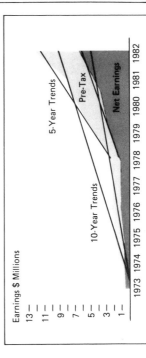

Earnings $ Millions

Figure 15–1A   Source: Apogee Enterprises Inc., *Annual Report* 1982, Wausau Corporation.

Return on Equity

Equity per common share rose 42.8% to $5.44. Total shareholders' equity now stands at $32.4 million. The return on beginning total equity in 1982 was 30.3%, our fifth consecutive increase. It compared with 26.3% in 1981. The five-year average ROE is 24.0% and the ten-year average is 19.7%.

Return on Assets

Total assets, which on February 27, 1982 totaled $60.1 million, have grown at a 10-year compound rate of 23.8%. Record earnings in 1982 produced a return on beginning total assets of 13.0%, a ten-year high. Over the last decade, ROA has averaged 9.6%, while over the last five years the average has been 10.4%.

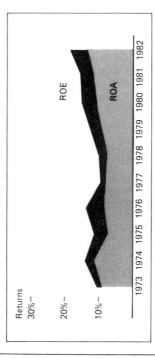

Return on Invested Capital

Fiscal 1982's return on beginning invested capital (long-term debt + deferred taxes + shareholders' equity) also is the highest in the ten years under review. ROI reached 18.5%, which compared favorably with the average for the last five years of 14.3%. The ten-year average is 13.0%.

While ROE, ROA, and ROI are generally accepted performance measures, they are external measures—useful to the outside analyst for measuring total company profitability and resource utilization. But our management philosophy also calls for measuring performance at the profit center level—our smallest stand-alone organizational level. For this purpose, we employ a measurement tool called "return on assets utilized." Returns are calculated to exclude the effects of those things outside of a profit center manager's direct control, such as taxes and interest charges, while assets utilized are measured in a way to encourage efficient working capital deployment by the manager. Each profit center must achieve, or in its start-up phase, demonstrate its ability to eventually achieve, returns on assets utilized of 30% or more. We monitor this internal performance statistic on a monthly basis for each of our operating units.

Significant Elements in Earnings Performance

While both sales and earnings increases for fiscal 1981 and 1982 exceeded our long-term goals of at least 20% in each, continuing cost pressures exist, as the accompanying table shows.

	1982	1981	1980
Net sales	100.0%	100.0%	100.0%
Cost of goods sold	81.2	81.0	80.6
Gross profit margins	18.8	19.0	19.4
SG & A	9.4	10.1	10.4
Interest	.4	1.2	1.2
Pretax profit margins	9.0%	7.7%	7.8%

Our stated goal has been to achieve and maintain a 9% pretax profit margin over the five-year period ending with fiscal 1985. This goal was reached in fiscal 1982, with help from the hefty sales volume increases noted earlier. As the table above indicates, gross profit has been declining slightly. This is due to a number of factors, including market conditions, sales mix and the effect of start-up costs.

In the past, pretax margin goals have been achieved primarily by increasing sales without a proportionate rise in overhead. However, an aggressive philosophy of expanding sales while at the same time improving operating

Figure 15-1A Continued.

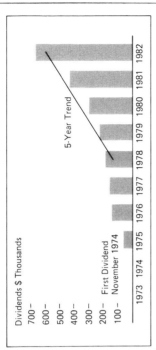

Dividends $ Thousands

700 –
600 –
500 –
400 –
300 –
200 – First Dividend
100 – November 1974

1973 1974 1975 1976 1977 1978 1979 1980 1981 1982

5-Year Trend

efficiencies has its risks. An example is our Bensenville glass fabrication facility, where we installed state-of-the-art technology in fiscal 1981. While progress with its horizontal glass tempering furnace has been encouraging, Bensenville has yet to achieve satisfactory utilization rates. This diminished operating profitability slightly in 1982.

Our oldest business is the distribution and installation of auto glass. Over the past few years, market conditions have slowed the growth of this business. Higher fuel costs have resulted in fewer miles being travelled, in smaller vehicles. Both the rate of breakage and the size of the windshield are down. Meanwhile, the cost of doing business has increased with the general level of inflation. Profit margins have been under pressure. We have responded with tight cost control, additional products and greater market penetration. We remain committed to the auto glass business, convinced that we have made the necessary adjustments and that the long-term outlook remains bright.

Our manufacturing operations, particularly custom fabrication of window frames and high-performance architectural glass, are currently the most profitable in terms of profit margins as well as return on investment. However, for growth they require significantly greater amounts of fixed capital than distribution and installation activities require. While we have systematically committed more resources to these businesses, we have also responded vigorously to an opportunity to establish ourselves as a major national contract installer of window systems. Contract installation is more flexible, requires less fixed capital, and can generate satisfactory margins and returns. We believe this two-pronged approach strategically balances our short- and long-term profit growth opportunities.

Dividends

Dividends have been paid quarterly since November 1974, and have increased an average 29% per year for the past five years. These dividend increases follow our policy of paying out dividends equal to 10-15% of the prior year's earnings.

In November, 1981 following a 4-for-3 stock split, the cash dividend rate was increased 14.3% to 12¢ a share annually.

Financial Resources for Growth

To help fund our sales growth, we have set an upper limit of debt to total invested capital of 45%. Last May's equity offering added $5.5 million to shareholders' equity and moved debt to 26.0%. However, the successful equity offering has meant our liquidity position is excellent during a time when headlines scream that other companies are overextended on short-term debt. Since the offering, we have not had to utilize our $4.2 million in short-term bank credit lines, and we had $8.3 million in cash and equivalents at February 27, 1982.

This highly liquid position is a guarantee to our customers that temporary negative cash flows will not cause us to shy away from the multi-million dollar projects that have begun to come our way. Furthermore, operations continue to provide substantial positive cash flow. Gross cash flow from operations (net earnings + depreciation + amortization) has increased an average 32.2% for the last five years.

Capital expenditures have totalled $15.3 million over the last five years and have been funded through a combination of long-term debt, new equity and internally generated funds. Fiscal 1983's capital expenditure budget is $6.5

Figure 15–1A Continued.

million. Approximately $3.8 million is aimed at improving productivity and reducing materials costs. The remainder, still under study, will augment and integrate existing product lines. At the same time, we continue to look at acquisition possibilities. Our cash reserves leave us secure in knowing that we have the back-up resources to take advantage of these kinds of opportunities should they arise.

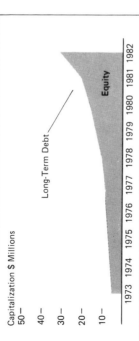

Outlook—Continuing Optimistic

Amidst a gloomy general economic climate, we remain confident that our future performance will stay true to our past trends. Our primary market, the non-residential building construction business, remains healthy. According to F.W. Dodge, the value of non-residential building contracts awarded during 1981—an indicator of future construction activity—was 11% ahead of 1980, totaling $58 billion. The first three months of 1982's contract awards are 7% below last year's comparable period. However, we are a small factor in this large market. Our backlogs are a strong $89 million going into fiscal 1983, compared with $56 million at the start of fiscal 1982. We expect to use the particular strengths of our separate operating units to gain market share during fiscal 1982.

Apogee's Strengths

In a market with hundreds of small competitors, Viracon, our glass fabrication division, has tried to differentiate itself by providing customers with product versatility and better service. This has enabled Viracon to emerge as one of six nationally certified fabricators of custom architectural insulating glass.

With a limited number of serious competitors at the high end of the aluminum window market, our window fabrication's Wausau Metals and Milco units have grown by giving customers high-quality engineering and products, backed up by reliable delivery schedules and the ability to solve problems that crop up in the field during installation.

The demand for capable firms to install windows and glass is great. Our branch operations division's Harmon Contract Glazing unit has expanded by providing architects with technical and design assistance supported by the financial resources to see multi-million dollar contracts through to completion.

Our strength requires a continuing investment in developing our people. In the past five years our growth has created nearly 700 new jobs in the communities where our operations are located. Our people are the foundation of our optimism for continued financial success.

Figure 15-1A Continued.

TO: Al Johnson   DATE: December 6, 1983
        Meg Petiowski
        Randy Webb

FROM: Ronald Smith

RE: Bidding Policy & Procedure

Please plan to attend a meeting in the WMC upstairs conference room on Monday, December 12th at 4:00 pm.

The purpose of this meeting is to define what our bidding policy and procedures will consist of and who will be responsible for supplying specific information so a decision can be made on the following areas:

1. Material costs
   A. Burden
   B. To-make including shipping hours
   C. Mark up

2. Engineering hours -- bid vs. actual

3. Outside services -- mark up and burden M.U.

4. Freight

5. Testing -- bid vs. actual

6. Escalation

7. Commision

8. Warranty

If you can't make it to this meeting, please let me know.

RS:rao

Figure 15-2A   Source: Interoffice Correspondence. Wausau Metals Corporation.

Wausau Metals Corporation

TILT CONTROL KNOB
FOR VENETIAN BLINDS

INSTRUCTIONS FOR
KNOB ATTACHMENT

1. Slide stainless steel wave washer (A) over the shaft of knob (B).
2. Position finger grip (C) parallel to pin (D) for proper engagement of locking barbs.
3. Push knob in firmly until locked in place.

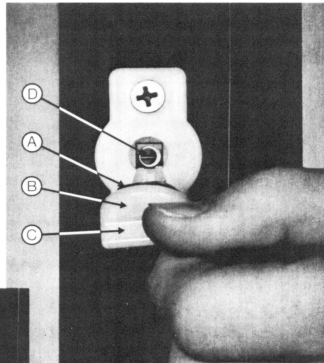

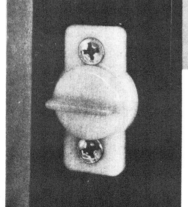

Our standard knob is snapped in place after erection forming a positive drive non-removable assembly.

1415 West Street • P.O. Box 1305 • Wausau, WI 54401 • 715/845-2161

Figure 15-3A Source: Wausau Metals Corporation.

Preread your article
     Title _____
     Author _____
Briefly describe the content of the article:

_____

_____

Skip read the article. Write one paragraph summarizing the article:

_____

_____

_____

_____

_____

_____

_____

Read the article carefully. What additional information did you learn?

_____

_____

_____

_____

_____

_____

_____

Record complete bibliographical information about your article: _____

_____

Figure 15–4A

PART VI Putting It All Together

EMPLOYMENT SCENARIO

"Guess what," Cathy said to Tom as he joined her for coffee in the employees' lunch room. "I just heard through the grapevine that Kearney & Trecher need a technician with an electronics background. Here's your chance to get back into industry."

"I've never heard of Kearney & Trecher," Tom said. "What do they do?"

"I don't know," Cathy told him. "Some kind of manufacturing, I guess. I've never heard of them before today either. Barb just said her husband, Dan, is quitting to take a job closer to their home and his boss is looking for a replacement. I thought you'd be interested. You're always saying that you like industrial work better than the retail trade."

"I do," Tom said enthusiastically, "and I am interested. Even though I've been promoted to sales manager, I still wish I could get back into industry.

"I'll look into it," he said happily. "Thanks for the tip."

Before Tom returned to his work area, he looked up Kearney & Trecher in the yellow pages and was surprised to find they were located near his apartment complex. "Maybe I should stop there on my way home," he thought.

When Tom left for the day, he was still undecided about stopping at Kearney & Trecher to check on the job, but as he passed the industrial complex, he impulsively turned into the parking lot.

"I'd better get a hair cut tomorrow," he thought as he quickly brushed the hair out of his eyes and rubbed his sweaty palms on his pants legs. After a full day at work, he felt hot and tired. His fingers were smudged with carbon from writing out sales receipts and his shirt and pants looked dusty from his forages into the stock room. But Tom didn't take time to stop at the washroom to clean up. He knew the offices would be closing soon and he wanted to get there before everyone went home.

"Hi," he said to the first person he saw. "I heard you have a job open."

"Not in this office," a burly young man said brusquely. "I intend to stay here awhile." Then he saw Tom's confusion, he added, "Why don't you try Personnel down the hall. Somebody should still be in the office."

When Tom finally found the office, a tall, blond man in a gray suit was putting a file away. He was the only person in sight.

"I heard about your job opening," Tom blurted even before the man had seen him.

"Did you have an appointment to see someone here?" the man asked as he closed the file.

"No," Tom said, feeling flustered. "I just stopped by on my way home from work."

"What's your name?" the man asked. "I'll look up your resume and application letter."

"My name's Tom Chenko," Tom stammered. "But I didn't send you a resume or application letter. I just heard about the opening today, and I hurried right over.

"I'd really like to work here," he added lamely.

"Well, my name's Mr. Amsrud. I'm the Personnel Director," Mr. Amsrud said.

"Lucky me," Tom thought. "I get to meet the person in charge right away."

"My secretary is gone for the day, and I'm on my way out," Mr. Amsrud said. "But," he added in a tired voice, "I suppose we can talk for awhile."

Mr. Amsrud remained standing, and he didn't write down anything Tom said. Tom thought this was a little unusual, but he decided that every interviewer probably had an individual style. The remainder of the interview went like this:

MR. AMSRUD: "Where do you work?"
TOM: "High Tec Equipment."
MR. AMSRUD: "How long have you worked there?"
TOM: "A year. My brother quit to go back to college, and I took over his job."

(By this time Tom was getting tired. Mr. Amsrud still had not asked him to sit down, so Tom leaned against the wall. After all day on the job, relaxing a little felt good.)

MR. AMSRUD: "Why do you want to work here?"
TOM: "I like industrial work better than retail. Customers drive me up the wall. They don't listen and they complain about every little thing."
MR. AMSRUD: "Did you ever work in industry?"
TOM: "Sure. I worked for L. M. Johnson. Our high school had a training program, and I was assigned to L. M. Johnson. After graduation, I just stayed on. I worked there full time and went to school part-time until I got my associate degree in electronics."
MR. AMSRUD: "Why did you leave that job?"
TOM: "I needed a change. My brother told me about the job. After I graduated from the Tech, I took over for him."
MR. AMSRUD: "Do you know anything about our business?"
TOM: "No, but I'm willing to learn. I'm a fast learner. I always got good grades in school."
MR. AMSRUD: "Do you have any references?"
TOM: "I'm sure my boss would give me a reference. I haven't asked him, but he probably would."

Tom looked at his shoes. Mr. Amsrud's steady gaze made him feel uncomfortable. He caught a glimpse of the director's shiney black shoes, and he wished he were wearing something other than his comfortable old sneakers.

"Well," Mr. Amsrud said, looking at his watch. "I'm late for a meeting, but I'll keep you in mind. We'll let you know if we have any openings. Thanks for letting us know you're interested."

"Sure," Tom said. "It was nice talking to you. Bye, now."

Mr. Amsrud was already stuffing papers in his briefcase as Tom turned to leave.

"Thought any more about the job," Cathy asked the next morning as she and Tom walked into the store together.

"I went over there after work," Tom said, "but I don't think they liked me much." He sounded unhappy.

"Oh, people always feel let down after an interview," Cathy said helpfully. "Why don't you call back in a few days and let them know you're still interested."

"That's a good idea," Tom said. But when he called back a few days later, Mr.

Amsrud was unavailable and his secretary didn't have any record of the interview. She didn't sound very encouraging.

Two weeks later Cathy told Tom what she had heard from Barb. "They hired someone for the technician's job at Kearney & Trecher, Cathy said. "I guess the guy is just out of school with no work experience. It seems like you were better qualified. I wonder why they hired him instead," Cathy said, sounding puzzled.

"I don't know," Tom said unhappily. "There's no explaining employers I guess."

DISCUSSION OF SCENARIO

Is Tom correct when he says, "There's no explaining employers?" Or did the way he conducted himself make Mr. Amsrud reluctant to offer Tom the job. If you had been Mr. Amsrud would you have hired Tom? Let's take a look at the circumstances that contributed to Mr. Amsrud's decision to pass over Tom's application as he screened prospective employees.

First Tom's decision to apply at Kearney & Trecher was spur of the moment. He did not know what the company manufactured or anything about their employment history, sales markets or working conditions. He did, however, have an excellent opportunity to learn about the company from Dan. Tom could have called Dan for general background information on Kearney & Trecher as well as specifics about the job opening. Perhaps Dan would also have agreed to let Tom tell Mr. Amsrud that he had learned of the job in a round-about way from him. Knowing particulars about the job would have strengthened Tom's position as an applicant.

Planning for the interview in other ways would also have helped Tom seem like a more serious applicant. Tom just "stopped in" to talk about the job. Instead, he should have called Mr. Amsrud's secretary to ask about the application procedure. Evidently Mr. Amsrud expected a resume and application letter on file. Surprising the Personnel Director at the end of the day made an unfavorable impression.

Tom may still have salvaged the interview and impressed Mr. Amsrud with his qualifications if he had known how to conduct himself in an interview. But Tom's body language and answers to Mr. Amsrud's questions all sent the wrong messages to the employer.

Tom's fingers were smudged with carbon, his clothes and shoes were dirty and his hair needed cutting. Because Tom had not taken the time to dress up for the interview, he sent a silent message to the employer that said, "I'm careless in my work habits, too."

The way he leaned against the wall and looked at his shoes also sent a negative message. Mr. Amsrud probably interpreted Tom's posture and lack of eye control as insecurity or laziness. Since employers look for ambitious, confident workers, Mr. Amsrud would use his body language as one factor in deciding against Tom's application.

The spoken messages Tom sent were as ineffective as his silent messages. Rather than emphasizing his education and work experience in industry, he complained about the people he met in the retail business. Mr. Amsrud probably thought, "This applicant may not get along with the other employees."

Tom also did not have a well thought out answer for wanting to leave his present job. "I need a change," he said.

Mr. Amsrud probably thought, "This applicant won't stay on the job long. We'll just get him trained and he'll leave."

Tom also didn't have any references. He thought his boss would give him a reference, but he hadn't asked him for one.

Altogether, the verbal and nonverbal messages Tom sends give Mr. Amsrud many good reasons for rejecting Tom's application.

Is Tom as unfavorable of an applicant as he appears to Mr. Amsrud? Probably not. Tom was chosen for a high school training program and was evidently good at the job because he was asked to stay with the company when he graduated. Since this job gave him experience in electronics, he should have emphasized his work experience at L. M. Johnson.

Although Tom sends nonverbal messages that make him appear unambitious, he must be quite ambitious if he held a full time job and went to school part-time until he earned an associate degree. Although we know Tom took over his brother's job as salesman at High Tec Equipment and was promoted to sales manager, Tom does not tell Mr. Amsrud this.

Tom may be an excellent worker, but he lacks knowledge and experience in job hunting. This is the first time he has interviewed for a job. Tom eased into his job at L. M. Johnson Company after graduation; therefore, he did not take an interview for that job. Then his brother recommended him for the job at High Tec Equipment and he was probably hired mostly on his brother's recommendation. In addition to his training in electronics skills, Tom needed some help with job seeking and communication skills.

HOW EFFICIENT ARE YOUR JOB SEEKING SKILLS?

Although Tom's experience is fictional, similar situations occur regularly. Often applicants arrive unprepared for interviews and appear unambitious or insecure. Nervousness can make us talk and act differently than we would in less stressful situations and especially tense applicants may actually misrepresent their work habits and attitudes.

Although some tension is normal in an interview, you can eliminate some uneasiness and present yourself more effectively if you know certain job seeking skills and prepare for the interview.

Are your job seeking skills up-to-date? To see how well you would do in an interview, study the picture on the next page. If you were an employer, would you hire this applicant? How many blunders can you identify? Compare your list of mistakes with the list on page 285; then read the chapter for more information of job seeking skills.

ABRAMS

1. Posture too relaxed.
2. Wearing jogging shoes.
3. Drinking coffee.
4. Needs a hair cut.
5. Should have a bound portfolio (at least he should have his papers in a folder).
6. Cigarettes showing.
7. Asks about money too soon and makes it sound like the foremost thought in his mind.

16

APPLYING FOR A JOB

After studying this chapter you should understand how to:
1. Organize a personal data sheet
2. Write a letter of application
3. Prepare for and participate in an interview

You can apply the skills and ideas we have discussed in this text to a variety of experiences in your personal and work-related life. They will be helpful to you in communicating with your friends and family as well as with your boss and co-workers. You can use them to improve your written and oral expression and to become more sensitive to the messages you receive as a reader and listener.

As a way of tying together the variety of ideas we have discussed, we will now talk about how these skills interact and how you can apply the concepts to one particular situation: the job-seeking experience. Although you will want to use the information you have learned from this book in all your daily experiences, the job-seeking situation is probably one of the concerns foremost in your mind now.

In this chapter we will discuss three areas of job seeking: organizing a résumé, writing a letter of application, and preparing for and participating in an interview. At the beginning of each of the three major sections you will find a list of the chapters that discuss the skills helpful in that particular part of the process. It is hoped that you will use those skills to communicate effectively during the job-seeking process and in other activities of your daily life.

ORGANIZING THE RESUME

Refer to the following chapters for helpful background information: 2, 4.

Résumé Defined

The résumé presents your work record and work-related experience in a clear and well-organized outline. It includes your educational background, work experience, awards, special interests, and unique experience that can make you an exceptional employee.

When you are preparing your résumé, you should keep two things in mind: (1) your audience, and (2) your purpose.

Your Audience

You should consider your audience as carefully when you are preparing your résumé as you do when you are preparing a talk or writing a letter. Put yourself in the employer's place. Today it is quite common for an employer to receive 50, 100, even 200 applications for one job, and the company may list 5, 10, or 50 jobs each year. When you think of a person reviewing hundreds of résumés, you realize that you must present exceptionally interesting information in an easy-to-read format in order to catch the employer's attention and earn a thorough look at your qualifications.

Your Purpose

Your purpose in preparing the résumé is to get an interview. When planning your résumé you should search your mind for special qualities you have that make you an outstanding worker. List work-related accomplishments that will help you stand out over the usual applicant and make the prospective employer want to discuss the job with you. Of course it is important to show that you have the basic qualifications for the job such as an Associate Degree or practical experience, but your résumé should also show that you have unique qualities that will help you do exceptional work.

Organizing the Résumé

Keeping your audience and purpose in mind, you can begin to organize your résumé. First make a list of all the items you think should be included. Mention educational background, work experience, special interests, awards, and memberships that will make you a better worker. This is the time to use your brainstorming skills. List everything you think is important. Then evaluate the things you have listed and add or cross out items. When your list is complete, organize your qualifications into a résumé you can send to an employer. Three résumé formats are generally accepted: the reverse chronological, the functional, and the combination.

Reverse Chronological The reverse chronological, shown in Figure 16–1, is the most common resumé format. In this organizational pattern you list the jobs you have held and the course work or degrees you have completed, starting with the

THOMAS CHENKO
1090 Dotter St.
Rothschild, WI 54401
(715) 359–8424

WORK EXPERIENCE	
6/85–present	HIGH TEC EQUIPMENT Rothschild, Wisconsin
	Sales manager. Hired sales personnel. Organized
	staff and did special ordering for customers.
1/85–6/85	HIGH TEC EQUIPMENT Rothschild, Wisconsin
	Sales person. Sold home computers, car stereos
	systems and other electronic equipment.
6/1981–12/1984	L.M. JOHNSON COMPANY Merrill, Wisconsin
	Technician. Repaired robots and other electronic
	machinery for packaging industry.
10/1980–5/1981	L.M. JOHNSON COMPANY Merrill, Wisconsin
	High school on-the-job training program. Worked
	three hours/day repairing robots and other
	electronic equipment for packaging industry.
EDUCATION	
1981–1984	North Central Technical Institute Wausau, Wisconsin
	Associate Degree in Electronics
1977–1981	Wausau North High School Wausau, Wisconsin
	Coursework included four years of math, science
	and English
	Elective course in electronics
	On-the-job training program in electronics
SPECIAL INTERESTS	Ham radio operator
	President of Northland Nordic Ski Club
	Volunteer with Big Brothers Association
AWARDS & MEMBERSHIPS	First class operator's license from the Federal
	Communications Commission
	2nd place in Wisconsin Contest for ham radio operators
REFERENCES	Transcripts and instruction references furnished
	upon request by North Central Technical Institute,
	Wausau, Wisconsin.

Figure 16-1 Reverse chronological résumé.

most recent experience and moving backward (in reverse) through your work and education activities. The advantage of the reverse chronological organization is that, since it is the most frequently used pattern, the employer will be familiar with it and view it as a straightforward account of your qualifications. The disadvantage of this format is that it quickly reveals any gaps in your work record. Extended periods of time when you did not hold a job or upgrade your skills with additional training are difficult to camouflage when you use this pattern.

Functional   The functional resumé is an innovative approach to personal data organization in which you describe your work experience and related training by job functions such as layout, proofreading or typesetting in the printing field. If you choose this format, you should brainstorm a list of the particular work-related functions you feel capable of performing under each job and give specific information about where and when you have performed these jobs, if you have.

From this list, organize the data according to types of job functions and write a paragraph giving specific information about your performance of these functions.

The obvious advantage to you of using this format is that you can camouflage time aspects of your work history that an employer might interpret negatively, such as extended periods of time when you did not work or go to school or a tendency to "job hop."

Employers, however, are aware that the functional format can be used to hide problem areas. For that reason, they often view this type of resumé with suspicion. You should be aware of this disadvantage and choose to use the functional resumé cautiously.

Combined   The third type of resumé organization combines the reverse chronological with the functional. Begin with a description of your special skills and accomplishments. Then list your work experience and educational background chronologically. This format allows you to draw the employer's attention to your strengths and at the same time it puts your work record up front. If you are applying for a job in a competitive market and have some special skills and experience that set you apart from other candidates, you might consider using the combination format.

Other Information

In addition to educational and work background you will want to include other information on your resumé. What additional data should you select?

Today, most people do not include age, height, marital status, and sex on a resumé. As a general rule, you should include only personal data that you feel will be helpful in getting you an interview. Remember that your purpose is to convince the employer to discuss the job with you. At this point do not volunteer any information that might be interpreted negatively.

Should I give my current salary or my preferred salary? Giving any salary information is usually not a good idea on a resumé. You may price yourself out of the market. Omitting all mention of salary is generally accepted as the best practice today.

Should I state why I left my past jobs? This information too is usually best left out. Many reasons for leaving jobs may be interpreted negatively. If you were fired, for example, you can handle that best by discussing it in person with the prospective employer. If you left your present job to accommodate your spouse, who received a tempting promotion, it will be more effective to assure the employer in person that you can make a commitment to the job now. Most significant reasons for leaving a job are better discussed in person.

Should I include references? A reference is a person who will vouch for your positive characteristics as a worker. Although you may list references on your resumé if you wish, most applicants today simply state that references are available on request. This is preferable for several reasons:

1. The prospective employer will have to contact you to get your references. That gives you an additional opportunity to talk with the employer or someone in the company. These extra contacts can be helpful in keeping your name in front of the employer.
2. You have more control over who is contacted and when they are contacted. If your resumé is not reviewed for several months, for example, you may change your mind about who to include as references. If you are scouting for job opportunities but don't want your current employer to know you are job hunting, you will probably prefer to withhold references until you know you are interested in the job.

What should I include under personal characteristics? You should include memberships, awards, and special interests that pertain directly to the job or show you as a well-rounded individual. Select information that will enhance your stature as an applicant. For example, if you are applying for a secretarial position and include an interest in needlecrafts under personal data, the employer might interpret this special interest positively because it shows that you enjoy working with your hands quietly and in an orderly fashion (characteristics that are admired in a secretary). If, on the other hand, you were applying for a job with a child care center and listed needlecrafts as a hobby, the employer would probably view this neutrally at best. The employer might even think someone who enjoyed the quiet, individual hobby of needlecraft would not cope well with the boisterous interaction of a child care center.

Rereading

When you have brainstormed your qualifications and organized them into a format that shows your special skills and work record in the most favorable terms, you should reread your resumé. Be sure you have stated facts only. Opinion statements such as "I get along well with people" and "I am an efficient worker" do not belong in a resumé. Your purpose in writing the resumé is to present facts; the prospective employer will interpret those facts.

When preparing the resumé, then, you should observe the planning, writing, and revising steps of the writing process. Keep your audience and purpose in mind and include only factual information. Organize your data so it highlights your special skills and presents your qualifications effectively.

APPLICATION LETTER

Refer to the following chapters for helpful background information: 2, 4, 10, 11, 13.

Along with your resumé you should send an application letter. The resumé is a list of personal qualifications that may apply to many different jobs, and you may decide to send the same resumé to several employers. The application letter, on the other hand, is written specifically in response to one particular job listing.

Application Letter Defined

Many of the techniques we discussed in Chapter 13 can be applied to this letter. The application letter is one of the most important letters you will write. It is really a cross between a letter of request and a sales letter; therefore, it combines the indirect and direct approaches used in these letters.

The letter begins with a direct request: "Please consider my application." Then it applies the technique of a sales letter (but this time you are selling yourself rather than a product or service) and concludes with a call for action: "Let's talk about my request further."

Introductory Paragraph

Although you can liven it up any way you want, the introductory paragraph of an application letter should include three things:

1. The position you are applying for
2. Where you learned about the position
3. A clear statement indicating that you want to be considered for the position

When you are writing the introductory paragraph, you must remember that the employer will be looking for people to fill several positions. Some personnel directors may be considering applicants for jobs as a typist, a floor supervisor, and a salesperson simultaneously. For that reason you must state clearly which position you are applying for.

Telling the employer where you learned about the position can be helpful for several reasons. First, it will give the employer a frame of reference. If you state,

"I learned about this opening from the placement director at Northwoods College," the employer will connect you with a particular school. If you state, "Mr. Jones, your night supervisor, told me about this opening," the employer will identify you with Mr. Jones. Especially if the employer thinks favorably of Northwoods College or Mr. Jones, your letter will be better received.

Finally, state specifically that you want to be considered for the position. A direct statement here indicates confidence, a trait employers appreciate.

Development Paragraph

Use the paragraph following the introductory paragraph to sell yourself to the employer. In these paragraphs you will mention important work experience, education, and personality traits that suit you for the job. Remember your purpose here is to prove to the employer that you are better suited for the job than anyone else. Telling the employer that you have an Associate Degree in Marketing does not set you apart from 200 other people graduating in the spring from Northwoods College with an Associate Degree in Marketing. On the other hand, telling the employer that you won an award for a window display while you studied for an Associate Degree in Marketing does set you apart.

Be sure to relate your qualifications to the specific job for which you are applying. Notice how the applicant in Figure 16–3 has matched his qualifications to the requirements mentioned in the ad (Figure 16–2). For example, your award in window display will be especially impressive if the job for which you are applying requires you to design window displays. Point out connections between your qualifications and the job. Don't expect the employers to make those connections for you.

Concluding Paragraph

The concluding paragraph is a call to action similar to those in other sales letters. Remember that the purpose of the application letter is to convince the employer to call you in for an interview. In the last paragraph, therefore, state that purpose clearly and make it easy for the employer to contact you. Express a willingness to meet at the employer's convenience and state how you can be contacted. Close with a friendly statement and hope for the best.

In Figure 16–3 you will see how these techniques can be combined for effective application letters.

JOB INTERVIEWING

Refer to the following chapters for helpful background information: 1, 2, 3, 4, 5, 6, 7.

If your letter and resumé are effective, you may be asked to an interview. The job interview is one of the most important applications of one-to-one com-

Figure 16-2 Source: Kearney & Trecher Corporation.

Electronic Technician

Kearney & Trecker
Customer Repair Center
(Butler Plant)

Due to expansion, we are looking for an individual with an Associate Degree in Electronics and possible 1-2 years' experience in a manufacturing environment. Background in DEC PDP/8A and PDP/8A® computers a plus.

We offer an outstanding benefit program, including paid health and life insurance, profit sharing/retirement plan, dental plan and educational refund program.

Please send employment history and salary requirements, in complete confidence, to the Employment Department.

Kearney & Trecker Corporation
11000 Theodore Trecker Way
West Allis, WI 53214
Equal Opportunity Employer M/F/H/V

munication in the business world. It is your first step to succeeding in the work place. Getting a job that interests and challenges you and one that lets you use your special talents depends on the impression you make when you first discuss jobs with a potential employer. Because effective interaction between the two of you is vital to job success, we will discuss two-person communication as it relates specifically to the employment interview.

The purpose of a job interview is: (1) to give the employer information about your personal characteristics and work-related qualifications, and (2) to give you information about the job. Job applicants often feel like they are in the spotlight and must prove themselves to the authority figure on the opposite side of the desk. That feeling may make you sound defensive and irritable during the interview. You

Figure 16-3

1090 Dotter St.
Rothschild, WI 54401
February 13, 1984

Personnel Director
Kearney & Trecker Corporation
11000 Theodore Trecker Way
West Allis, WI 53214

Dear Director:

The opening you advertised in the Milwaukee Journal for an electronics technician sounds like just the job I am looking for. I have an Associate Degree in electronics and experience in an industrial setting so this position is especially interesting to me. Please consider my application for the job in your Customer Repair Center.

My Associate Degree from North Central Technical Institute gives me a firm background in production and repair of electronic equipment. My course work includes a course in digital integrated circuitry and one in Control Circuits and Systems which emphasized industrial electronics. I also took an elective course in Microprocessor Fundamentals which was especially helpful when I worked for L. M. Johnson Company repairing industrial robots and computers.

My work experience has given me excellent background in electronic repair and in working with people. I have worked as a salesperson for High Tec, where I sold home computers, car stereo systems, and other electronic equipment for cars and home. I know how to listen to people and pay attention to customer needs. When I worked for L. M. Johnson Company, I was able to apply many of the things I learned in school and gain hands-on experience in repairing industrial computers and computerized equipment.

I am an independent, outgoing person with a special interest in electronics. I enjoy being a ham radio operator because I can combine my knowledge of electronics with my interest in people. I am comfortable talking to customers and responding to their concerns. My job as a sales manager gave me experience in planning my work day effectively. I had a lot of responsibility there and learned to work independently.

I enjoyed my job in industry and would like to return to that work environment; therefore, I hope we can discuss this position in more detail.

If you think my qualifications meet your requirements, please let me know. I can come to your office for an interview at your convenience and look forward to talking with you about the electronics position.

Sincerely,

Tom Chenko

Tom Chenko

should remember that the employer is as interested in hiring an employee as you are in finding a job. You are both pursuing a common goal. Keeping that in mind will help you be open with the interviewer and establish the feeling that you are both working together to fill the opening.

If you are relatively new to the job market, you may also have the idea that you should take the first job offered to you. You have lived on a student's income long enough and you may be more interested in drawing a regular paycheck than in finding a challenging job where you can develop your unique talents. This attitude can also hinder your job-seeking success. Remember the second purpose of an interview: to learn about the company. During the interview you should show the employer that you are interested in finding a job that matches your qualifications and a place where you will work effectively. In a polite way you are also interviewing the employer. Keeping in mind these two purposes, let's look closely at the interviewing process.

Organization

Like any other two-person communication, a job interview has a beginning, a middle, and an end. We have already looked closely at these three stages as they relate generally to two-person talks. Here we will discuss techniques that are applicable to each of the three stages of a job interview. In each stage you and the interviewer send and receive both verbal and nonverbal messages. We will talk about these messages as we discuss each stage.

Opening the Interview

Purpose   Like other two-person talks, an interview begins with casual, neutral comments. The purpose of this stage is to exchange basic background information and establish rapport between you and the interviewer.

Verbal Signals   The interviewer may start with questions about your trip to the office and your educational background. These should be nonthreatening questions which are easy for you to answer with factual information. This is an appropriate time for you to compliment the employer on the appearance of the building, the community in general, or some interesting item in the office. Choose the item carefully and word your compliment wisely so you sound sincere and interested rather than too personal or overeager.

Answer questions completely, but don't ramble on with long involved answers. Throughout the interview, knowing when to stop talking is as important as knowing what to say. Often interviewers will not signal you when they have heard enough. They will wait for you to finish talking. You have heard people who repeat themselves in an effort to fill a silence and finally run down like a tired clock spring. Short silences can be beneficial in an interview. They give both you and the interviewer time to think about what has just been said and to collect your thoughts before going on to the next topic. Stopping when you have given a sincere, complete answer is one indication that you can make decisions and act on your own.

Nonverbal signals   Nonverbal signals are especially important during the first stage because they create a subtle impression that will last throughout the interview. Often we are not sure why we feel uncomfortable or seem instinctively to dislike a person. Careful analysis may reveal that body language is responsible for our negative or positive reaction to a person. Because you are especially eager to impress the employer positively, you should be particularly aware of the nonverbal signals you send. Although you will certainly feel some nervousness, don't show it by drumming your fingers on the desk, swinging your foot to an inner rhythm, or clearing your throat repeatedly. These actions may make the employer wonder how you will react to on-the-job pressures. They will also probably heighten tension for the interviewer and hinder concentration for both of you. On the other hand, don't try to cover up your nervousness by acting overly casual. Slumping in the first chair you see, crossing your legs, and lighting up a cigarette in an attempt to appear "at home" will surely send negative signals to the interviewer.

You should dress neatly and conservatively, observing the particular etiquette of the company. In business, for example, men and women usually wear suits or blazers in conservative colors. You will want to show, through your appearance, that you can fit into the company. Avoid overdressing. Sometimes attempting to impress, we might wear extra jewelry, higher heels, flashier clothing, or heavy fragrances. Remember you are going to work, not to a party. Your dress should say, "I'm ready to do the job."

You can start the interview effectively by arriving on time and greeting the interviewer politely. You should follow the interviewer's lead. Wait until the interviewer offers to shake hands; sit down only when you are invited.

Early in the interview you will also want to establish eye contact with the employer. Look directly at the interviewer during the greeting and when you answer questions. Use eye contact to show that you are listening closely to the questions and comments.

Second Stage of Interview

Purpose   When the initial greeting and exchange of casual comments and background information are finished, you move into the second stage of the interview. This is when the interviewer gets down to the business of finding out if you are the best candidate for the job. This is also the time when you should find out if the job is right for you. During this stage the interviewer will be interested in your education and training and your work experience as it relates specifically to the job. The interviewer will also use this time to evaluate personal characteristics which may help or hinder your job performance. You should show the employer that you understand the basics about the job and have some background information about the company. Relate to the employer's needs and show how you can benefit the company. Tom Jackson in his popular book *Guerrilla Tactics in the Job Market* says:

The message that is irresistible to an employer is the message that makes him feel confident of two things:

- Your ability to contribute to the solution of problems he faces. Your skills or aptitude.
- Your willingness to do what is necessary to get the job done. In other words, your attitude.[1]

Verbal signals   Answer questions positively. Rather than saying, "I don't have much experience in this field but I'm willing to learn," say, "I am looking forward to the chance to apply the technical skills I have learned in school to a job in (marketing or drafting)." Use every opportunity to show your interest in the job, to relate to the employer's needs. For example, you may be asked, "Why should I hire you?" and you may be tempted to say, "Because I need a job"; this will not impress the interviewer, though. Prove instead that if you are hired you will be an asset to the company because of your training, past experience, or personality traits.

Although you should prepare for the interview, avoid trite responses such as the following.

Q: Why should I hire you?
A: Because I get along well with other people.
Q: Why did you leave your last job?
A: For advancement.

Answers like this will tell the employer that although you have been coached in the interviewing process, you are not relating specifically to this job. Strive to answer questions directly as they relate to your particular experience and the particular job you are seeking. Remember that an interviewer may talk to hundreds of candidates during a year. Your main purpose during this stage is to prove that you will involve yourself with the job and the business the interviewer represents.

During this stage you should also ask questions about the job. Like your responses to the employer's questions, your own questions should show your involvement with the job. Ask questions about the type of work you will do and the way important projects are handled. This is not the time to ask about salary, benefits, or vacation days. Wait until you are offered the job to ask about these areas.

Nonverbal signals   Nonverbal signals are also important during this stage. Continue to show sincerity with eye contact and keep in mind the importance of your appearance.

Reading the nonverbal signals the interviewer sends you is another important part of this two-person communication. Remember what you have learned about body language and use it to evaluate the impression you are making on the

---

[1] Tom Jackson, *Guerrilla Tactics in the Job Market* (New York: Bantam, 1978), p. 239.

employer. Does the interviewer remain open to your conversation (palms up, coat unbuttoned, glasses on)? Or does something you say make the employer take off the glasses, button the coat or fold the arms? Does the interviewer nod and smile or frown and clear the throat? An awareness of these signals will help you to continue if they are favorable or to change tactics if they are not.

Answering difficult questions   Even when you have planned carefully for an interview, you may find some of the questions difficult to answer. Your personal goals may be unclear, you may be embarrassed by occurrences in your working past, or you may have difficulty discussing your personal strengths with another person. Anticipate questions that you may have trouble answering and plan your responses carefully. The less you are caught off guard, the more smoothly you will be able to respond to troublesome inquiries. Some difficult questions you may be asked along with suggested answers are listed below.

Q: I notice you have changed jobs four times in the last three years. What is the reason for these frequent job changes?

A: I did change jobs frequently before I went back to school. I was looking for challenging and rewarding work. Studying mechanical design is very interesting for me and I expect to find a job in that field equally challenging. When I am involved in my work I won't have a reason to job-hop.

Q: Why did you leave your last job?

A: *(In this case, if you were fired, you will have to answer the question honestly. Try to phrase your answer as positively as possible. Play down personality conflicts and emphasize the idea that you have learned from your experience and you think that you can make a worthwhile contribution to a company now.)*
I lived ten miles from my job and I had difficulty getting to work on time. I realize now how important it is to be punctual and I am prepared to move so I can be close to my work.
(If the decision to leave was entirely yours, be careful that you are not too flippant with this answer. Make the point that you are looking for a company where you can get involved and grow as a worker.)

Q: What do you expect to be doing five years from now?

A: *(With this answer you want to show that you are motivated to get ahead, but don't sound so aggressive that you frighten the employer. You will not, for example, tell the employer you hope to own a competitive company.)*
I would like to use my training and work experience to move into a supervisory position with a forward-looking company such as yours.

Q.   If you are hired, how long will you stay?

or

If you are offered the job, will you accept it?

A.   *(You may be tempted here to promise anything to get the job offer, but you should be careful about promising too much. If you tell the employer you plan to stay forever and leave six months later when your wife receives an attractive job*

offer in another city, the employer may remember you negatively despite your
outstanding job performance.)
I am looking for a job I can become involved in. I like to finish projects I start
and I would like to stay in this location. For those reasons, if I were offered this
job and accepted it I would intend to stay with it. I don't see any reason now
why I would leave the job in a short time.

or

If I am offered this job, I will consider it seriously.

Q: How old are you? Do you intend to have children?

A: *(Although most interviewers know they cannot legally ask these kinds of questions, you may encounter one who forgets or is uninformed and asks questions
that discriminate among applicants. You can call the error to the interviewer's attention with an answer like the following.)*
That's illegal.

or

I refuse to answer that.
*(However, these answers won't make you very popular. You might choose instead
to answer the question without revealing private information.)*
My maturity and variety of job experiences will help me bring a balanced
perspective to this job.

or

I think it's possible to enjoy both a rewarding career and a fulfilling family life.
I'm here because I think I can handle the dual role.

Other difficult questions may be:

Q: What are your strengths?
Q: What are your weaknesses?
Q: You worked with Mrs. _____.
     How did you get along with her?
Q: What salary do you expect?

Anticipate questions that you may feel uncomfortable answering and plan
responses carefully. Most colleges and technical schools have career counselors. If
you need help planning an interviewing strategy, consult these counselors.

Concluding the Interview

As the interview draws to a close, you should remember the purpose of concluding a two-person talk. This is the time to ask for feedback from the interviewer:
"Do my qualifications seem to fit your needs?" "Have I answered your questions
adequately?" Express your interest in learning the employer's decision and show appreciation for the opportunity to discuss the job. Show your willingness to conclude
the interview by following the employer's nonverbal lead. As the interviewer leans

forward, shuffles papers, or puts down a pen, you too should gather your papers together, move forward in your chair, and be ready to stand when the interviewer stands. Although you may still prefer to wait until the interviewer offers to shake hands in parting, you may also find the close of an interview an appropriate time to initiate this friendly gesture.

Applying the techniques of two-person talks throughout the interview, maintaining eye contact, and remaining sensitive to the nonverbal signals you both send and receive will help you communicate effectively during this rather stressful time.

Table 16–1 outlines the stages of an interview and the verbal and nonverbal communications that occur.

SUMMARY

Many of the communication skills we discussed in this text can be applied to the job application process. Use your brainstorming and organization skills to plan and prepare the resumé. Keep your audience (a prospective employer) and your purpose (to get invited for an interview) clearly in mind as you organize your resumé. Choose the organization pattern (reverse chronological, functional, or combination) that allows you to play up your strong points and downplay the weaker aspects of your work-related characteristics.

You will send the same resumé to many different employers, but the application letter included with the resumé should be tailored to a specific job listing.

Table 16–1 Comparison of Verbal and Nonverbal Signals

STAGE I: BEGINNING	
VERBAL	NONVERBAL
Interviewer:	
• "How are you this morning?" • "Did you have any trouble finding us?" • "Where did you go to school? How did you like it there? Did you know _____? That school has quite a hockey team. Do you play hockey?" • "Where are you from?"	• Establishes eye contact • Extends hand to shake hands • May proceed you into the office or may motion you ahead • Motions you to a seat
Interviewee:	
• Answer questions completely and sincerely • Use voice and silence to show definite end to each answer	• Dress appropriately • Establish eye contact • Follow interviewer's lead to shake hands and sit down • Sit comfortably—not tense or slouched in chair • Do not smoke or drink coffee • Refrain from nervous movements

(Continued)

Table 16-1 (Cont.)

STAGE II: MIDDLE	
VERBAL	*NONVERBAL*

Interviewer:
- "I notice that you have taken courses in _____. How will these courses help you do this job?"
- "How do you feel about working weekends?"
- "Why did you leave your last job?"
- "Why should I hire you?"
- "If you did work for us, what problem do you think you might have on this job?"
- "Where do you expect to be five years from now?"
- "What do you like to do in your spare time?"
- "Why are you interested in this type of work?"
- "What salary do you want?"

- Continues to make eye contact
- May nod and smile to show approval or frown, clear throat, take off glasses when disapproving

Interviewee:
- Answer all questions sincerely and completely
- Ask technical questions about the work:
  - "How is mail distribution handled in this office?"
  - "What are the specific duties of this job?"
  - What is your policy on employee education?"
  - "How many accounts do each of the people in this department handle?"

- Maintain eye contact
- Maintain upright, relaxed posture
- Use items from your portfolio to support your assertion that you have unique qualifications for the job
- Avoid nervous movements like finger tapping, head scratching, or feet shuffling

STAGE III: CONCLUSION	
VERBAL	*NONVERBAL*

Interviewer:
- Concludes interview
- Gives an indication of when you will hear from them again
- "Do you have any more questions about the job?"

- Will begin sending concluding signals such as shuffling papers, closing notebook, leaning forward

Interviewee:
- This is the time to ask for feedback:
  - "From what I have told you, do you think I have a chance for the job?"
  - "Is there anything else you would like to know?"
  - "Will you be notifying me of your decision?"

- Wait until interviewer starts sending concluding signals, then follow the lead: begin collecting your papers, leaning forward, showing a willingness to conclude
- Stand up when the interviewer does
- Maintain eye contact throughout
- Shake hands if initiated by interviewer or if you feel comfortable at this point in initiating it

Mention particular characteristics that you think will be important to the specific job and relate them to the job opening for which you are applying. The application letter combines the techniques of a direct letter of request with a sales letter. With the application letter you are selling yourself.

We hope that an effective letter and résumé will result in a job interview. This interview is one of the most important applications of one-to-one communication in the business world. Its purpose is: (1) to give the employer knowledge about your personal characteristics and work-related qualifications, and (2) to give you information about the job.

An interview usually opens with nonthreatening questions and comments which call for basic information and which establish rapport between you and the interviewer.

Anticipate difficult questions prior to the interview and be prepared to answer them during the middle stage of the interview. During this stage you should also ask questions about the job. As the interview nears an end, ask the interviewer for feedback about your qualifications.

Throughout the interview pay attention to body language both as you send to the interviewer and as you receive. Give the interviewer direct eye contact and know when to stop talking. Pay attention to how you greet the employer and how you sit during the interview. Use the communication skills you have learned from this text to find and keep the job you want.

REVIEW QUESTIONS

1. What is the purpose of a resumé? How is it different from an application letter?
2. What are the three ways you can organize your resumé? What are the advantages and disadvantages of each?
3. What pattern of resumé organization do you think would fit your work history and qualifications best? Explain the reasons for your choice.
4. How is the application letter similar to a sales letter? What characteristics about your work record and related qualifications do you think are worthy of highlighting in your application letter?
5. What are the three stages of the interviewing process? What goes on during each stage?
6. How does body language relay information during an interview? Give specific examples.

ACTIVITIES

1. If you were an employer, how would you evaluate the resumé in Figure 16–1A? Indicate problem areas, then rewrite the resumé to show Mary Owens' qualifications in the best way. Choose a format that deemphasizes the problems you spotted in Mary's resumé and be prepared to explain why you selected that particular pattern.

Mary Owens
114 Prince Avenue
Merrill, Illinois 68218

PERSONAL DATA SHEET

Work Experience:

June 1984–June 1985	Holland's Gourmet Foods Waitress Reason for leaving: moved
December 1983–June 1984	Karlan's 5 & 10 Sales Clerk Reason for leaving: advanced to a job I liked better
May 1983–December 1983	Kentucky Fried Chicken Check-out Reason for leaving: terminated
May 1982–May 1983	Jack's Fine Foods Waitress Reason for leaving: moved

Education:

1980–1982	North Central Technical Institute Associate Degree in Marketing
1976–1980	Wausau North High School

Personal Data:

Marital Status:	Divorced
Family:	2 children
Sex:	Female
Age:	26
Health:	Good
Special Interests:	I enjoy movies and reading President of PTA I like to talk to people and get along well with different personalities.

References:

Maxine Olson
1080 Spruce St.
Cambridge, Illinois
Position: friend

Reverend Robert Jackson
1084 Wilson St.
Cambridge, Illinois
Position: Pastor of Cambridge
                Lutheran Church

Figure 16-1A

2. Prepare a resumé of your qualifications. Organize it to highlight strengths that you now have as a worker and minimize problem areas in your work history. Be prepared to discuss your resumé with your instructor and other members of your class.

3. Page through trade journals, newspapers, and employment agency listings. Select a listing for a job that interests you and for which you believe you are qualified, and write a letter focused on that particular job. Be sure to follow the format discussed in this chapter, and highlight your strong points.
4. Exchange your letter and resumé with a classmate. Imagine that you are the employer and evaluate your classmate's application. Your classmate will do the same for you.
5. Using the job listings that you and your classmate applied to, role-play the interview situation. You interview your classmate, then reverse roles. Let the other members of your class comment on the interviews.

INDEX